Non-Western Theories of Development

RIZONS IN
TIVE POLITICS

Non-Western Theories of Development

Regional Norms versus Global Trends

Edited by Howard J. Wiarda

**Professor of Political Science, and the Leonard J.
Horwitz Professor of Iberian and Latin American Studies
University of Massachusetts/Amherst**
and
**Senior Associate
Center for Strategic and International Studies
Washington, D.C.**

With Contributions By
**Steven Boilard, Dale S. Herspring,
Peter R. Moody, A.H. Somjee, Anwar Syed,
Howard J. Wiarda, and Lana Wylie**

Harcourt Brace College Publishers
**Fort Worth Philadelphia San Diego Orlando San Antonio
Toronto Montreal London Sydney Tokyo**

Publisher Earl McPeek
Acquisitions Editor David Tatom
Project Editor Michael E. Norris
Production Manager Linda McMillan
Art Director Garry Harman

*This book is printed on
acid-free recycled paper*

ISBN: 0-15-505366-3

Library of Congress Catalog Card Number: 97-74698

Copyright © 1999 by Harcourt Brace & Company

Cover photo: Corel Professional Photos

Address for Editorial Correspondence:
Harcourt Brace College Publishers
301 Commerce Street, Suite 3700
Fort Worth, TX 76102

Address for Orders:
Harcourt Brace & Company
6277 Sea Harbor Drive
Orlando, FL 32887-6777
1-800-782-4479

Website: http://www.hbcollege.com

Printed in the United States of America

9   0   1   2   3   4   5   066   9   8   7   6   5   4   3   2

Table of Contents

Preface

In the 1950s and 1960s, many American social scientists thought that social, economic, and political development in the non-Western or Third World would largely follow and echo that of the West. In both Marxian and non-Marxian models, the modal patterns were the Western or already-developed nations; the developed nations showed to the undeveloped the socioeconomic and political mirror of the latter's future.

Then in the 1970s the idea of indigenous or home-grown models of development caught hold in various areas of the Third World. Rather than slavishly and retardedly imitating the West, the non-Western nations were attracted to the idea of fashioning their own systems of politics, economics, and social organization based on native and recently rediscovered values and institutions. There would be, conceivably, an east Asian or Confucian model of development, a south Asian model of development, an Islamic model of development, a sub-Saharan African model of development, and perhaps also a Latin American model of development. Latin America presented a particularly difficult case because, while it was predominately Western, it represented a semifeudal fragment of the Western tradition dating back to pre-1500.

Today the situation is more complex, more confusing, and therefore deserving of a serious study and updating. On the one hand, some groups and individuals (the Iranian mullahs, prime ministers Lee Kwan Yew of Singapore and Mahathir bin Mohamud of Maylasia, Col. Mu'ammar al-Qaddafi in Libya, and Julius Nyerere in Tanzania, among others) continue to assert the advantages of non-Western theories of development. But many others in these same countries have become disillusioned with indigenous theories and institutions, seeing them as romantic visions, unrealistic, unworkable, the products of intellectual thinking but not necessarily in accord with their own peoples' wishes or practices. The argument has been tipped recently by the mammoth and probably irresistible impact of Western influences (Coca

Cola, blue jeans, rock music, consumerism, and—not least—democracy, human rights, and free-market capitalism) on the non-Western world. Meanwhile, the end of the Cold War means not only the collapse and discrediting of one of the main alternatives (Marxism-Leninism) to Westernization, but also the end of the Third World's ability to play the United States off against the Soviet Union and, thus, to preserve a larger degree of their own autonomy and independence.

All these changes, new currents and countercurrents, make it imperative that we reassess, in this new national and international context, the argument between local or regional and global or universal models of development. To what extent in today's circumstances can indigenous models and movements hope to survive? Will they not be overwhelmed by what MIT political scientist Lucian Pye once called the "world culture" of Western values and ideas? Or, paradoxically, might not the end of the Cold War, rather than producing only one model, provide opportunity for a great variety of indigenous ethnic, religious, and national groups in Asia, Latin America, Africa, the Middle East, Russia, and Eastern Europe to assert more strongly their own indigenous solutions, ethnic pride, and ideas of separatism? Could we not see a continuum of countries, ranging by degree from those with strong indigenous cultures, such as Japan, India, and China, able to borrow *selectively* from the Western tradition, versus countries with weaker, local cultures that are likely to be overwhelmed and/or submerged by Western influences?

This book wrestles with the question of whether there is now only one (mainly Western, democratic, capitalist) model of development, or is there still room for two (socialist), three (mercantilist, statist), or many (Islamic, African, Confucian, Latin American, etc.) more models of development? What kinds of blends and overlaps exist between the Western and non-Western models? With the end of the Cold War and the seeming triumph of the neoliberal model, is it still possible to envision multiple routes to development, or is there now only one path? Must indigenous groups like those in Mexico or Guatemala give up their struggle and resign themselves to being absorbed into Western ways, or can they still hope for some degree of autonomy?

The topic is freighted with heavy issues that resonate both intellectually in terms of the models we use to interpret non-Western countries, *and* practically and politically as regards the future development of Third World countries and the indigenous movements within them. In the cases of Russia, China, and Japan, the debate between Western and non-Western models involves important security issues as well.

The book examines these issues by focusing on the change process in all the world's major, non-Western or partially Western areas. The authors of each chapter are recognized authorities in their respective areas. Each author was asked to speak to a common set of questions: How Western or non-Western is the area? What are the indigenous traditions of development and what is their influence? What is the blend of Western and non-Western? What has been the impact of the end of the Cold War and the new neoliberal orthodoxy? And what are the prospects for Western versus indigenous models of change? What fusions may emerge? The use of a common outline for each chapter facilitates comparison; the addition of an introduction and conclusion by the editor helps tie the volume together as an integrated *book* rather than just a loose anthology.

The editor of this volume would like to thank his current "home" institutions for their continued support of this and other projects: the Department of Political Science of the University of Massachusetts, Amherst, and the Center for Strategic and International Studies in Washington, D.C. David Tatom, acquisitions editor at Harcourt Brace College Publishers, not only encouraged this effort but also provided crucial continuity to the "New Horizons in Comparative Politics" series of which it is a part. Barbara Ciesluk assisted with the typing and provided useful editorial advice. The usual disclaimers apply; only the authors and editor are responsible for the analysis that follows.

HOWARD J. WIARDA
Washington, D.C.
Spring 1997

1
—

Introduction: The Western Tradition and Its Export to the Non-West

—Howard J. Wiarda

Howard J. Wiarda, editor of this volume, is professor of political science and the Leonard J. Horwitz Professor of Iberian and Latin American Studies at the University of Massachusetts at Amherst. He is also a senior associate of the Center for Strategic and International Studies in Washington, D.C. He is the author of Introduction to Comparative Politics, American Foreign Policy, Latin American Politics and Development, Corporatism and Comparative Politics, Politics in Iberia, New Directions in Comparative Politics, *and* Ethnocentrism in Foreign Policy: Can We Understand the Third World?

During the 1960s the fields of comparative politics, comparative sociology, and economic development studies were largely dominated by what came to be called "developmentalism." Developmentalism in turn derived from earlier studies in the fields of cultural anthropology and sociology, and from greater dynamism and analysis of change processes in political science. Developmentalism encompassed the study of economic, social, and political development in the Third World of emerging nations. The study of development was further fueled by the emergence of a host of new, formerly colonial nations onto the world stage in the late 1950s and early 1960s, and by the rising preoccupation in American foreign policy to fashion an attractive, noncommunist model of development that would serve as an alternative to Marxism-Leninism.[1] In the 1960s the study of social, political, economic, cultural, even psychological development became *the* dominant paradigm in the social sciences.

The development model generally posited that all societies go through similar if not identical processes of economic development, social change, and political modernization—the latter not always well defined but usually implying

1

greater pluralism, democracy, and social justice. Once the great motor force of economic development begins, it produces some quite predictable social changes: the rise of a middle class, a working class, and the mobilization of the peasantry. These social transformations in turn help produce greater political pluralism, more democratic politics, and the need for more effective public policy.[2]

The process was usually portrayed in nice, antiseptic phrases like these, implying a happy ending—thus ignoring the wrenching, often bloody disruption and chaos that accompany such major change processes. Moreover the developmental approach suggested that hated fascism and communism were "diseases of the transition" that could be overcome or vanquished through development, and that the end-product of this unilinear, presumably universal development process was a society that looked just like we do: happily democratic, pluralist, and socially just. How comforting that conclusion was both to the scholars of developmentalism and to U.S. foreign policy makers! Unfortunately it was not an accurate portrayal either of development or of the Third World nations starting out on the development path.

Then came the war in Vietnam, the assassinations of John F. and Robert Kennedy and Martin Luther King, upheavals in American cities and universities, and Watergate. These events shook our faith in the inevitability and even the desirability of the American model on which so much of the development paradigm had been based. In addition, it turned out that much of the earlier development literature was written by theorists who had never visited the Third World. Furthermore, after a decade of actual experience with and study of development in Third World nations, policy makers and theorists realized that the main institutions and processes involved often failed to conform to the model. The result during the 1970s was strong criticism of the prevailing development model, the assertion of alternative approaches (dependency theory, corporatism, bureaucratic-statism), and the dawning realization that the Third World would not and could not imitate the developmental experiences of the West (the United States and Europe).[3]

One of the alternatives put forward in the 1970s and then blossoming in the 1980s was the notion of a home-grown or indigenous, Third World model of development. After the numerous failures of developmentalism and the coming to power of a whole wave of repressive, human-rights-abusing regimes in Africa, Asia, the Middle East, and Latin America, the idea of a native or indigenous theory of development was enormously attractive. Presumably these home-grown models would be more closely attuned to local conditions than the imported and often ill-fitting Western ones. There would therefore have to be an east Asian, perhaps Confucian theory of development, an Indian and presumably Hindu theory of development, a sub-Saharan

African theory of development, a Latin American theory of development, and—particularly after the Iranian revolution of 1979—a distinct Islamic theory of development. There were, probably, still universals in the development process but now each Third World region would do it, to use the title of the Frank Sinatra song, "my way."[4]

During the decade of the 1980s, the idea of a home-grown theory of development was very popular among Third World intellectuals. Not only did it offer an attractive alternative to the often (in their contexts) dysfunctional Western model but it also promised a Third Way between democracy and authoritarianism, between capitalism and communism. Unfortunately the countries where an indigenous theory of development was seriously embraced (Iran, Tanzania, Cambodia) turned out to be not very attractive places. There were other serious problems with indigenous theories of development as well, which are discussed at length in the book. Suffice it here to say that these indigenous, home-grown ideas and models of development proved to be (except perhaps in east Asia) no more effective in actually promoting development than earlier theories had been, and they were often downright harmful.

Then came the collapse of the Soviet Union, the end of the Cold War, and a new international world where every basic foreign policy assumption of the preceding forty-five years required reexamination. This transformation in international politics took place at precisely the time in the 1980s and 1990s when the "Third Wave"[5] of democracy seemed to be triumphing worldwide and representing the wave of the future,[6] when free market or neoliberal economic policies acquired the cachet of a new orthodoxy, and when what MIT political scientist Lucian Pye once called the "world culture" of consumerism (Coca-Cola, blue jeans, rock music, and—not least—democracy and human rights) seemed to become universal.

So what then in this context becomes of the idea of an indigenous theory or several indigenous theories of development? Is this idea still viable and attractive or has it now been overwhelmed by Western influences? Is it possible to blend or to select, retaining what is good and useful of indigenous practices but also accommodating to powerful Western ways? Or are the Third World and its institutions bound to be submerged in the Western onslaught? Are there some countries (Japan, for instance) that are so important and powerful that they can successfully blend and fuse Western and indigenous ways, choosing selectively among the best features of each, while there are other countries less wealthy and less self-confident that will simply be overwhelmed by Western culture? What kinds of blends and fusions are possible? And what implications do all these trends have for the social sciences, both for our theories of development and even for the notion of a universal social science?

These are the large and intriguing questions explored in this book.

Comparative Politics and the Development Literature

Through the mid-1950s, the field of comparative politics was dominated by what came to be called the "formal-legal" approach. That is, scholars focused on the more formal and legalistic aspects of comparative political systems: their constitutions, laws, federalism, local government; the powers of the executive, of parliaments, the courts; rules and bureaucracies. Not only was comparative politics largely confined to these subjects but the field was also limited to a narrow range of countries: those in North America (United States, Canada) and Northwest Europe (Great Britain, France, Germany). Because of these emphases, the field was criticized as being narrow, ethnocentric, parochial, and boring.[7]

But then four major transformations occurred that made comparative politics the premier field within the political science discipline. Two of these transformations were academic and intellectual while the other two were in the realm of practical politics or "on the ground." The first of the scholarly transformations was in the larger discipline of political science: toward greater emphasis on the dynamic and informal aspects of politics—political parties, interest groups, public opinion, political processes, political behavior, decision making. The second of the academic transformations occurred in the subfield of comparative politics itself: away from formal-legalism and Eurocentrism toward the study of political processes, toward greater analysis rather than mere description, real comparisons rather than case studies of single countries, and focused on nations and areas—including the Third World—not previously studied by the discipline.

On the ground, the changes refocusing the comparative politics field were no less significant. The first major change in the late 1950s and early 1960s was the sudden emergence of a large number of newly independent nations in Africa, Asia, and the Middle East onto the world's stage. Suddenly, within a few years, the number of countries available as "living laboratories" for the study of comparative politics and development had more than doubled. The opportunity to do research in new countries that no one had ever seriously studied before was very heady stuff and attracted some of the best young minds in the country to the study of developing nations. Within a decade there were more, especially younger, scholars studying Africa, Asia, and Latin America than there were in the more traditional field of European studies. The most exciting, innovative approaches in the field tended to come from the study of developing areas.

Accompanying this revolution of new nations was a shift in American foreign policy. During the early years of the Cold War American foreign policy had largely focused on the possibility of a direct confrontation with the Soviet Union; hence Europe and the North Atlantic Treaty Organization (NATO) had received most of the attention. But during the late 1950s and early 1960s, with such important countries in mind as Egypt, Iran, Indonesia, the Philippines, the Congo (later, Zaire), and Cuba (then experiencing the revolution of Fidel Castro), U.S. policy began to realize the main locus of Cold War conflict was likely to be the Third World with its guerrilla revolutions, Marxist nationalism, and anti-imperialism—often in proxy wars using local forces as stand-ins for the United States and the Soviet Union. Moreover, the U.S. government quickly realized that it knew next to nothing about most of these Third World countries; further, that it had little in the way of an attractive model to offer the developing nations as an alternative to Marxism.[8] Hence the U.S. government began during this period the sometimes frantic creation or subsidy of new international centers at leading American universities to study Third World issues, the sponsorship of fellowships to encourage young scholars to enter Third World studies, and the search for an alternative model to Marxism that would be attractive to Third World elites.

Where to find such a non-Marxian model? The alternatives were few. Hardly any American economists, sociologists, or political scientists at that time had studied the Third World closely, much less lived there or come to know its regions intimately. Hence the elaboration during this period of developmentalism, a model that bore a striking resemblance to the societies that these scholars knew best, Western Europe and the United States itself: liberal, democratic, pluralist, capitalist or mixed economy, middle class, middle-of-the-road, pragmatic, noncommunist, socially just. It was a model that, perhaps unsurprisingly given the times and circumstances, looked just like we do—or as we imagined ourselves to be.

It should be said immediately that by no means were all the scholars who wrote on development issues during the 1960s in the pay of the U.S. government or simple stooges for its policies. A handful were, but the vast majority of "developmentalists" were not on the U.S. government payroll. Most of them wrote out of sheer conviction that a developmental model that followed the American/Western European example of democratic pluralism was also best for the Third World. However even those scholars of development who were not subsidized by government funds tended to believe overwhelmingly that there was no incompatibility between the developmental goals of the Third World and American foreign policy. They believed that the two could go together in harmony, indeed that through such then-innovative programs as the Peace Corps, the Alliance for Progress, and the newly created Agency for International Development (AID, the chief U.S. foreign aid agency) the United States could assist Third World development while serving U.S.

foreign policy goals at the same time. Remember, this was the era of the early 1960s, of John F. Kennedy and Camelot, of Lyndon Johnson and the Great Society, before Vietnam and Watergate, of close cooperation between America's universities and U.S. government policy, of "pay any price, bear any burden," and "ask not what your country can do for you but what you can do for your country." In these halcyon and, let us face it, rather naive years, one did not actually have to be on the government payroll in order to believe the American dream that our institutions were the best in the world and that they were also the most appropriate for the Third World.

Three academic disciplines were the main contributors to the developmentalist model that came to prevail: economics, sociology, and political science. The economists, led by scholar and future presidential adviser Walt W. Rostow, argued that all the world's countries went through several stages of development, from underdevelopment, to take off, to drive to maturity, to modernity.[9] Naturally we (the United States and Western Europe) were already in the "modern" category; other countries could catch up with us by following our lead and example of progressive capitalism and democracy. *All* countries had to go through Rostow's stages, which were seen as both inevitable and universal. Although communism was portrayed as a "disease of the transition" from underdeveloped to developed, the final product of the process was bound to be liberal, democratic, and "just like us." Rostow's analysis with its antiseptic processes and happy ending had a major impact not only on scholars studying development but also on the reorganization of the U.S. foreign assistance program, of which he was the chief architect.

Sociological writings on development largely derived from Harvard scholar Talcott Parsons.[10] Building upon the work of the great German sociologist Max Weber, Parsons set forth a series of characteristics, called "pattern variables," that he thought defined the differences between traditional and modern societies, as follows:

Traditional	Modern
Ascriptive (who you know)	Achievement, Merit
Particularistic (narrow, village-based)	Universalistic
Functionally Diffuse (militaries or churches may also play political roles)	Functionally Specific (separation of church and state, professionalized militaries)

Presumably, as they developed, all societies moved from being ascriptive, particularistic, and functionally diffuse to being achievement-oriented, universalistic, and functionally specific. Note that once again the definition of a modern society looked just like we did—or as we imagined ourselves to be.

Another sociological insight incorporated into development theory was that of Seymour M. Lipset.[11] Lipset and his colleagues gathered data on the educational and literacy levels, levels of economic development, and political beliefs and attitudes of *all* the countries in the world. Next he correlated these rankings with whether a country was democratic or not. He found, unsurprisingly, that countries with higher education levels, higher levels of economic development, and more positive and participatory attitudes toward governmental action tended to be more democratic. Poorer and less educated countries tended not to be democracies. These are important findings, but note they are *tendency statements*, not laws of causation, and there were numerous anomalies: Costa Rica was a poor country and yet a democracy, while Argentina was wealthy and well-educated but not a democracy. Lipset's findings suggested only a *correlation* between economic development and democracy, not that economic development caused democracy. Later scholars and many U.S. foreign aid officials were not always so clear as Lipset in maintaining this important distinction, suggesting often mistakenly that somehow economic development *caused* democracy to flower.

The political science contribution to developmentalism was led by Gabriel A. Almond and the Social Science Research Council's Committee on Comparative Politics (SSRC/CCP). Almond's 1960 edited volume, *The Politics of the Developing Areas*,[12] was a pioneering contribution to development studies—even though Almond later admitted that at that time he had never visited or studied a developing nation. In his oft-cited introduction, Almond took Parsons's pattern variables and applied them to political institutions and behavior; he also suggested a seven-part categorization of political functions that presumably all countries perform or need to perform:

1. Political Socialization—the teaching of political values and norms
2. Interest Articulation—the setting forth of different groups' interests
3. Interest Aggregation—the bringing together of these interests presumably through political parties
4. Political Communication—communication of these interests to government officials
5. Rule Making—presumably what a Congress or Parliament would do
6. Rule Administration—presumably what an executive would do
7. Rule Adjudication—presumably what a Supreme Court would do

Political development in this formulation consisted in the growth and institutionalization of these seven functions. Note that in Almond, as in Rostow, Parsons, and Lipset, the movement from traditional to modern is both inevitable and universal (all countries must follow this formula); note also how closely Almond's seven functions correspond to the workings of the U.S. political system and its division of powers.

The Almond framework spawned a host of studies in the 1960s on political parties and development, interest groups and development, bureaucracies and development, militaries and development, religion and development, labor unions and development, etc.—all using this particular, America/Europe-based paradigm. In addition, hundreds of newly minted graduate students fanned out to Africa, Asia, Latin America, and the Middle East in the 1960s armed with the Rostow, Lipset, and Almond categories, all looking for "development."

They seldom found it—and certainly not in the form Rostow, Almond, and the others had prescribed. They found little of the "inevitable" and "universal" march toward democracy and development prescribed by the model, few of the institutions the framework suggested ought to be present, and few of the seven functions described by Almond. Instead what they found was a large number of poor countries, often with not very effective political systems, with confused, messy, overlapping fusions of both traditional and modern features, struggling to cope with (among other things) all these American officials and scholars seeking to remake them in America's image. Quite a number of these scholars returned to write path-breaking new books not only pointing out the flaws and ethnocentrism of the Rostow-Lipset-Almond analysis but often suggesting new and alternative models.

The criticisms of the Almond approach may be summarized as follows:

1. It was ethnocentric, based on American or European models that often had little relevance to the Third World.

2. It lumped all Third World areas together, like trying to compare apples, oranges, and peaches, making little allowance for the social, cultural, and historic difference between Africa, Asia, Latin America, and the Middle East.

3. It suggested that all good things (economic, social, and political development) go together; in fact, we have learned that economic and social modernization often *disrupt* political stability.

4. It was too antiseptic, ignoring class conflict and the possibility during the transitional stages of revolution and civil war.

5. It ignored international factors and influences such as transnational religious bodies, global market forces, multinational corporations, foreign embassies, and international lending agencies.

6. It misrepresented the role of traditional institutions, which did not give way or disappear under the impact of modernization but *adapted* to change.

7. It ignored the differences between those nations that developed earlier (the United States and Western Europe) and today's developing nations where the timing, conditions, sequence, and stages of development are

both very different and highly telescoped.

8. Its logic and methodology were flawed, especially the pattern variables and the functional approach.

9. It often did actual harm to Third World nations by destroying traditional institutions before newer ones had been consolidated (as in Vietnam).

10. It was too tied to American foreign policy goals of creating stable, friendly, middle-class societies, which compromised its usefulness as a serious comparative politics approach.

11. It sucked us deeper and deeper into the Vietnam war, led to the Americanization both of the war and the Vietnamese political process, and thus demonstrated the bankruptcy of the developmentalist approach.

These criticisms were devastating. By the end of the 1960s developmentalism was thoroughly discredited. Except for a handful of scholars who continued to follow this model, and U.S. foreign aid which continued to be based on the Rostow analysis, most scholars in the 1970s began to employ other approaches. During the 1990s, as the spread of democracy and the acceptance of a neoliberal economic model made the developmentalist approach look more accurate in long-range terms than it had looked from the perspective of the Vietnam war era, a modified developmentalist approach made something of a comeback. But during the 1970s and 1980s developmentalism was seldom employed in the study of the Third World.

In its place came a variety of new approaches. These included dependency theory, the corporatist approach, bureaucratic authoritarianism, organic statism, and political economy. We cannot here summarize all of these approaches.[13] But we do need at least to list them because it is from this context of challenges to developmentalism and the emergence of alternative approaches that the idea of an indigenous or home-grown theory of development also emerged.

Indigenous Theories of Development

The idea of an indigenous, local, or home-grown theory of development is undoubtedly attractive. It proved to be enormously influential among intellectual elites and some political leaders in the Third World during the 1970s and 1980s—and in some countries it is attractive today. The fashioning of indigenous models of development was particularly attractive to Third World leaders given the apparent failures or unattractiveness of the main alternatives, both Marxism and the U.S.-favored developmentalist approach. Both the Marxian and the non-Marxian models are, after all, based on the particular developmental experience of a select group of countries in Western Europe (Germany, France, Great Britain) and the United States. But by the 1970s it was clear that *neither* of these two major alternatives was necessarily appropriate for or had much relevance for the Third World. Hence the newfound interest in fashioning a home-grown model that *did* reflect indigenous cultures and institutions.

Our purpose here is not to present a complete analysis of the indigenous, Third World models set forth in the 1970s and 1980s; we leave that up to our contributing authors. Instead, our purpose in this introduction is to provide the broader context in which these ideas and approaches emerged and to offer a brief synopsis of them.

In Africa, for example, following the hopeful and optimistic euphoria that accompanied independence in the early 1960s, political as well as economic collapse and disintegration set in. Neither the Marxian nor the developmentalist approach provided adequate answers. Both approaches seemed to suggest that getting rid of tribalism or ethnicity (seen as a "traditional" institution) was necessary for development to occur. But the tribe or the ethnic group provided one of the few institutions that helped hold African society together, providing security, police protection, education, and other essential social services that no other "modern" institution seemed capable of supplying. Hence instead of eliminating tribalism as the earlier development literature suggested, many African leaders began to look on it more benignly. Instead of dysfunctional centralized regimes, some African political leaders began to envision a more decentralized or even federal regime in which localized ethnic organizations would be utilized rather than snuffed out. Incompletely, by fits and starts, and not without misgivings, some African leaders began to consider a political system that dealt realistically with persistent tribalism rather than trying to eliminate it in the name of "modernization."

In India some parallel developments occurred. Not only did India have a long tradition of philosophical and religious thought quite different from that of the West, but it also had traditional institutions that stubbornly refused to give way under the impact of modernization. Indian caste associations, for instance, proved to be not just parochial, ascriptive institutions in the Parsons-Almond mold fated to disappear, but adaptable and even modernizing forces, taking on many of the functions of interest groups and political parties. While India did not wish to jettison the liberal-democratic institutions inherited from earlier British colonial rule, it did need to adapt its imported models (by now including both democracy on the political side and more open markets on the economic side) to Indian ways of doing things.

Much the same can be said of east Asia. Here we have an area that has strong indigenous (Confucian, Shintoist, Taoist) traditions and culture. At the same time, east Asia (Japan, South Korea, Taiwan, Hong Kong, Singapore, now China, Indonesia, the Philippines) has been the most successful non-Western area in adapting Western ways to Asian practices and traditions. Japan, for example, produces cars, pianos, and all manner of high-tech instruments, and plays Beethoven often better than the West. Much of Asia's success, in fact, has come not from abolishing traditional institutions but from adapting these to Western practices. More recently Japan and other east Asian countries have held up *their* development experiences, not America's or Europe's, as models of economic growth and governance for the world to emulate.

It is similar in the Islamic world. In Islam we have a long religious and philosophical tradition comparable to Buddhism, Confucianism, or Christianity. The modernization literature argued that such traditional institutions as the Islamic religion should fade under the impact of development and secularization; instead it has flourished. Not only is Islamic fundamentalism growing and, especially since the Iranian revolution of 1979, becoming more militant and aggressive, but increasingly whole societies and polities are being recast in the Islamic mold. On the other hand—and unlike east Asia—there are as yet *no* examples of a successful and specifically Islamic *economic* model; and in the political sphere, in non-Moslem countries, there is little admiration for an Islamic theocratic state.

Latin America, Eastern Europe, and Russia represent variations on these themes. Latin America is primarily Western in its main institutions, but as an offshoot of Spain and Portugal of the Middle Ages, it represents a particular, semifeudal fragment of an earlier West and is now seeking to catch up both economically and politically. For decades Latin America has been searching for a political and economic model that reflects both its Westernness and its particularly Hispanic past—and has not found it yet. Some Latin American countries also have large indigenous, Indian populations, so when we speak of an "indigenous model" of that area we need to know if we are speaking of the assertion of Indian rights or of a distinctive Hispanic framework. For a time Latin American intellectuals also put forth dependency theory (see chapter 4) as their own creation but that assertion faded as democracy and integration into the world economy grew.

Eastern Europe is similarly divided. Some countries of the region (the Czech Republic, Slovakia, Poland, Hungary, Slovenia, perhaps Croatia) are mainly Western in their histories, peoples, languages, and religion; since the collapse of the Soviet Union and its communist satellite regimes in Eastern Europe, these countries have become increasingly interconnected with the West, both politically (democracy) and economically (free markets). But other countries of the region (Bulgaria, Romania, Serbia, Albania, Macedonia, Bosnia) are, by the same criteria of language, ethnicity, culture, and religion, more mixed, often both Western and Eastern. Unlike the other regions surveyed, however, a distinctly Eastern European model of development—or even much agreement on what "Eastern Europe" now means or if it has a separate identity—has not been seen here. Instead we have witnessed, especially in southeastern Europe, a great deal of confusion, even chaos and instability in some countries, and uncertainty as to what precise directions to take either politically or economically.

Russia is an especially interesting case not only because of the divisions over its identity and future directions but also because it is such a large country with so many nuclear weapons. In that respect, the West has high strategic stakes in the outcome. Russia has long been divided between its pro-Western and Slavophile loyalties, divisions that were often hidden or submerged during its long, seventy-year period of communist dictatorship. But with the collapse of communism these divisions have resurfaced, made more complicated by the new forms of electoral politics as well as foreign policy considerations. President Boris Yeltsin has been identified with democracy and the West and has received strong support from the West; his opponents, both Vladimir Zhirinovsky and more moderate Gennady Zyuganov, have put forth an oftentimes anti-Western and Slavophile political agenda, complicated by the fact that they were the candidates of a revived Communist Party which the West (the United States and its NATO allies) sees as threatening. The Slavophiles often emphasize authoritarianism, top-down rule, a strong state and military, and a more collectivist economy; but it is as yet unclear whether this constitutes a full-fledged and distinctive, indigenous *theory* of development.

The idea of an indigenous or home-grown theory of development thus became very popular in the 1970s, 1980s, and on into the 1990s. In one form or another, the idea of building a development model on local or native institutions and practices—as distinct from imported ones, whether stemming from Western or communist practices—gained popularity in virtually all areas of the globe. These efforts to fashion a model based on native institutions reflected not only dissatisfaction with existing models but also nationalistic, cultural, and ethnic pride in utilizing "our own" institutions and practices.

While undoubtedly attractive, the idea of an indigenous model or models of development presents a variety of problems and questions. We raise these questions here in preliminary fashion for our readers to think about as they read the chapters that follow; we return to these themes in the conclusion:

1. Who will define these indigenous models for each area and country; what *precise* ingredients will be included?

2. What if conflict arises (as in Russia) between two or more conceptions of a home-grown model or between ethnic groups with competing indigenous conceptions, and how would such conflicts be resolved?

3. What if the intellectual elites favor an indigenous model but their peoples want what the West has to offer: rock music, blue jeans, Coca-Cola,

consumerism, and democracy?

4. What if some aspects of the indigenous model (e.g., the Latin American tradition of authoritarianism or the Islamic treatment of women) are uncomfortable or unacceptable to outsiders or to some within their own culture?

5. What if some elements in power *manipulate* indigenous symbols to enhance their own positions—e.g., those who unscrupulously wrap political agendas in religious mantles?

6. Must a country or region opt *entirely* for indigenous solutions or can it (like Japan) pick and choose among Western and its own traditions? What form(s) will such fusion take?

7. If we accept the notion of indigenous models, does that mean there are no universals, only country-, or culture-, or region-specific policies and institutions? What then happens to such hoped-for universals as democracy, human rights, and open markets, among others?

8. If we have a separate east Asian, Islamic, African, etc., model of development, does that also mean we need a separate east Asian, Islamic, African, etc., social science? And what are the larger implications of such specialization?

9. What if the indigenous models of development prove no more workable or productive of positive results than earlier, imported models?

10. Is the Western cultural influence in *all* its manifestations (economics, politics, society, fashion, music, behavior) now so powerful that no indigenous culture can stand up against it? Or are we still likely to see various blends and fusions of Western and non-Western influences?

Just this preliminary listing indicates that, though attractive in many ways, an indigenous model of development is not without many traps, difficulties, and problems of its own. Now, let us add a further complication.

Indigenous Models and the New World Order

It is perhaps more than coincidental that these new, usually Third World, indigenous models of development flowered and flourished during the last, waning decades of the Cold War when the two major superpowers and the rival systems they represented, capitalism and communism, both seemed to be in trouble. The so-called nonaligned movement of Third World countries that refused to align themselves with either Cold War bloc—and asserted their own foreign policies and developmental models—was at the same time an expression of greater nationalism and independence. So long as the Cold War was on, the nonaligned countries could seek to play off one superpower against the other, and meanwhile assert their own independent ways of doing things. But if the advancement of indigenous models and of independent foreign policies was related to the Cold War, then once the Cold War ended, presumably the context and opportunities to put forward homegrown models of development would change as well. And that is precisely what happened.

To begin, the end of the Cold War and the collapse of the Soviet Union mean that the developing nations can no longer play what has been called the "Third World game." That is, in the absence of the Soviet Union, nonaligned countries can no longer play off the West against the Soviets, meanwhile getting more from both camps in the process. The ideological battle is over and the West has won; the Soviet Union is no more and Russia has largely withdrawn from the international playing field. Third World nations now have far less choice in models; at some levels they *must* conform to Western ways and the new international power configuration. Such conformity will probably entail some, perhaps considerable, sacrifice of indigenous ways. It may be in the future that Japan, China, or other emerging powers will become developmental exemplars for the world, but for now at least and for most of the Third World the West is about the only game in town.

Second, since the mid-1970s (and thus concurrently with the growing assertion of indigenous models) the world has witnessed an enormous surge of democracy. This recent wave of democracy began in southern Europe (Greece, Portugal, Spain), then encompassed Latin America (nineteen of the twenty countries are now democratic), next spread to east Asia (South Korea, Taiwan, the Philippines), now includes Eastern Europe and Russia, and has made inroads in Africa and the Middle East. Note that many of the countries and regions listed are the same ones that were attracted to notions of an indigenous model of change. Now, a country can have democracy, or it can have an indigenous model, or perhaps some murky combination of both. So we have asked our contributing authors to wrestle with this theme as well: whether democracy can coexist with indigenous traditions, values, and institutions that are sometimes less than fully democratic.

Third, there is culture, in its broadest sense. We are now in an era of global communications and transportation; the older isolation of nations and peoples is rapidly breaking down. The new era features movies, radio, television, VCRs, satellites, cell phones, the Internet, home fax machines, electronic mail, and teleconferencing which reach into the most distant countries and remotest villages. It is virtually impossible now, even if one wants to (and few do), to block out this global revolution in communications; virtually every previously isolated peasant and locality can now tune in this global network. The result is a virtual onslaught of global cultural trends (primarily Western) of dress, styles, music, behavior, and beliefs—including democracy, human rights, and consumerism. The relation of all this to our theme is obvious: how can the Third World continue to be an advocate of indigenous (usually poor and miserable) ways of doing things once it's seen the wealth and glamour of *Dallas, Melrose Place*, or *Beverly Hills 90210*?

The fourth area of change corresponding with the end of the Cold War is economic. It has never been entirely clear, in the Third World and in our discussion here, whether in advancing indigenous models of development we were speaking of only politics, or economics or of both. Earlier we raised the question of whether, with democracy now sweeping the globe and enjoying unprecedented legitimacy and popularity, indigenous models can (or should) stand up against this democratic onslaught. Now we also need to ask, in the wake of the apparently near-universal global triumph of capitalism, free markets, and neoliberalism, if it still makes much sense to speak of diverse, indigenous economic models. For we now know far more than we did in past decades what *works* in development. The answer is: free markets, stable and democratic governments, infrastructure (education, roads, electricity), and effective social policies. So if we now know the general formula to produce economic growth, what logic is there in advancing a particular indigenous model that only perpetuates poverty?

These sweeping changes in the post-Cold War world compel us to reassess the possibilities for indigenous models of development that are at the heart of the analysis in this book. Can the indigenous models that have grown up in recent decades survive, let alone thrive, under the impact of the seeming globalization of Western values and institutions? Or, paradoxically, might not the end of the Cold War, rather than producing only one homogenized world culture and developmental model, instead unleash now a great variety of indigenous, ethnic, religious, and nationality groups—unfettered by the constraints of the Cold War—free to do their own thing? Certainly the conflicts, upheavals, and civil wars in the former Yugoslavia, Somalia, Rwanda, the Crimea, the Urals, Northern Ireland, Mexico, Guatemala, the Sudan, Peru, and other divided countries lend support to the thesis that, even within the new *global* world order, there is still ample room for the assertion of indigenous rights.

So let us keep open for now the issue of whether there is but one, or two, or many routes to development, and what kinds of blends or fusions may exist.

The Book: A Preview

Not all individual countries or regions can be treated in this book, but certainly the major ones are analyzed. We begin with what is arguably the most successful effort to date to absorb Western ways and accommodate them to indigenous institutions: east Asia and the Confucian tradition as it has adapted to modernity, as analyzed by Peter R. Moody, professor of government at the

University of Notre Dame. Next, Indian scholar A. H. Somjee of Simon Fraser University in Canada analyzes the complex case of India, with its similarly powerful indigenous religious and philosophical traditions, its ongoing commitment to liberal democratic values, and its recent shifts in economic policy from socialist to more free market forms. The case of Latin America, analyzed by the book's editor, comes next: an area that represented a premodern, semifeudal offshoot of Western Europe, but is now trying desperately to catch up both politically and economically, still often uncertain about its proper role and destiny.

The discussion then turns to sub-Saharan Africa, as analyzed by Lana Wylie of the University of Massachusetts. Ms. Wylie explores Africa's colonial heritage, its desperate but often frustrated efforts to achieve development, and its recent attempts to find in its own traditions new models of social and political organization. Next, Anwar Syed, professor of political science at the University of Massachusetts, examines the Islamic tradition of political thought and wrestles with the issue of whether a separate Islamic theory of governance and development is either viable or desirable.

The final two country- and area-specific chapters deal with Eastern Europe and Russia, respectively. Professor Dale Herspring, chair of the Political Science Department of Kansas State University and a former high-ranking State Department official, pushes the divide which once separated the NATO and Soviet blocs farther east, drawing a new line across Europe that incorporates some of the Eastern European countries within the Western systems of society, politics, and economics, while characterizing others as mixed, divided, and often confused about their futures and destinies. Similarly in Russia, Professor Steven Boilard of the University of Western Kentucky paints a picture of a country deeply divided by language, ethnic, and nationality differences, agonized and torn between its Western and its Slavophile tendencies, and often going in both directions at once.

To provide unity and coherence to the book, each of our authors has been asked to address so far as feasible a common set of issues. The very diversity of the countries and regions analyzed, and their distinct histories, cultures, and connections to the West, make this a difficult task. So, without forcing any of our authors into a rigid straightjacket that distorts their analysis, we have nevertheless requested that they respond to a common set of questions and to use a common outline as set forth by the editor. The use of a common outline not only facilitates comparisons between these several regions but also enables us to draw systematic conclusions from them. The common set of topics each author was asked to address is as follows:

I. Introduction to the country or area: brief description and statement of chapter thesis

II. The Western Impact: What kind (colonialism or other)? What time period? To what degree and how has the country been Westernized? How has the indigenous culture responded? What developmental mixes and overlaps have evolved? What have been the consequences of independence?

III. An Indigenous Way Asserted: What form did this model of development take? Is it home-grown? How successful were these independence movements?

IV. The End of the Cold War: Have democracy and neoliberalism now triumphed, along with Western culture? Have indigenous movements weakened or disappeared? Has their strategy changed? Is there a new post-Cold War balance of local and imported institutions?

V. Conclusions: Has Westernism triumphed? What are the strength and status of indigenous movements? Is there a home-grown model of development or has it been submerged under the impact of Westernism? What is the current and future balance between Western and non-Western ways and influence?

These are the questions our authors have been asked to answer.

It is a fascinating set of chapters with large themes, important and provocative ideas, and well-informed authors who write well. In the conclusion the editor returns to an assessment of the controversial themes and questions raised in this introduction.

Endnotes

1. For an overview see Howard J. Wiarda, *Introduction to Comparative Politics* (Belmont, CA: Wadsworth Publishing, 1993); also Irene Gendzier, *Managing Political Change: Social Scientists and the Third World* (Boulder, CO: Westview Press, 1985).

2. For some representative literature, see C. E. Black, *The Dynamics of Modernization* (New York: Harper and Row, 1968); and Robert J. Heilbroner, *The Great Ascent* (New York: Harper and Row, 1963).

3. The critical literature includes: Sidney Verba, "Some Dilemmas in Comparative Research," *World Politics* 20 (Oct. 1967): 111–27; Mark Kesselman, "Order or Movement: The Literature of Political Development as Ideology," *World Politics* 26 (Oct. 1973): 139–53; Philip H. Melanson and Lauriston R. King, "Theory in Comparative Politics: A Critical Appraisal," *Comparative Political Studies* 4 (July 1971): 205–31; Geoffrey K. Roberts, "Comparative Politics Today," *Government and Opposition* 7

(Winter 1972): 38–55; Sally A. Merrill, "On the Logic of Comparative Analysis," *Comparative Political Studies* 3 (Jan. 1971): 489–500; Robert T. Holt and John E. Turner, "Crises and Sequences in Collective Theory Development," *American Political Science Review* 69 (Sept. 1975): 979–95; R. S. Milne, "The Overdeveloped Study of Political Development," *Canadian Journal of Political Science* 5 (Dec. 1972): 560–68; Philip Coulter, "Political Development and Political Theory: Methodological and Technological Problems in the Comparative Study of Political Development," *Polity* 5 (Winter 1972): 233–42; Ignany Sachs, "The Logic of Development," *International Social Science Journal* 24, no. 1 (1972): 37–43.

4. Howard J. Wiarda, *Ethnocentrism in Foreign Policy: Can We Understand the Third World?* (Washington, DC: American Enterprise Institute for Public Policy Research, 1983); and A. H. Somjee, *Parallels and Actuals of Political Development* (London: Macmillan, 1986).

5. Samuel P. Huntington, *The Third Wave: Democratization in the Late Twentieth Century* (Norman, OK: University of Oklahoma Press, 1991).

6. Francis Fukuyama, "The End of History," *The National Interest* 16 (Summer 1989).

7. Roy Macridis, *The Study of Comparative Government* (New York: Random House, 1955).

8. Max F. Millikan and Walt W. Rostow, *A Proposal: Key to an Effective Foreign Policy* (New York: Harper, 1957).

9. Walt W. Rostow, *The Stages of Economic Growth: A Non-Communist Manifesto* (New York: Cambridge University Press, 1960).

10. Talcott Parsons, *The Social System* (Glencoe, IL: Free Press, 1951); Parsons and Edward Shils, eds., *Toward a General Theory of Action* (Cambridge, MA: Harvard University Press, 1951).

11. Seymour M. Lipset, "Some Social Requisites for Democracy: Economic Development and Political Legitimacy," *American Political Science Review* 55 (Sept. 1965): 495–514.

12. Gabriel A. Almond and James S. Coleman, eds., *The Politics of the Developing Areas* (Princeton, NJ: Princeton University Press, 1960). For the SSRC/CCP series, "Studies in Political Development," see Lucian W. Pye, ed., *Communications and Political Development* (Princeton, NJ: Princeton University Press, 1963); Joseph LaPalombara ed., *Bureaucracy and Political Development* (Princeton, NJ: Princeton University Press, 1963); Robert E. Ward and Dankwart A. Rustow, eds., *Political Modernization in Japan and Turkey* (Princeton, NJ: Princeton University Press, 1964); James S. Coleman, ed., *Education and Political Development* (Princeton, NJ: Princeton University Press, 1965); Lucian W. Pye and

Sidney Verba, eds., *Political Culture and Political Development* (Princeton, NJ: Princeton University Press, 1965); Joseph LaPalombara and Myron Weiner, eds., *Political Parties and Political Development* (Princeton, NJ: Princeton University Press, 1966); Leonard Binder, James S. Coleman, Joseph LaPalombara, Lucien W. Pye, Sidney Verba, and Myron Weiner, eds., *Crisis and Sequences in Political Development* (Princeton, NJ: Princeton University Press, 1971); Charles Tilly, ed., *The Formation of the National States in Western Europe* (Princeton, NJ: Princeton University Press, 1975).

13. See the author's summaries of these approaches in *Introduction to Comparative Politics*; also Howard J. Wiarda, ed., *New Directions in Comparative Politics*, 2nd ed. (Boulder, CO: Westview Press, 1991).

2

East Asia: The Confucian Tradition and Modernization

—Peter R. Moody, Jr.

Peter R. Moody, Jr., teaches in the Department of Government and International Studies at the University of Notre Dame. He is also the author of Tradition and Modernization in China and Japan, Political Opposition in Post-Confucian Society, *and other works, and is editor of the* China Documents Annual.

"East Asia" in this essay refers to those societies in which Confucianism has been the dominant or official system of thought: China (including, at least for cultural purposes, Taiwan), Japan, Korea, and Vietnam. Singapore, with its large ethnically Chinese population, should also be included in this group. Although the original cultures of these societies were quite different from each other and their spoken languages unrelated, their "higher" cultures all derived from the Chinese.

It is no easier to summarize Confucianism than it is Christianity or any other rich, complex, and enduring system of ideas, and any brief description risks caricature. Confucius lived from about 551 to 479 B.C., a period of social change, in which China was divided among numerous small warring dukedoms. He deplored what he took to be the collapse of order and justice, reflected in the loss of a sense of ritual. In endeavoring to restore what he took to be the proper ritual of ancient times, he redefined the concept so that, in Confucian thinking, ritual becomes the proper way in which human beings should interact with each other. True ritual, as distinct from its ceremonial forms, is the outward manifestation of *ren*—love, humanity, the virtue which makes us human beings.

In Confucian thinking all human beings are intrinsically equal, but most human *relations* are hierarchical, with people relating to each other through roles based on age, sex, family relationship, or political and social status; ritual then becomes the way in which persons in their varying roles relate to others. Confucian ethics are personalistic and situational, in that while, say, everyone should behave with love and justice toward everyone else, the specific content of love and justice depends upon the circumstances and the relationship. Confucianism enjoins the constant moral and spiritual development of the self through study, with the goal that, as Confucius put it, by the time he turned seventy he could follow his heart's desire without departing from the correct path. Political authority is instituted by Heaven for the benefit of the people. The exercise of political authority is the duty of those who have most fully developed their moral consciousness; in actuality, though, the measure of this enlightenment in traditional China came to be, in a very liberal concession to practical reality, the ability to pass a civil service examination on points of Confucian teaching.

The Confucian societies share more than a Confucian heritage (all, for example, eat with chopsticks, a practice found nowhere else), and each society has its own type of Confucianism. Also, Confucianism is not the entirety of east Asian culture. The style, say, of Singapore, with its harsh punishments and meddlesome laws, may reflect Legalism, another more autocratic Chinese system of political thought. This essay will explore the possibility that the economic success of east Asia does reflect a generically Confucian influence, particularly reflected in a pattern of state-society relations and in the continuing importance of personalistic relationships in society at large.

Modernization, or self-sustaining economic growth, did not occur spontaneously in east Asia, but no other non-Western region has developed more successfully, and some may judge on balance that development in east Asia has been more successful than in the West. Some east Asian societies not only enjoyed rapid economic growth but also continued to show relatively equal distributions of income—"growth with equity." Development in east Asia has not been without its pernicious social consequences, but they may be less severe than elsewhere—less social decay, less inflation, less unemployment, stronger family structures, lower crime rates. East Asia was, prior to the troubles of 1997, spectacularly successful in economic development in the second half of the twentieth century, where that development has been unhindered by either socialism or civil war.

Asian statesmen and spokesmen, at least until the 1997 Asian financial crisis, have come to proclaim a distinct "Asian model" of development, superior to that of the West. This theme is often used to rationalize political autocracy and to enforce social conformity, or as a way to counter unwelcome American attention to the policies of the east Asian states. The assertion may nonetheless still have some merit. The east Asian experience has not exactly been neglected, but it has not received all the scholarly attention it deserves.[1] Area specialists, along with the official Asian spokesmen, are inclined to look to culture for explanations of east Asia's performance. Others, recalling that a generation ago it was more common to adduce culture as the main explanation for east Asia's *failure* to develop, believe references to culture are confessions that the expounder has no clue about what is really going on.[2]

Yet those who accord primacy to other factors disagree about what those might be. One influential explanation has been that the east Asian states are skilled at implementing "neoliberal" policies: governments provide public services and otherwise let the market work its magic. This may apply to Hong Kong, but growth elsewhere is more plausibly explained in terms of an active, even entrepreneurial state, which shapes the economic environment in a way favorable to business interests while itself remaining immune from the more parochial or short-sighted influence of the business community or "traditional" elites. The most promising hypothesis, perhaps, is that in east Asia development is associated with *strong states* which do not themselves directly manage the economy. A strong state here is one which, whatever its policies, is able to enforce those policies it does adopt, while at the same time keeping general order in the society.

A related hypothesis is that these states tend to be "autonomous," in the sense that they are not controlled by particular social interests. An old Marxist phrase has the state as the "executive committee" of the ruling social class, the instrument whereby the ruling class—whether landlords, bourgeoisie, proletariat—enforces its interests against other social classes. Thus, in a capitalist country, the courts, the police, the army, the legislature, the executive, the regulatory agencies all serve the interests of the capitalists. In east Asia, however, the political order has instead stood on its own, shaping and even "determining" the social order. This is not always the case elsewhere, say, in southeast Asia. In Malaysia, for example, political power is mainly concentrated in one ethnic group, the Malays, while the Chinese, despite programs favoring the Malays, continue largely to dominate the economy. In the Philippines, whether in its democratic or autocratic phases, the political system tended to serve the interests of the "oligarchy" of powerful land-holding families.

I am inclined to treat this state autonomy (but not, of course, state strength) as an east Asian cultural trait. In traditional China the ruling class was produced through a system of government administered examinations, with those who passed the highest level of examinations eligible for civil service appointments. Those who passed any level of examination constituted a "gentry" granted special privileges and access to local government, and expected to perform various local leadership services. The impact of early modernizing influences in east Asia affected the political order more profoundly than the social order. Since society was structured by the political system, political decay also implied social disruption. The modernization process has centered on the re-strengthening of the state. These measures hardly guarantee economic development, but where the state is strong and autonomous, there are few effective social interests to hinder economic development. Development, then, may be fostered relatively easily where policies (which may vary) suit the interests of those in control of the state.

There is certainly some merit to the neoliberal proposition that governments may facilitate but rarely *cause* development; and given the apparent diversity of government policies, a complete explanation would have to look to the society itself. Here I would stress another cultural trait, the apparently non-modern or anti-modern patterns of particularism which remain important in east Asian society. Perhaps the most evident manifestation of this is a tendency toward pervasive political corruption; but in its non-pathological forms, particularism may foster economic development while cushioning the disruptive psychological and social consequences of rapid modernization.

East Asia and the World System

The east Asian state was challenged most directly with the region's incorporation into the world system shaped by the industrial revolution of the nineteenth century. The loose hypothesis asserted above was that development may be served by a strong, autonomous state. The two adjectives are not meant to be redundant: a strong state is an effective state, while an autonomous state is not captive of particular social interests. It was China's misfortune, in particular, to be exposed to the new world order—more bluntly, imperialism—at a time of state weakness.

In 1839 the Chinese government attempted to stop opium smuggling by British merchants. These gentlemen induced their own state (which was not autonomous in the sense used here) to go to war with China. By 1839, England was becoming an industrialized power, while the Chinese state was tending toward decay: chronic fiscal crisis, spreading corruption, and social unrest (with the endemic opium addiction also evidence of a broader social or moral crisis).

China had sometimes suffered military defeat—indeed, the imperial house from 1644 to 1911 (the Qing dynasty) was Manchu, not Chinese (that is, Han). But the Manchus were able to rule China because they adapted completely to the dominant Confucian culture. In the modern West, China met a militarily superior enemy disinclined to make any concessions to Chinese culture—determined, rather, to make China adapt to *its* ways. After the Opium War, England (and then other Western states, sometimes through war, sometimes through most-favored-nation treaties) imposed a series of "unequal treaties" on China, depriving the Chinese government of effective control over portions of its own territory and numbers of its own subjects. One consequence was a bifurcation of Chinese culture. Certain "concessions" or "treaty ports," especially Shanghai, mostly along the eastern and southern coasts, became open to Western investment and were governed by Western law, providing an alternative to the Confucian order. The treaties legalized Christian missionary activity throughout China. The missionaries set up Western-style high schools and colleges, again, mostly in the treaty ports, providing an alternative to the traditional Confucian education. On balance the exposure to the West may in fact have led to economic growth, but it was culturally and politically corrosive. Sun Yat-sen, the father of the Chinese Republic and founder of the Nationalist Party (Kuomintang or KMT) said China had become a "semi-colony," worse off than a real colony such as India: in India the British at least had to take some responsibility for the In- dians' well-being, while in China foreigners collectively enjoyed all the bene- fits of colonial overlords with none of the responsibility.

An autonomous state can promote modernization—but only if those in charge of the state want to. Even if it had had the power to do so (and the weakness of the Chinese state may make the point irrelevant anyway), the Chinese ruling elite was disinclined to pursue modernization. Modernization would have ended the power and privilege of the Confucian gentry and— narrow personal or "class" interests aside—would have required the Confu- cian gentry to embrace a system of values in many ways contrary to that which defined their entire moral outlook: the Confucian state, in principle, was about love and justice (*ren-yi*), not wealth and power (*fu-qiang*) (how- ever much love and justice translated into the wealth and power of those in charge). As Manchus, the imperial household may have been more commit- ted to a conservative Confucianism than a native Chinese dynasty might have been, in that, unable to appeal to Chinese nationalism, the Manchu rulers had little choice other than to identify themselves as the embodiments and defenders of human (that is, Chinese) culture.[3] Among the general popula- tion, the bureaucracy and the gentry at large owed their status to their com- mand of the Confucian classics. To modernize would have meant granting status, say, to soldiers, or engineers, or businessmen, or scientists, or special- ists in management. Were China to train such specialists, it would have to reward them with social status; and even were the authorities to insist that they also acquire a Confucian mentality along the way, this Confucianism would be something extraneous to their functions.

The traditional Confucian order lost prestige among younger genera- tions as those who exemplified that order proved incapable of defending the country from foreigners. Those who received a Western education came to identify more with China as a nation, and a scandalously put-upon one at that, rather than as the center of human culture, and came to identify the higher Confucian tradition as a large part of the reason for China's weakness.

The Qing dynasty collapsed, finally, in 1911, and was replaced by a republic. The republic soon became a military dictatorship, and, after the death of the dictator, fell into warlord anarchy as his various former subordinates, ensconced in provincial commands, fought with each other for control of the center. At the local level, power and social conditions probably remained much as they had been in the last decades of the Qing. In these circumstances, Western influences acquired an increasingly radical import. As a slogan of the 1910s and 1920s had it, China should get rid of the "shop of Confucius and Sons" and take its business instead to those modern Western gentlemen, Mr. Science and Mr. Democracy. A tension between traditional Chinese culture and a modern Chinese nationalism became an enduring theme of contemporary Chinese thinking on development.

In Japan modernization and tradition were much less in tension. The Japanese elite, in contrast to the Chinese, carried out an astonishingly successful program of defensive modernization partly by making constructive use of the Japanese tradition to legitimate what they were doing.

Japan had certain accidental advantages over China. Japan was poorer and so attracted less rapacious attention from foreigners. The effective chief of government (as distinct from the emperor, who enjoyed a sacred aura and, in principle, ultimate authority but exercised little if any real power) was the shogun ("general"), a hereditary office held by the head of the Tokugawa family. Tokugawa policy kept Japan isolated from the rest of the world until it was forced open in the 1850s; and the Japanese government, stronger than that of China, was able better to control the pace of events. Japan, from the sidelines, was also able to take advantage of the experience of China and India, and so better able to reflect on what an appropriate reaction to the intrusion of the new world order should be.

Japanese society was also different from China's. The political offices in the Tokugawa regime were staffed by a hereditary warrior class (*bushi* or, more popularly in the West, *samurai*). The presence of a hereditary ruling class might normally be taken to indicate a non-autonomous state, except that in Japan the hereditary practice was a deliberate policy of the state, rather than an intrinsic part of Japanese society—there had been considerable social mobility prior to the Tokugawa and, after the Tokugawa, feudal privileges were abolished with extraordinary ease. The warriors were on top of the social order, with merchants, in principle, occupying the bottom position. Yet the long Tokugawa peace created conditions conducive to internal commerce. Many merchants grew quite wealthy, and collectively the class had more influence and even prestige than its legal position would indicate. Chinese society, with status based on achievement and the expectation, in the abstract, of social mobility might seem considerably more modern in spirit than the Japanese; but the relatively archaic Japanese social structure was more propitious to modernization. In China, a rich merchant would invest in land, a more respectable and safer outlet than commerce, and then try to educate his sons for the examinations. In Japan, a merchant had no choice but to plow the profits back into the business. When Japan was finally forced out of its long isolation, it was poised for economic takeoff.

This takeoff probably could not have occurred under Tokugawa auspices, as the necessary social changes would have gone against that regime's principles of legitimation. The rapid collapse of the Tokugawa (particularly when juxtaposed against the protracted collapse of the Qing) also served Japan's interests. A new imperial reign, that of the Meiji emperor, began in 1868, and at the onset of that reign the anti-Tokugawa forces joined together to force the shogun's resignation and "restore" the power of the emperor. Those same forces, samurai from fiefdoms historically hostile to the Tokugawa family, rapidly established a modern state and a modern social system. There was no revolutionary overthrow of the old system but, rather, a coup by one coalition of the ruling class against the previously dominant coalition. The new rulers were then able to use the strong state to impose a revolution from above.

The Chinese emperor ruled by the Mandate of Heaven, as Heaven's agent in carrying out the Way. If the emperor failed in his duties, whether through personal vices, political incapacity, or extraneous circumstances, he was in danger of losing this mandate. In practice, this contingency meant that the emperor and his dynasty were most secure when they presided over a stable Confucian society (since the ethos of the gentry defined what was just and what was not). The Japanese emperor did not have any heavenly mandate. Rather, as a direct descendant of the Sun Goddess, the patroness and protectress of Japan (the "root of the sun"), he and his family were sacred in their very being. To overthrow the imperial house would be (in Western terms) not merely treason but blasphemy: there has been no dynastic change in Japan. A corollary of this was that since the emperors were, in effect, incapable of being held responsible, they had in practice been deprived of direct political power. After Japan's opening to the world, the emperor was available as a source of traditional legitimacy alternative to the existing system. The Meiji-era reformers set up what amounted to a constitutional monarchy masquerading as an absolute despotism. Real power was exercised by the government or by informal cliques. The sacred emperor, representative of the Japanese people and state, showed continuity despite radical change, his aura and authority not restricted to any particular type of social or political system.

The Japanese elite, able to keep a strong state, were soon participating in the new world order on their own terms rather than on terms set by foreigners.[4] Japan adopted a modern military system and set up an industrial base to support it. Japan's enduring pattern of state-business cooperation dates to the Meiji era. The Japanese economy would remain mainly under native rather than foreign ownership. To support modern industry Japan established a modern educational system, with compulsory primary education for both girls and boys.

The strong state was certainly no unmixed blessing. State intervention in the economy may sometimes be advantageous in developing countries, but it may come at the cost of liberty. The Japanese state was strong enough to allow the ruling elites to ignore social problems they should have faced and social movements they should have attempted to co-opt. By the 1920s the Japanese political system was evolving toward a parliamentary democracy. At the same time there was growing resentment among workers for having to labor in wretched conditions and among poor peasants for having to bear the costs of modernization while receiving none of the benefits. British conservatives a half century earlier met similar problems by addressing the interests of the poor. Japanese conservatives, ruling a stronger state, had the luxury of being able instead to pass legislation to allow the police to repress the expressions of the discontent.

Nor was Japan's modernization entirely without cultural stress. As Japan's economy developed there were inevitably those who wondered whether the country had not lost its soul. There were more objections, of course, to the non-material consequences of modernization—liberalism, socialism, democracy, modish new notions of the proper relations between the generations and the sexes—than, say, to airplanes, radios, or tanks. The Great Depression hit Japan hard and the atmosphere turned against Western influences. The new sentiment was articulated by small cliques of radical right-wing nationalists, some of them in the army. Japan gradually came under military domination, ruled as a police state on the basis of the repressive legislation adopted during the previous decade. The extreme nationalist leadership took the country into war and destruction.

Far from being a victim of imperialism, Japan was a major perpetrator. In 1895 Japan acquired its first colony, the Chinese province of Taiwan. Taiwan previously had been something of a frontier area, part of the Chinese empire but not well-incorporated into it, while at the same time rather well-developed commercially. Taiwan continued to prosper under Japanese control, with the economy geared toward producing fruit and other foodstuffs for Japan. The Taiwanese were never exactly overjoyed to be under Japanese rule; they put up stiff resistance at first and later there were sporadic outbreaks of Chinese nationalism. But overall they adapted to the situation relatively well.

Korea became Japan's more important colony. In 1895 Japan destroyed Chinese influence in Korea and eliminated that of Russia in 1905. In 1910 Japan took Korea as a colony. When growingly outspoken Korean nationalists resisted, Japan responded brutally. By the mid-1930s Japanese policy was directed toward wiping out traditional Korean culture, with Koreans being forced to take Japanese names and forbidden education in the Korean language. Development, as in Taiwan, was directed toward Japanese interests, with the colonial experience remaining much more bitter for Koreans than it seems to be for Taiwanese.

Vietnam, in the meantime, had come under French domination. At various times during its history Vietnam had been occupied by the Chinese. As in Korea, elite culture and even much of folk culture were taken from China. The Vietnamese political system was a replica of China's. But unlike other southern peoples the Vietnamese were not absorbed permanently into the Chinese state, and China to this day remains the "hereditary enemy."

Proto-nationalism honed in conflict with China blossomed under French hegemony, even among those who attempted to assimilate themselves into French culture. The style of French rule encouraged a chronic sense of dissatisfaction. French imperialism in Vietnam may have been marginally less brutal than that of the Japanese in Korea, but it was similar in style. Both colonial overlords attempted to foster cultural assimilation. Both encouraged industry and commercial agriculture, eroding the basis of the traditional communities. In both Korea and Vietnam even the lower ranks of the colonial civil service, and, for that matter, even relatively menial jobs, were held by nationals of the mother country, at, of course, higher pay than could be commanded by the locals.

France was itself a liberal state, and in Vietnam there was somewhat more opportunity for political and cultural expression than in Korea. The Vietnamese, with their baguettes and café au lait for breakfast, may also carry less resentment of their former masters than do the Koreans. Since Vietnam was under foreign control, by foreigners who tended to have a rather exalted view of their own culture, patriotic Vietnamese could appeal to the Vietnamese tradition (in contrast to Chinese nationalists, who tended to see their traditional heritage as a source of backwardness). The French, for their part, did not extend their toleration of opposition to active resistance. By about the time of the outbreak of the Second World War, French repression was thorough and tough enough to stifle overt or organized nationalist resistance in Vietnam by all except the communist movement.

East Asian Ways of Development

After the collapse of the Qing, China devolved into warlord anarchy. From 1926 to 1929 military forces organized by the KMT, led by Chiang Kai-shek, established a superficial semblance of unified rule. Chiang also defeated, without annihilating, the armed forces of the Communist Party of China (CPC), his one-time allies against the warlords. China did begin to make considerable progress in economic and political development, but this came undone after 1937, when Japan invaded in full force. The KMT and CPC again joined together, now to fight Japan. Once the conflict reached stalemate, they spent more energy preparing for the showdown against each other. Civil war broke out after Japan's surrender, and the Nationalist forces disintegrated with surprising speed. On October 1, 1949, the communist leader Mao Zedong proclaimed the founding of the People's Republic of China, while Chiang Kai-shek retreated with the remnants of his following to Taiwan, which had returned to Chinese control after the war. For the first time since the fall of the empire, the Chinese mainland had a strong, effective central state.

Both the Nationalist and Communist parties were initially products of that part of China most connected with the world system. The KMT leadership came mainly from southern China and the areas around Shanghai, those regions most exposed to the world economy. The KMT was perhaps too modern in composition and outlook to gain control over China's "traditional" society (and in those areas where it made alliances with the traditional forces, it became perhaps too linked to the local structures of wealth and power). The KMT had some appeal to modern-minded Chinese, at least until it bogged down in corruption, sloth, and incompetence, but had difficulty attracting a mass base. Chiang Kai-shek's attempts to monopolize political power alienated liberal opinion. Given China's internal divisions, its weak state, and the Japanese invasion there was no time during which Chiang could reasonably have been expected to loosen up, and perhaps educated public opinion might have been more understanding had there been more of a show of an attempt to do a good job. Especially after World War II, the KMT tended to govern through police-state methods but without police-state effectiveness.

The CPC had been founded in the treaty port of Shanghai, with the help of Comintern agents, by modern-minded young Chinese intellectuals. The KMT, however, eventually destroyed the Party organization in the modern cities, and the Party survived by shifting its base to the countryside, building up military power and gaining local political control by appealing to peasant discontent. In its early years the Party had been under the Soviet Union's supervision. After 1935, however, Mao Zedong, one of the Party's more successful peasant organizers, began to consolidate his leadership. He was not exactly opposed by the Soviet Union, but neither did the Soviets help him; and his rivals included communists trained in Moscow. During the war against Japan the CPC supplemented its social appeal with Chinese patriotism. Mao and his publicists touted Mao's "Thought" as the application of the "universal truths" of Marxism-Leninism to China's special circumstances. The communist victory in 1949 seemed like a nice solution to China's cultural contradictions—a modern-minded elite had been able to win the support of the traditional society.

Yet in the early years of the People's Republic, China did not adopt an "indigenous" path of development but followed instead the Soviet model, based upon state ownership of industry and collective agriculture. China broke away from dependence upon the world economy, partly to end "imperialist" leverage over the country, and partly because, given American sanctions imposed at the time of the Korean war, China had little choice. This method had perhaps been successful for a time in Russia, despite its brutal human costs. It was not as effective in China, where the economic base was much lower and the agricultural sector more important.

As economic growth slowed in the mid-1950s, Mao proposed modifications of the Soviet model, asserting China should find its own path. In 1958 the Chinese elite embarked on the Great Leap Forward, requiring the total political mobilization of the people, instilling in the population a selfless enthusiasm for the socialist enterprise (as it was called), and repudiating all personal desires or claims. In its early stages the Leap entailed the complete collectivization of agriculture. Because overly rigid plans were thought to stifle the enthusiasm of the masses, much of the central planning system was broken up and its functions devolved to the local level. The economy remained politicized, so market forces played no part; production and distribution were controlled, not by the central state, but by local party organizations. By the end of 1960 China was caught in perhaps the most severe famine in its long history, and the Leap had obviously failed.

The Party establishment undertook to modify Leap policies, and in the early 1960s China slowly recovered. The problem was, however, that Mao had become so personally committed to the Leap that an overt and systematic repudiation of it would seem a repudiation of his leadership. At the same time, everyone, including, certainly, Mao himself, knew that the policies would not work. The inherent tension led to the disruption and terror of the Great Proletarian Cultural Revolution in 1966.

A guiding slogan of both the Leap and the Cultural Revolution was that politics (not economics) takes command. Politics in this context meant "class struggle," the relentless persecution of those defined as enemies of the proletariat. During the Cultural Revolution ideological correctness came to imply even a kind of hostility toward economic development: increased prosperity, it was urged, would take the edge off class struggle and would be a symptom of a return to capitalism.

All of this development was "indigenous" enough, if only in the sense that it was imposed upon the Chinese people by a Chinese regime acting for Chinese reasons. It had little connection, however, with any Chinese tradition, except, perhaps, for a certain affinity with earlier anti-Confucian millenarian movements; nor did it have much to do with the country's real needs and capabilities.

After the end of World War II until the 1980s, Japan grew to become the second largest economy in the world. China's development was influenced by communist ideology, whereas Japan's did in fact reflect more traditional cultural patterns. Japan, unlike People's China, was incorporated into the world economy—even one-sidedly so, on its own terms. It was also protected, to the extent it needed protection, by its security relationship with the United States. The Japanese pattern was hardly liberal. Japanese business counted on easy access to the broader world economy for exports and investment, while remaining relatively immune from foreign competition at home. Japanese business continued to accept guidance from the professional civil service—with government taking as its central mission the promotion of Japanese prosperity, and the promotion of Japanese business abroad as a means to this end. Business and bureaucracy were closely connected to the Liberal Democratic Party (despite its name, a conservative organization), which held a majority in Japan's Diet (parliament) from its founding in 1955 to 1993 and which, after a brief interruption, continued to dominate the political leadership. Business accepted bureaucratic guidance and financed the LDP; the bureaucracy fostered business interests; and the LDP-controlled Diet passed laws desired by bureaucracy and business.

Although Japan has been Asia's only long-term stable democracy, it was hardly, even after the breakup of the LDP in 1993, a *competitive* democracy. The LDP kept power not because its principles or vision had great appeal but because the party was able to indulge strategic social sectors (such as agriculture) and because the individual Diet representatives, acting more on their own than as agents of the party, were adept at constituency service. The Japanese economy was structured more to keep the LDP in power than to assure economic efficiency.[5] In strict neoliberal logic, for example, Japanese agriculture should perhaps have folded, with Japan importing its food. But farmers voted for the LDP and the LDP, in turn, protected Japanese agriculture. LDP policy fostered neighborhood stores and other small businesses, as the proprietors and their families tended to vote conservative. Japan's success was paid for by the Japanese consumer: the standard of living remained lower than might be expected in an economy of Japan's size, and the cost of living was very high. At the same time, however, it is fair to say that the Japan produced by LDP rule reflected genuine cultural biases. To put it in neoliberal terms, the social gains from such policies were held to be worth the costs.[6] Although Japan was a democratic country, the LDP's monopoly over the government permitted it to act as if it were "bureaucratic authoritarian": in the formulation of policy there was plenty of consultation among the various agencies involved and with the interests that would be directly affected, and a certain amount of consideration for just how much the public would stand, but not much need to worry about effective broad-based popular opposition to the policies adopted by "Japan, Inc."

Business style also reflected traditional influence. Much of what is known as the Japanese management style seems to be of postwar origin, and may even reflect the influence of occupation-era American management specialists, their ideas having gotten a warmer reception in Japan than at home. The style is consonant with broader cultural patterns, on its face going against what are supposed to be the prescriptions of classical economics. These practices are probably more effective in Japan than any attempts to apply them elsewhere.[7] The system of lifetime employment ties the worker to a single company and inhibits labor mobility, but also creates a sense of mutual obligation and interest among employees and between employees and employers. The organization of firms into the *keiretsu* (interlinked sets of companies engaged in different kinds of enterprise) assures supplies of materials and outlets of products regardless of market conditions, and the ability of firms to borrow from banks in the *keiretsu* keeps interest rates low. In classical economics firms are expected to maximize profits, but Japanese firms are said instead to maximize market share. Japanese firms are excellent at tactical adaptation although, despite their long-range perspective on profits, not necessarily good at strategic planning, and are limited in their ability to rethink a systematically deficient program of action—the kind of limitation that produced the Pearl Harbor attack: the brilliant implementation of a fundamentally flawed design.

In some of its more interesting aspects the Japanese system functions almost as a reverse image of how modern society is supposed to work. Modern society is thought to be impersonal, centered on voluntary, contractual relationships, with no person having power over another except as defined by law, and decisions made according to either law or the cold operation of the market. In contrast, the Japanese system reproduces the dynamics of the traditional society, maintaining social control through the working of reciprocal duties, obligations, and benefits among well-defined superiors and inferiors, with relations among firms in the system functioning in ways analogous to relations among connected persons. The system works (when it does) because persons feel responsibility toward those they stand in direct relationship to, or, if they do not *feel* this responsibility, find they have no way to escape it. Politicians support the faction leader because of his position, not necessarily from any policy or ideological agreement with him, just as you might support your dad simply because he is your dad. You will buy from the neighborhood store even if you can get a better price elsewhere, because the proprietor is a neighbor (and because he will make allowances should you become temporarily unable to pay). A firm will buy from the supplier in the *keiretsu* because the supplier is part of the group.

Asia's tiger economies (Taiwan, South Korea, Hong Kong, and Singapore) were, like Japan, part of the U.S. security system (South Korea and, until 1979, Taiwan explicitly so, Hong Kong and Singapore implicitly and "functionally"). They were also part of Japan's general economic sphere. The tigers profited from their incorporation into the America-centered world economy, most directly from the spending required for the conduct of America's Asian wars. Hong Kong and Singapore, given their size and geography, could thrive only if they were trading ports, whatever else they might be. Taiwan and South Korea received American aid during the early Cold War years, although economic aid to both was terminated in 1965 on the pretext that they no longer needed it. When the Taiwanese and South Korean governments began encouraging exports to replace the foreign exchange given in aid, their economies really began to take off. As in Japan, export promotion supplemented rather than replaced import substitution since eagerness to sell abroad was not matched by an equal enthusiasm among consumers to buy locally produced goods. While the economic policies in South Korea and Taiwan resembled those of Japan, there were interesting differences as well. One plausible element in Japan's postwar growth is low military spending, freeing money and talent for the civilian sector, but Taiwan and South Korea have grown rapidly despite huge, even exorbitant, military budgets.

The South Korean economy, like the Japanese, centers on relatively few large combinations of firms. In Taiwan and Hong Kong the more dynamic economic actors are small firms, usually family-owned and interlocked with other family firms. Hong Kong was virtually completely open to foreign investment (and is supposed to remain so under Chinese rule), and Taiwan also encouraged investment from abroad, particularly from overseas Chinese. The Korean government has preferred to finance investment through foreign borrowing, building up a burden of debt it found difficult to carry by the late 1990s.

Early in the postwar period the tigers, like Japan, resolved through land reform the problems of rural poverty and potential peasant discontent (questions by their nature, of course, not particularly relevant to Hong Kong and Singapore). The state helped develop the rural infrastructure, bringing in roads, health care, elementary education, clean water. Over time the agricultural sectors became less internationally competitive, prompting nearly all rural families to find ways of supplementing their income from farming. Governments nonetheless continued to attempt to protect agriculture, partly because, as in Japan, the peasantry more often than not gave conservative support to the existing political order.

Those who study development disagree on whether land reform in itself contributes to development. The larger point, however, may be that land reform reinforces state strength and autonomy by eliminating a potentially powerful landlord class, a class whose position would not be furthered by rapid growth. The capacity of state elites to foster growth unhindered by social interests does not mean that they will in fact do so, but during the Cold War the tiger governments had every reason, for the sake of their own survival, to follow this policy.

With the post-Mao economic reforms, China became part of the east Asian economic boom. Some contemporary theorists of the reform in China, namely the neoauthoritarian and neoconservative schools, were directly influenced by the tigers, taking them to exemplify the benefits of economic liberalization in the context of tight political control. By the time Mao died China was ready for a radical change of policy, with both people and rulers weary of endless political campaigns and economic stagnation. The consolidation of the power of Deng Xiaoping, who was historically a political hardliner but a pragmatist on economic issues, meant a turn toward a market economy. The mainland takeoff in the reform period, like that of Taiwan earlier, began with land reform. The rural reforms generated a food surplus available for both consumption and investment. Later reform of the state-owned industrial sector was not as successful, but in the meantime China developed an economy based upon numerous small firms, particularly in the countryside and rural townships. The reform also included "opening" to the world economy, in the hope of attracting foreign investment, advanced technology, and markets for exports.

There was the question from the beginning of how much a liberal economic system could coexist with an autocratic polity; yet South Korea and Taiwan managed this for decades. The deeper issue was which type of autocracy. Carried to their logical end, the reforms required the separation of the economic from the political sector, and this would have rendered many of the functions of the Communist Party unnecessary and also revealed too bluntly the irrelevance of its ruling ideology. The great crisis of 1989, the student-led democracy movement and its brutal suppression, is evidence that the reform from within had gone as far as it could without a change in the system itself.

But there was no returning to the old path, either. In the aftermath of the suppression the party hard-liners, worried by the political, cultural, and social consequences of reform, attempted to reassert administrative controls over economic activity. Deng Xiaoping, himself somewhat in eclipse, was blamed by the hard-liners explicitly for creating the conditions which led to the unrest and tacitly for the brutality of its suppression, reasserted himself in the spring of 1992. By means of a well-publicized tour of the boom areas of southern China, he personally appealed over the heads of the party leadership for even more radical economic (but not political) reform. After Deng's southern tour (*nan xun*—the term used to be applied to imperial visits to that region) Chinese economic policy moved unequivocally toward building a "socialist market economy." Deng sharply and irascibly asserted that the market and all the reforms were inherently socialist. Socialism did not necessarily mean central planning and public ownership; rather, socialism was anything that contributed to the development of the economy. This became Deng's "theory of socialism with Chinese characteristics."

In the 1990s, China grew faster than any other country. Some Chinese scholars abroad, however, find the mainland economy more to approximate a

Latin American model than an east Asian one. The argument is that the mainland now is, surprisingly, ruled by a weak state which needs to make concessions to the dominant elites, in this case the cadres of the party-state apparatus, increasingly in alliance with a newly rich capitalist class which depends for its wealth on its connections with the party-state. Those in political positions and with political connections were well-placed to take advantages of the new opportunities for making money. Even the small rural and "township" industries depend upon the state, in that local governments may help finance them—or, more perniciously, refrain from harassing them—in return for a cut of the take. Economic decentralization makes local leaders, with their sources of income from local taxes, profits, or graft, less under the control of the central authorities than they had been. The center is less able than in the past to stultify local initiative, but also less able to control irrational local expenditures or check the rapacity of local tyrants. In Chinese conditions, the personalistic connections which prevail in other east Asian societies also contribute to economic growth, but take an inevitably corrupt coloration.

The tiger economies and Japan are known for state guidance of economic growth, and also have more than their share of corruption. There is, however, a clear separation of official from non-official functions and positions. In China the state and economy remain highly interpenetrated. Chinese neo-conservatives speak of a "rent-seeking state": that is, while the state may not be particularly good at performing what might be considered its normal functions (enforcing agreements, punishing criminals, providing basic public services), its functionaries are quite skilled at extracting revenue from the economic sector without themselves contributing to productivity. The failure to separate economics and politics is exacerbated by the lack of a developed legal system and the unchallenged dominance of the Communist Party. The rent-seeking state is obviously compatible with economic growth—given the dominance of the Communist Party, it may even be the price society has to pay for growth—but maybe not with long-term stability.

Vietnam and North Korea, like China, remained communist. In Vietnam the victors in the long civil war which ended in 1975 imposed typical communist policies—collectivized agriculture, expropriation of private business. Hardly recovered from its American war, Vietnam became bogged down in conflicts with Cambodia and China, while keeping the hostility of the United States and Thailand. It remained impoverished and dependent upon the Soviet Union. By the mid-1980s the USSR was having its own problems and was also again eager to make friends with China. The changing international situation reinforced the Vietnamese rulers' decision to embrace reform and by the 1990s Vietnam may have been developing into a tiger-type economy fashioned after the Chinese south. The Vietnamese reforms also seemed to have many of the same social and cultural consequences as the Chinese, although by the mid-1990s the effects on legitimacy had not become as traumatic as in China.

North Korea remained in a Stalinist rut. That part of the country had prospered more in the 1950s than the South, but subsequently the regime impoverished itself through decades of extreme "self-reliance" (*Juche*). After the death of the dictator Kim Il Sung in 1994 the true locus of political authority remained obscure: presumably it was with Kim's son and designated successor, Chong Il, but the army high command may have held at least a general veto over policy. By 1996, after two years of natural disasters exacerbated by bad policy, there were reports of famine in the North (although the closed nature of the society made it difficult to know just how extensive this was). As the economy deteriorated the North remained given to random acts of international provocation, such as deliberately creating the impression that it was developing nuclear weapons or conducting commando raids against the South. Such behavior was probably marginally rational, in that it did allow the regime to coerce international respect that it had otherwise lost: America, for example, could not but take a reckless North Korea seriously. There were timid moves toward economic reform, but there was also fear in the South especially that it was too late: the northern regime may have been heading for collapse and, who knew, might be tempted, with its military capacities, to take the South along with it; and even without war, the South at best could have only mixed feelings about attempting to reabsorb the North, whose economic situation seemed many times worse than that of East Germany at the time of the destruction of the Berlin Wall.

Since the Cold War

In east Asia the end of the Cold War reinforced trends already evident. The east Asian experience may itself have had a role in the end of the Cold War, in that the prosperity of the conservative Asian states and the Chinese reforms made it difficult to take ideological communism seriously.

The fall of the Soviet Union encouraged Asian states to distance themselves a little from the United States: the elimination of a common threat exposed more clearly differences over trade and, more deeply, over culture. Until the last years of the Cold War America looked on Asian prosperity as a force against communism, and in the early Cold War was willing to suffer minor economic disadvantages to serve the larger political goals. With the relative decline of American economic supremacy and the end of communist power, these priorities changed.

Economic policy in east Asia since the end of the Cold War may have become marginally more "neoliberal" than before. In part, this is a result of American hectoring; in part it has to do with the greater international presence of Japanese and tiger economy firms: with their own commitments abroad, they had less of a narrow interest in protection at home. A more profound transformation, however, may be the increasingly articulate resentment of what were taken to be America's attempts to foist is own political culture on everyone else, a resentment felt both among elites and public opinion generally.

Around the mid-1980s public opinion, even in the communist countries (although with North Korea, who knows?) tended to be friendly toward the United States, American power, and the American way. This began to change toward the end of the decade, the main occasion being trade disputes. The United States, facing huge budget and balance of payments deficits and protectionist pressures from threatened industries, couched the argument in terms of a level playing field. Asian spokesmen (most articulately, the Japanese) came to show an increasing tendency to trace their problems with the United States not to anything that their own countries did, but to the deficiencies of American culture: Americans had become unproductive spendthrifts unable to keep even minimal order in their own society but still given to ignorant and arrogant pronouncements about how everyone else should live.[8]

East Asia participated in the late-Cold War, worldwide tendency toward democratization. Americans tended to see the spread of democracy as one more vindication of the American way, and American policy sometimes fostered the process—directly in the Philippines, less directly in South Korea, tacitly on Taiwan. Asian democratization, however, did not necessarily feed admiration for America, but coincided with a growing popular anti-Americanism. Some of this derives from specific past incidents (such as the supposed American complicity in the 1980 Kwangju massacre in Korea), and much of it is fed by the presence of American troops. The perception of American high-handedness in trade negotiations also contributed to anti-American sentiment. Even democrats who might welcome American support against local tyrants could be ambivalent about their own government's vulnerability to U.S. pressure.

The Chinese case is especially complicated. The opening to the outside made totalitarian thought control an even less realistic goal than before, and access to capital and technology from abroad brought with it cultural influences deemed insalubrious by the country's rulers.[9] In the years following 1989 this was generically grouped as "pornography," the term ranging from the real stuff to thoughtless adolescent hedonism to liberal political attitudes to Western religious belief. The Chinese regime spoke of a deeply laid

American plot to bring about the country's "peaceful evolution" toward capitalism; but while the Chinese democrats of 1989 often voiced their demands in a political idiom influenced by the American example (the "Goddess of Democracy" as a variation on the Statue of Liberty), they came to their opinions more through daily experience of an intrusive dictatorship than from any abstract study of Western liberalism or political institutions.

The popular enthusiasm for America cooled during the early 1990s. The economic boom which resumed in 1992 did not lead to greater admiration for the current rulers, but it nourished Chinese patriotism and pride in country and bred resentment against American actions hostile to China, even actions advocated by the democrats of 1989. A turning point may have been in 1993, when Sidney was chosen over Beijing as the site of the Year 2000 Olympics. In the course of the discussion, the U.S. Congress had passed a resolution (with no legal weight whatsoever) that China, with its dismal human rights record, did not deserve such an honor. Whether fairly or not, the Chinese government and public both blamed the United States for the Olympic committee's ultimate decision, which both government and public, fairly or not, treated as a deliberate humiliation. The aware Chinese public, perhaps surprisingly, also resented America's tacit intervention in favor of Taiwan during the 1996 crisis, when China, hoping to intimidate the Taiwan public, fired test rockets over the Taiwan straits and the United States sent two aircraft carrier groups to "observe" the exercise. The American action was interpreted not as a defense of democracy but as arrogant imperialistic intervention in China's domestic affairs.[10] In 1996 *The China That Can Say No*, a not very competent and perhaps not entirely serious anti-American diatribe in imitation of the earlier Japanese attempt, became a best-seller in China.[11]

Much of the Chinese criticism of America strikes a chord in countries traditionally friendly to the United States. In 1993 a caucus of Asian states meeting in Bangkok prior to a general human rights conference asserted that the "Western" interpretations of human rights have no universal validity, that human rights vary according to culture, history, and level of economic development, and each country (political regime, in practice) must resolve its own problems in its own way. This pronouncement was accepted by all attending except for Japan and the Philippines. Certain Asian analysts have taken to pointing out that America, with its racial discrimination, its crime rate, its deplorable educational system, its divorce rate, its sexual promiscuity, its improvident ways, its narcotics epidemic, is not necessarily qualified to set itself as the model for the world.

Toward the end of the Cold War Francis Fukuyama published his famous essay on the "end of history,"[12] history culminating in the victory of liberal democracy. This looks like a revival of a theme from American academic modernization theory of the 1950s and early 1960s, that the world was moving toward a "world culture of modernity," conforming suspiciously to the tastes of late-twentieth-century-vintage American liberals.[13] It is, in fact, impossible to deny the way in which modern Western influences have permeated daily life in all parts of the world, and difficult to deny that much of the Asian criticism of this is born of "*ressentiment.*" But it is also less evident now, given east Asia's economic and social successes, that modern Western culture is in fact normative for everyone, or that all of its precepts are unquestionably rational and valid.

An Asian Model?

The notion of an Asian model of development is certainly ideological, but so, too, is much of the American perception of the world. Some Chinese commentators have "constructed" what they take to be the inner logic of post-Cold War American ideology, combining Fukuyama's end of history with Samuel Huntington's equally famous "clash of civilizations."[14] At first blush, this seems an unlikely compound, for in part Huntington's essay was an explicit rebuttal of Fukuyama. The Chinese interpretation, however, takes Fukuyama and Huntington less as expounders of the way things really are than as ideologues developing a rationale for American cultural (and perhaps other) aggression. In this purported American ideology (analyzed in a way eerily similar to certain older conservative interpretations of communist ambitions), the Americans are said to think their way is destined to universal triumph; on the other hand, the other "civilizations" refuse to accept their fate, however, and so "clash" with the Americans—justifying a hostile attitude by the United States toward those not willing to accept its example and leadership. The appropriate "Asian" reaction, then, is to see clearly the weaknesses of American pretensions and guard their own integrity. Anti-Americanism, of course, is nothing new; but in post-Cold War east Asia, even in communist China, it tends to be conservative and traditionalistic, rather than radical.

Objectively, there is certainly no single "Asian" model of development, even if, as in this essay, we confine ourselves to the post-Confucian societies. If the east Asian states do share a common trait, it may be more cultural than economic or political. In the "Asian values" arguments there is often a contrast made between Western individualism and Asian collectivism, and allowing for the simplifications this contrast contains some truth. The social pressures in east Asia militate against the kind of individualism characteristic, if not of "the West" as a whole, at least the United States. "Collectivism," however, is an overly broad term for the alternative, and Confucianism may be helpful in understanding just what the operating ethos is.

As a complement to the strong, autonomous state, east Asian societies tend to have a weak "civil society": there are few effective and powerful secondary groupings autonomous from the state and able to make demands upon the state.[15] This helps explain how, despite a general affirmation of democratic principles among both the public and elites, these societies remained autocracies for so long; and it also helps explain the particular features of east Asian democracy when it does take hold. On the other hand, primary ties in these societies have remained strong during modernization, and more socially and politically relevant than in the post-industrial West.

The classical modernization paradigm, whether elaborated by Karl Marx, Max Weber, Talcott Parsons, or the political scientists formerly funded by the Social Science Research Council, identifies modernization with the replacement, for purposes of public life, of personal ties based upon sentiment or custom with contractual relationships based upon instrumental rationality, objective criteria based on merit, operating according to impersonal rules which treat everyone alike. This may be valid as far as it goes, although even in American society we still hear of the importance of "connections." There have certainly been pressures toward impersonal rationality in the east Asian societies (and, for that matter, there were attempts to incorporate such pressures into the structures of the pre-modern states), but in many respects the modernization of the region has taken a different path.

Confucian ethics are explicitly and rationally personalistic. In the Chinese tradition there is precedent for the modern Western vision of human relations in the Mohist and Legalist schools, ancient systems of thought which have found favor among many contemporary Chinese who aspire to the more conventional vision of modernity. Mohism advocated universal love on largely utilitarian grounds, giving it something of a Puritanical flavor (similar, perhaps, to the kind of Protestantism Max Weber thought propitious for modernity). Legalism is best known for its advocacy of despotism and harsh punishments. As a system of political science it recommends rule through law, clearly stipulated, equally applied, energetically enforced; merit should be rewarded and shortcomings punished, and the standard of merit should be performance, particularly performance beneficial to the state. From the Confucian perspective, both Mohism and Legalism were repudiations of justice. Abstract laws which take no account of particular circumstances operate unfairly. Universal love is overly abstract—love for everyone in general and no one in particular. In the Confucian view, we learn to love in the context of particular human relationships, especially those of the family, and greater love grows from these relationships: Mohist love lacks roots.

Explicit Confucian philosophy may be making a comeback, but it has been out of fashion among educated east Asians for most of the twentieth century. The practical implications of Confucian ethics remained a part of the fabric of society, however. In the West, the growing influence of impersonal forces—technology, the market, bureaucracy—was (with many misgivings) regarded as part of the development of liberty, the freedom of the individual from the arbitrary power of other individuals. No classical liberal theorist explicitly praised rootless, detached, affectless, isolated individualism as a desirable human condition, but this may be a tendency in "actually existing" liberal society, particularly in its post-industrial or post-modern phase.

In east Asia, "society" (to continue in this mode of shameless reification), operating through the family and other primary groups, provides support for the individual in the midst of radical changes in material ways of life while at the same time holding the individual accountable to standards set by society. Whatever generalizations we make about collectivism and individualism, there may be a more refined sense of individual responsibility in east Asian society than in the more litigious regions of the West, as well, for better or worse, as greater toleration for the petty injustices dealt by life—as a consequence of the informal pressures groups are able to place upon the individual.

The east Asian pattern should certainly not be idealized. The claim is certainly not that east Asians are more virtuous than Westerners: rather, they are under greater social constraint to behave in a virtuous way.[16] The pattern as a whole perhaps suits the old, the male, and the comfortable, and can be repressive of those not sharing those traits. In politics, personal connections contribute to unprincipled factionalism and to corruption. As a cultural pattern it cannot be duplicated in detail elsewhere, and if it could many would not choose to do so. Yet the east Asian case presents an alternative to the dominant modernization paradigm, one reflecting genuine human achievement and a set of values not entirely contemptible.

Endnotes

1. For various insights, see, among many other works, Ezra Vogel, *Japan as Number One: Lessons for America* (Cambridge, MA: Harvard University Press, 1970); Kent Calder and Roy Hofheinz, *The Eastasia Edge* (New York, 1982); Stephen Haggard, *Pathways from the Periphery: The Politics of Growth in the Newly Industrialized Countries* (Ithaca, NY: Cornell University Press, 1990); Chalmers Johnson, *MITI and the Japanese Miracle: The Growth of Industrial Policy, 1925–1975* (Stanford, CA: Stanford University Press, 1982); Peter Evans, *Embedded Autonomy: States and Industrial Transformation* (Princeton, NJ: Princeton University Press, 1995). For an interesting survey and critique of various scholarly approaches, see Robert Wade, "East Asia's Economic Success: Conflicting Perspectives, Partial Insights, Shaky Evidence," *World Politics* 44, no. 2 (Jan. 1992): 270–320.

2. For example, it is fairly common now to identify Confucianism or some variation of it as a functional alternative to Max Weber's "Protestant ethic," supposedly a major factor in Western modernization. Weber himself, however, long ago attempted to test that hypothesis, and concluded

that is precisely what Confucianism was not. *The Religion of China* (New York: Free Press, 1951). To the extent that east Asian societies had modernized, prior to the 1980s it was more usual to use that progress as an indication of how much they had left behind their traditional cultures.

3. That being said, it is worth remembering that at least one emperor, the "next-to-last" one, was personally strongly committed to a program of radical reform—and was kept under house arrest for the last decade and more of his life in part to prevent him from acting on this program.

4. On state strength as the main difference between China and Japan at the time of their incorporation into the world economy, see Frances V. Moulder, *Japan, China and the Modern World Economy: Toward a Reinterpretation of East Asian Development ca. 1600–ca. 1918* (New York: Cambridge University Press, 1977).

5. Chalmers Johnson, *MITI and the Japanese Miracle: The Growth of Industrial Policy, 1925–1975* (Stanford, CA: Stanford University Press, 1982). For an update and revision, see also Chalmers Johnson, *Japan: Who Governs? The Rise of the Developmental State* (New York: Norton, 1995).

6. Such attitudes are hardly peculiar to Japan. Compare the hostility in certain smaller American towns to the intrusion of Wal-Mart, Meijer, or other superstores. In Japan, however, state policy reinforces the more conservative cultural preferences, while in America state policy generally does not.

7. Compare, for example, Laurie Graham, *On the Line at Subaru-Isuzu: The Japanese Model and the American Worker* (Ithaca, NY: Cornell University Press, 1995).

8. Perhaps the most famous example is Ishihara Shintaro, *The Japan that Can Say No* (New York: Simon and Schuster, 1991). Similar points were even raised, slightly more politely, by Japanese negotiators in the structural impediments talks of the late 1980s and early 1990s.

9. There was a greater influence on popular culture, though, from the other east Asian societies than from the West in general or the United States in particular. In 1989, especially, rock music came to be identified with political dissent, but I think it remains for most Chinese (of all ages) a somewhat exotic curiosity. Popular music seems to be a variation on the Japanese adaptations of pre-rock-and-roll Western popular music, in China's case filtered through Taiwan and Hong Kong adaptations. The more popular Western singers are those whose style most approximates the modern east Asian taste: John Denver, for example, or Simon and Garfunkel.

10. One Chinese student in America, of impeccably democratic sentiments, found herself surprised to discover how "patriotic" deep down she really

was. Ordinary Chinese perhaps readily see why the Taiwanese compatriots may not be too eager to unite with the crowd currently in control in Beijing, but still do not want to eliminate the possibility of eventual unification; nor do they want other countries meddling in the affair.

11. Chinese patriotism, however, is an ambivalent thing. In the twentieth century, popular attacks on Japan have often been ways of criticizing the Chinese government for being so cowardly in the face of powerful foreigners while being so brutal to the people under its rule. A recent example is the criticism, by the people in Hong Kong of all places, of the supposed failure of Beijing to stand up to Japan in 1996 on the claim to the Diaoyutai islands in the East China Sea. The general message was that Beijing has no business saying the people of Hong Kong are not good patriots simply because they do not want to be ruled by the People's Republic, and the rulers in Beijing themselves are afraid to defend the country's interests.

12. For the developed version, see Francis Fukuyama, *The End of History and the Last Man* (New York: Maxwell Macmillan International, 1992).

13. For a useful epitome, see Lucian Pye, *Aspects of Political Development* (Boston: Little, Brown, 1963).

14. Samuel P. Huntington, "The Clash of Civilizations?" *Foreign Affairs* (Summer 1993): 22–49.

15. Japan, of course, has well-developed interest groups, but these tend to operate in a corporativist rather than pluralist manner, in cooperation with the state rather than as independent influences upon it. Hong Kong, as it changes from colony to Special Administrative Region, also seems interesting, as the new governing authority seems eager to court the favor of the most wealthy businessmen, while they in their turn are anxious to place themselves on the side of the new order. The example, I think, would repay further study.

16. Although Confucian societies have a deserved reputation for courtesy, public manners (waiting your turn in line, obeying traffic regulations, saying please and thank you while transacting business with strangers, not throwing trash all over the place) are, I think, better developed in the United States than in at least the Chinese-type societies.

3
—

India: A Challenge to Western Theories of Development

—A. H. Somjee

A. H. Somjee is professor emeritus at Simon Fraser University in Canada and has been an associate fellow of Queen Elizabeth House, Oxford. His published works include Political Capacity in Developing Societies, Parallels and Actuals of Political Development, Development Theory: Critiques and Explorations, *and (with G. Somjee)* Development Success in Asia Pacific.

Introduction

India, the world's largest democracy, happens paradoxically to be non-Western. And its democratic and development experience in the half century since it achieved independence has posed far-reaching implications for theory construction which cannot be ignored. The existing corpus of theoretical knowledge, both in democratic and development theory, tends to treat India's experience as an *exception*, irrelevant to other non-Western societies. Such a body of knowledge continues to treat the corresponding Western experience and its theoretical implications as *archetypal*, with little or no need to take seriously the experiences of other regions, both in the field of democracy and development.[1]

In a sense such an attitude was the product of an era of economic and intellectual dominance by the Western world and of the Cold War compulsion for closing ranks against variations in the Western model of democracy and development. Half a century of the Cold War nevertheless generated enough historical and empirical knowledge related to the non-Western world to suggest a much needed refinement, replacement, and even reformulation of our theoretical knowledge in the fields of both democracy and development.

In this chapter I shall argue that India and south Asia generally tried first to graft Western liberal legal and political institutions, practices, and ideals onto their own social and political institutions and then recently to begin paying attention to various normative-pragmatic balances that the neighboring countries of east and southeast Asia have struck in their policies of economic growth and social development.[2] In both these respects, as could be expected, each of the south Asian countries came out with its own borrowings, fusions, and persistent incompatibilities. What was evident in all of them, nevertheless, was an increasing pragmatism that they belatedly learned from their Asian neighbors and for which they had to wage their own internal battle against entrenched economic interests, bureaucrats, and politicians. Thus, for the countries of south Asia there were two sources of development stimulus: the Western world, with its liberal legal and political institutions, modern education, science, and technology; and the Asian neighbors, with their pragmatic policies leading to stunning economic growth. The latter source also allowed south Asian nations to customize their own balances between what they thought was normatively desirable and politically or realistically possible.

The scene in south Asia is thus one of development plurality as a result of individually customized strategies and priorities. And, for the sake of a closer look at one of them, I shall confine myself to contemporary development in India, a country where I have done field research over three decades in its grassroots communities. Moreover, India also represents a challenge to the corpus of our theoretical knowledge, which is almost entirely rooted in the development experiences of Western societies.

In the case of India, however, the Cold War provides a poor guide to determining the country's ideological grouping. India shunned not Western political liberalism but absorption into the Western (or Eastern) power bloc. The sensitive nationalist leaders of independent India saw the creeping hand of neocolonialism in the superpowers' efforts to pull emerging countries into their own warring camps. India, therefore, decided to shun membership in the Western bloc without giving up on its liberal political ideology. At the same time, however, its attempt to participate in building a bloc of nonaligned countries, to trade with Eastern bloc countries, and to criticize some of the weakest emerging countries for getting involved in the Cold War resulted in India's marginalization in international politics.

Furthermore, what forced the Indians to take a hard look at their own tortuously slow economic growth and persistent poverty was not the end of the Cold War, but the stunning, come-from-behind economic success of its Asian neighbors. Their repeated pragmatic course corrections attending to the problems of economic growth, education, housing, health, sanitation, public transport, and infrastructure, together with their importing of advanced technologies through links with multinationals, made the Indians realize the loss of several years' development. Such realizations were at the root of the Indian economy's liberalization. Simultaneously, India wanted neither to compromise on its liberal political commitments nor to give up on what I have called a "many-sided development." In the Asian development scene, where tigers and dragons occupy the center stage, the Indians decided to make their country a development tortoise so as to avoid the future nemesis of neglecting the participatory aspect of their overall development. In the following pages I shall go into the details of these and other issues and explore their significance for theory construction.

The Western Impact

Like China, India is one of the world's most complex societies, where different external encounters have left behind different layers of deposit which have neither totally merged nor ceased to influence the Indian people. W. H. Morris-Jones, a perceptive scholar of Indian politics, called India a country where "centuries coexist." In a real sense, therefore, it has a *multilayered* society, the analysis of which requires a much more sophisticated conceptual framework than the tradition-modernity or Western and non-Western dualism permits.[3] Reinhard Bendix often bemoaned the fact that since the end of World War II, we have largely sought to explain the emerging world, including societies in Asia, with the help of the intellectual capital that we generated to explain Western societies.[4]

Indian civilization, unlike most others, has maintained a remarkable continuity and influence on its people despite wars, conquests, external cultural influences, and prolonged periods of social destabilization. Since its classical civilization dealt with the problems of the human mind and spirit, rather than with material things, neither the sheer passage of time nor intrusions of outsiders could diminish the interest of its people in non-material things. Consequently, even the oldest layer in its political society continues to have meaning to some people as some more recent layers have for other people.

The classical civilization of India left a many-sided legacy. It gave rise to six schools of philosophy and took great pride in cultivating subtleties of intellectual effort and canons of reasoning. For such a civilization, cognitive effort did not stop at identifying and solving intellectual puzzles but extended to the human spirit and laws governing it. Consequently, despite the passage of time and exposure to rival philosophical ideas, cultivation of the human spirit is still considered to be worthwhile.

Then there is the prevalent characterization of material objects and social situations as impermanent, insubstantial, and illusory; of spiritual goals and objects as timeless, real, and therefore worth pursuing. Such an attitude was severely criticized by Indian social and religious reformers of the nineteenth and twentieth centuries. One such critic was Mahatama Gandhi who exhorted the Indians to take social and political reality seriously. He maintained that political subjection and degradation prevented any effective pursuit of higher purposes.

What helped bring social and political issues to the center of attention, especially in the nineteenth and twentieth centuries, was the revival of the spirit of criticism. The habit of critical discourse and criticism was an integral part of classical civilization, albeit confined to a small section of Indian society. Towards its revival, however, the contact with the West, and Western education itself, were of inestimable value. Such a resource was used against the harsh comments of colonial rulers and claims to moral superiority by Christian missionaries. The spirit of criticism and its increasingly bolder expression were finally used for demanding constitutional reforms and political independence itself.

In the field of law and liberal politics, the British influence on India had been immeasurably great. The founding fathers of the Indian republic were constitutional lawyers who had deeply assimilated British common law, Anglo-Saxon jurisprudence, and social and political ideals thrown up by the discourses that had preceded the American, French and Russian revolutions. They had brought into the center the individual, provided him or her with a list of fundamental rights, and then charged the courts with protecting those rights. Such an emphasis came in conflict with the norms of hierarchy and became the source of social change in India since independence was achieved.[5]

In a sense the emphasis on the individual in Western political liberalism struck a responsive chord among educated Indians. This is because Hindu beliefs had already sensitized them to the importance of individuals and their inner experiences. At the other extreme, there was emphasis on group compliance to norms of various castes. Such a basic dichotomy between emphasis on the individual in the belief system and on his conformity to the norms of his caste within the social organization has led to an extreme form of individualism in some matters and unquestioned group compliance in others. The Indian elite hoped that eventually, with the influence of the social organization reduced to cultural essentials, a relatively freer individual would emerge. After independence was achieved in India, it was this vision of the elite which seems to have won the day.

The six schools of philosophy which India produced by and large led to plurality in thought, culture, and religion in society. They also favored the inclusion of the incompatibles within intellectual, philosophical, and social systems. In other words, instead of regarding the presence of contradictions as a mark of imperfect reasoning or condition, Indian philosophy viewed it as a situation requiring special intellectual effort and categories so as to be able to include and accommodate the differences in thought, religion, and society. In that respect the course of Indian intellectual development was different from the rationalism of Western Europe, right from Socrates to Immanuel Kant. To European thinkers the presence of contradictions in reasoning was illogical, imperfect argument and the mark of intellectual immaturity in general. Later, in the ideas of Hegel and Marx, contradictions came to play an important role as a necessary logical or a social idiom through which a higher intellectual or social evolution became possible. Indian philosophical thinking couched some of its major ideas in terms of plurality, contradictions, coexistence, and attainment or non-attainment of the state of higher unity.

Far from being snuffed out during the Western encounter and British rule, and after independence was achieved, the cultural heritage of the Indians has continued to make them the assimilators and synthesizers of what came from the outside, often grafting onto what they already had. This was also true of the assembly principle. Unlike the growth of the assembly principle, which developed in Europe with the growth of guilds, parliaments, church councils, and other groups, the Indian indigenous legislative experience remained too closely tied to canons and customs, giving enormous importance to kings and their advisers. Moreover, the assembly principle, particularly for sharing political power, had a slim chance of development in India because of constant invasions, conquests, and social destabilizations.

What was developed in the most enduring fashion was the institution of *panchayat* (local council), which embodied the theory and practice of the grassroots assembly principle. These *panchayats* had been filled by venerated old men of villages and enjoyed considerable revenue, judicial, and administrative powers. Along with village communities, they survived through a succession of political regimes in Delhi and other regional capitals.[6] The *panchayats* embodied the principle of decision making in public matters by means of discussion and consensus. After the 1950s the Indian constitution revitalized and reconstituted them by means of the one man-one vote principle. Universal adult suffrage and enforced equality before law and in electoral politics began to radically alter political relationships in rural India. Thus, instead of creating rival or alternative courses for social action or models, it created an assimilative disposition in which things fit and also remain essentially Indian.

The Assertion of Indigenous Ways

In the countries of the West, liberal political systems owe their origin to specific economic and historical forces of the eighteenth and nineteenth centuries. Those forces reshaped the legal as well as political institutions on both sides of the Atlantic. One of the major players in that was the growth of capitalism which needed greater room to operate and therefore directly came in conflict first with the feudal and later with the regulatory mercantilist state. During those two centuries of encounter with capitalism, as Max Weber reminded us, divergent factors converged. These factors included a fresh drive for profit, the religious justification and organizational means needed to realize it, the growth of cities, bureaucracy, new policies governing land tenure, newly defined notions of innate individual rights, and relaxed state authority over individual enterprises. Together these factors gave further support not only to capitalism but also to the liberal democracy that sustains it.

By contrast, democracy in emerging societies grew largely from demands for constitutional reforms, movements for national independence, assimilation of the liberal political ideals by Western-educated elites, and then the tortuous learning process of how to use democratic process itself to protect one's individual and group interests. Moreover, such a process had to take place within the social and historical contexts of each developing country. It often created an interaction between the indigenous social organization, based on the norms of hierarchy, and the new legal and political institutions, based on the norms of equality. It also created a problem for the traditional authority that depended on compliance. Even after being elected to public office, elected deputies remained uncomfortable with the questioning political culture and demand for accountability. Above all, it created the need for the growth of political capacity of the citizenry to be able to make use of the new political process. Finally, new political institutions were emulated from outside and required the learning and assimilation of the often unarticulated dos and don'ts of their own operations.

The newly introduced democratic institutions and practices in India faced a peculiar problem—they had to operate in a society with an entrenched hierarchical social structure characterized by a deeply rooted cohesion in its various castes and religious subgroups. Such cohesion had existed since the dawn of Indian civilization. Consequently, deeply entrenched social institutions based on the norms of hierarchy came into direct conflict with new legal and political institutions and their claims to equality. The democratic process finally won by nibbling away at the social cohesion that had extended itself from traditional to nontraditional concerns. Voters in the same castes registered increasing diversity in election after election.[7]

The political society of India, especially at the grassroots level, had to undergo some major leadership changes in order to respond to the introduction of the principle of one man-one vote and to the general idea of a questioning political culture. Such a change was reflected in the bifurcation of leadership which followed: the old and venerated leaders of the village, who were mostly from higher castes and relatively affluent economic background, relinquished their political leadership and settled for the status of caste leaders; then younger men, who were mostly from the same families, moved in to take over political leadership of those communities. Such a bifurcation also introduced an element of political opportunism which was unheard of before. The younger men entered into all kinds of cynical deals with those who agreed to support them. Unhinged from the traditional normative constraints of their elders, these younger men introduced an element of political flexibility, and, at times, cynical opportunism, in the pursuit, use, and retention of political power. When some of the leaders of this generation entered state assemblies and/or *Loksabha* (parliament), they carried with them a predilection for horse trading and floor crossing for office or cash. In 1995–1996, some members this political class, which made up state assemblies and *Loksabha*, were even accused of hiding their criminal records from their constituents.

The Indian democratic process also made deep inroads into social and political privileges that had been traditionally enjoyed by the upper strata of its hierarchical society. Given the overwhelming numerical superiority of the middle and lower strata of the traditional society, individuals from the lower middle and lower castes of society were able to get themselves elected to public bodies within two decades of the introduction of universal adult suffrage and enjoy some of the highest public offices. In that sense the Indian democratic process had given to people of traditional lower social status the means to circumvent disadvantages imposed by traditional society. The democratic process thus served, and is serving, a much wider purpose in India than in other political societies. For one thing it has just about become a potent instrument in the hands of those who were condemned to socially and economically disadvantaged positions for centuries.

The operation of democratic institutions in India, uninterrupted over the last fifty years, has also placed before the students of society and politics two major issues: the evolution of citizens' *political capacity*, on the one hand, and the learning of the unarticulated dos and don'ts of running fragile democratic political institutions, on the other. Unlike the countries of Western Europe and North America, India came to have its liberal political institutions, adult suffrage, freedom of speech and association, fundamental rights and independent judiciary in advance of popular demand and therefore before a commensurate political capacity to be able to use them effectively existed. That, however, was not the case in the countries of the West. In Europe and America, human political capacity grew along with liberal legal and political institutions. It sometimes even preceded such growth and then engaged in demand and political agitation to secure rights and freedoms. In other words, when legal and political provisions were put in place in the West, a human political capacity to make use of them already existed. It was the other way round in the case of India. It took Indians close to three decades to learn to use the power of the vote effectively to send messages to the political class, and more than half a century to bring in the judiciary to play its role in guarding individual rights and public interests with which the founding fathers of the Indian republic had entrusted it. The Indian democratic experience thus also suggests that it is not enough to hold elections or to have the privilege of a plurality of political parties. You also need to make elected deputies represent your interests and be accountable while in public office. The real problems of democracy thus begin after the deputies are elected.

Then there are the problems of dos and don'ts for the people on both sides of the political divide. Britain, the United States, and France were able to develop their own traditions of democratic governance. These included respecting the verdict of the electorate, respecting the right of the majority to govern and of the minority to debate and criticize those in power, and having leaders willing to face the press and the public on all major policy issues. In all of these exercises too many democratic dos and don'ts are involved. The example of India shows that while the Indians learned a lot about the British parliamentary process, they were not always able to use that knowledge effectively. Even now, for instance, no minister is obliged to face the press or meet the demand for information that media or citizens may want. Public accountability is still not an established part of the tradition of governance in India.

Democratic political societies are sustained by means of shared notions of what is fair and what is not in the political field. Not all such notions, which seek to civilize a vital segment of human activity and competition, can be written up. Nor can one fully articulate what is fair or unfair in the treatment of one's political adversaries. Furthermore, you cannot fully define the gray areas of legality, propriety, or morality which govern the separation of private and public interests. People join democratic politics for power, status, glory, indirect material gain, public service, and other reasons. In order to make citizens' involvement in democratic politics more realistic and worldly, it is important that the notions of proper "fit" between public and private interests are widely discussed and shared.

The process of democratic maturation in the half century since India won independence registered some gains. But it also identified some major problems. Ironically enough, rural dwellers, despite their limited literacy, registered greater interest in the democratic process than did urban dwellers. Furthermore, the bulk of India's vast middle class, currently estimated to be somewhere between 200 and 300 million, which had benefited enormously from the country's development since independence was achieved, did not think that it was worth its while to get involved in the democratic process. Only a small segment within it, which had learned to benefit from it materially, remained interested in it.

India has regularly held all of its elections and has also firmly established in the psyche of its people the idea that the only route to political power is through the ballot box. In its 1996 general election, with a staggering electorate of more than 600 million people, India was able to secure a voter turnout of a little less than 60 per cent. That indeed was a remarkable achievement for any democracy. What it could not do, however, was to bring into the electoral fray the best of its professional, technological, managerial, academic, entrepreneurial, and social activists. The people of this class remain deeply committed to democratic system of government, but they do not want to help run it. India has paid heavily because of their withdrawal from its democratic life in general. The quality of the people attracted by civic, state, and national bodies has declined; people with criminal records have gained access to governing bodies. The *Vohra Committee Report* on crime and politics made a shocking statement on the extent to which the level of India's democratic politics had sunk.[8]

Instead of overseeing the performance of public officeholders and making them accountable for the use or abuse of public authority, as happens in the mature Western democracies, the burgeoning Indian middle class remained politically indifferent and uninvolved. The democratic performance in Britain and the United States improved when that class took on the responsibility of overseeing the fair and just implementation of public policy and offered its services by running for public office. The politically uninvolved component of the Indian middle class now has only a limited understanding of this responsibility. Wherever such a realization has dawned, its first choice is for voluntary, non-government activities. As a group, it still shuns public office.

Since before India became independent, the middle class had put an enormous emphasis on education, character-building, hard work, and personal integrity. It had held onto most of its traditional values, albeit in a diluted form. As a group it had succeeded an earlier middle class that had believed in "simple living and high thinking." Nevertheless, its recent affluence has not totally unhinged it from its commitment to traditional values. So great had been this group's continued emphasis on education and the fear that the deteriorating situation in India held out little hope for the future of its children that it had, through personal involvement of both the mother and father, transformed the generation of their children into a professional class of great preparation and excellence, ready to compete with the best in the world. Its goal for its children is to send them abroad for further education and then settle them in North America or Europe. This class, which has achieved so much for itself and its children and has the educational and moral resources for reshaping India's democracy, is only marginally interested in its democratic process. So far it has kept up its unrelenting criticism of falling standards in public life but has had very little impact on the quality of public life itself. If it involves itself in the democratic process in a big way, it might make all the difference to it.

The distinguished Indian jurist K. Santhanam had once identified the three arms of corruption as politicians, administrators, and business people. They were the principal beneficiaries of the development that had taken place since India won its independence. But what was worse was that they also created an air of invulnerability for themselves and helplessness on the part of the average Indian. Such helplessness was often expressed in the Hindi language as *chalta hai* ("this will go on"). Corruption in India has been so pervasive that until recently publicly funded investigative agencies and various governing bodies charged with enforcing the law were working hand-in-glove with those involved in corrupt practices. Segments of society that continually publicized abuses were the Election Commission, media, social activists, and, since the early 1990s, an activist judiciary, particularly in the highest courts. And they have indeed earned the gratitude of Indians. But that is not enough. Unless the best of the Indians get involved in the democratic process of their country, of which they are deeply proud, and acquire a more active role in overseeing the uses and abuses of public authority, Indian democracy will not produce the desired results.

The End of the Cold War

Distress with the Rate of Development

The end of the Cold War evoked different responses from India. Ever since its independence, India has been a liberal democracy in the strictest Western sense of the term. Barring two or three states in different parts of India, the bulk of the Indians did not even think that Marxism had been a suitable ideology for India. What India had, instead, was a mixed economy with Fabian style "socialism" as its goal. But that had disastrous consequences, too. For nearly forty-five years after independence was achieved, more and more Indians sank below the poverty line, at times close to 40 percent; income disparities widened; and the country came to have one of the largest, most obstructionist bureaucracies in the world. During that period the country's growth rate rarely exceeded 2 percent. Indian-style "socialism" had become a huge embarrassment.

Politicians, bureaucrats, industrialists, economists, and other vested interests got so deeply entrenched around socialist policies that any criticism of such policies, let alone a departure from them, became very difficult. The credit for changing the mind-set of the Indians and, thus, opening the way for increased liberalization of the economy and for seeking investment and advanced technology from abroad went to former Prime Minister P. V. Narasimha Rao, and Manmohan Singh, who had been Rao's finance minister. But there again it was not the collapse of the Soviet Union which brought in the necessary changes in its economic policy but the conditions imposed by the International Monetary Fund, on the one hand, and the stunning economic growth continually registered by the neighboring countries of Asia.

Asian Comparisons and Shocks

After a prolonged, flattering self-assessment, the Indians got a shock when they discovered that the smaller countries of southeast Asia, whose cultures had been historically influenced by India, had gotten twenty-five to fifty years ahead, at least in economic growth and modernization. Educated Indians, who were more likely to feel the hurt, did not want to believe what they read in the press for a long time. But then their travels, especially to shop in Singapore, and the search by industrialists for new markets convinced them that South Korea, Malaysia, Thailand, and the other, smaller south Asian nations had surpassed India.

The second shock was much bigger, and that was at the hands of China. Given the problems between the two countries, the Indians did not want to believe for a long time that the Chinese growth rate was phenomenal, ever since Deng began experimenting with various kinds of modernization. Indian newspapers and journals were slow to record what was going on in China. Even to this day, print media still report that China's great progress cannot be all true, given China's limited credibility and frequent tendency to play with figures. But when international organizations such as the World Bank, IMF, and OECD started talking about it, Indian media had no alternative but to lend credence to it. Given the frosty relationship between India and China, very few Indian scholars have tried to go to China and see for themselves what is happening out there.

Whatever was the level of perception or contact with Asian neighbors, there was a feeling of dismay for being *left out* in this game of development. Other countries, big and small, had bypassed India. The proud Indians, with a self-image as perhaps intellectually the best in the non-Western world, could not help their own country keep in step with some of the rapidly developing countries. India was left behind even by countries such as Indonesia and the Philippines, even though they also had many similar problems. They now did not know whom to blame for this: Democracy? Decline in the moral fiber of the Indians? Western powers? The middle class? Politicians and bureaucrats? Academics? Who else? None of these made enough sense.

"Exclusion from Asia"

The third shock concerned India's "exclusion from Asia." India has been different in some respects from other Asian nations which tend to view the region of south Asia and, in particular, India as not quite Asian. They see in

India characteristics different from what they think are the pan-Asian characteristics. Such a judgment about India, despite the prolonged cultural influence of Hinduism and Buddhism on it, is based largely on the similarity of India's languages, intellectual life, and political institutions to their Western counterparts. Throughout Japan, China, Indonesia, Malaysia, and other Asian countries, there is a perception that India is not completely Asian. At best it is south Asian, which in their way of thinking is not quite Asian. For a number of years I asked that question in all of those countries. In Japan, India was considered intellectually too close to the West. In China, India was criticized for the renunciation of Buddhism, which the Chinese considered *the* religion of Asia, and for its decision to opt for Western-style democracy. In Malaysia and Indonesia, people felt religious conflicts in India put it outside the pale of Asia where people do not kill one another in the name of religion. International trade and regional security considerations may still change the way that other Asian countries perceive India. As of now, India could not go beyond the status of a dialogue partner in the Association of Southeast Asian Nations.

The Delayed Search for Normative-Pragmatic Balance

Since it achieved political independence, India focused on the social and economic issues of poverty and inequality. It was natural, therefore, that it should have taken seriously the political ideology of socialism that claims to address those issues. There was another equally strong ideological commitment on its part, namely, liberal democracy. That was borne out of the long national struggle for independence which was also waged in the name of the liberal political ideals that Britain claimed to have. During the early days of Indian independence, the Labor Party held power in Britain. The party's socialist ideology addressed precisely those issues. Added to this was a generation of Indian elites educated in Britain and exposed to British socialist ideology and its Fabian roots. Fabianism addressed itself to the twin issues of social equality and liberal political participation. It appeared to be much more progressive to the political mind of the 1940s and 1950s in India than Marxism did.

So while India had seen Marxism in action for nearly three decades in the Soviet Union, it did not have the similar benefit of seeing British socialism in action. It was coeval with Indian independence itself. India, in that respect, did not have the benefit of Singapore and Malaysia which were also drawn to British Fabianism but soon found out that it was not suitable for them. Prevailing in Singapore, particularly, was a much sharper pragmatic sense that viewed critically what was happening in Britain during the 1950s. By 1965, when Singapore's founding fathers were embarking on policy making for their city-state, socialism in India was two decades old and had created its own vested interests in the form of politicians, bureaucrats, industrialists, and credulous intellectuals who had not learned to critique public policy boldly in light of actual results. As opposed to that, Singapore, which had become a "superpragmatic society," continually examined its policies and discarded those that did not produce the intended results. Being a micro-state, it remained obsessed with the problem of security. It sought to improve security by export-led growth, bringing into decision making the best technocrats and producing a virtual *meritocracy* which never failed to give dividends. Malaysia delicately balanced the economic dynamism of its 30 percent Chinese population, which owned more than 60 percent of national assets, with the demands of *bhumiputera* (sons of the soil) for affirmative action for the then left-behind Malays. Indonesia produced a fascinating kind of "social pragmatism," first, and then applied it to economic growth. Thailand put to pragmatic use the emphasis on practical result in the Theravada brand of Buddhism to which its people subscribed. One could multiply examples of Asian countries striking their own unique normative-pragmatic balance.

In India, given an emotional commitment to the ideology of socialism, and the powerful vested interests which grew round it, the shift away from it was halting and fraught with the dangers of reversibility. But, as stated earlier, former Prime Minister Narasimha Rao and his associates forced the Indians to look at other Asian countries which by the 1990s had far surpassed India. They sensitized the Indians to be more and more pragmatic. What convinced Indians across the political spectrum was what China, India's rival, and the smaller countries of southeast Asia had achieved. Moreover, when some pragmatic policies which were put in place bore quick results, Indians decided to try economic liberalization.

But what finally did the trick was the creative energies of the Indians—entrepreneurial, technological, and managerial—which started bearing fruit in the economy. So far, such energies were giving good account of themselves abroad, but now they were making the much needed difference at home for everyone to see. Thus, only recently has India taken seriously the impressive economic growth in other countries of southeast and east Asia. What has dominated their policies, both economically and politically, is what I have called a balance between what is *normatively desirable* and *politically possible* for them. Such an awareness is now beginning to influence the utopian commitments of the Indians which had continued, at least at the formal level, since independence was achieved.

In its delay in striking such a balance, India not only missed the possible fruits of a pragmatic revolution, which had achieved results all over Asia, but it also strained, and at times weakened, the democratic roots of its polity. This often made thinking people wonder whether it was caused by its being a democracy. That uncertainty and its possible harm to Indian democracy could have been avoided.

Western education, liberal political ideals and institutions, and, above all, Western culture as seen through various television channels did not make as much difference to India in recent years as did the lure of consumer goods, on the one hand, and the learning from the normative-pragmatic balances struck by neighboring countries of Asia in their own rapid economic growth, on the other. Unlike its Asian neighbors, India continues to be suspicious of multinationals that might take the enormousness of the Indian market more seriously rather than bring India's technology up to date and also help it realize its economic potential. Consequently, whenever there is a demand to protect indigenous industrial or commercial concerns, politicians and industrialists of all kinds join in.

To conclude this point, the end of the Cold War, no doubt, saw an acceleration in the process of economic liberalization. Nevertheless, such a process was inspired more by what was happening in neighboring Asian countries than by the triumph of the Western economic and political system over the Marxist model. This is because neighbors who envy one another often tend to learn from each other more than they care to admit.

Conclusions

The Liberal Route to Development

Ever since attaining its independence, India has been one of the few non-Western countries to have approached its development through a liberal route in which emphasis on human freedom and participation received the same importance as economic growth. Not only that, even to an institution builder like Jawaharlal Nehru, India was going to benefit as much from freedom and released energy of its people as it would from the economic initiatives undertaken by the state. Such a route to development came closer to some of the approaches followed by the three major Western democracies—Britain, France, and the United States.[9]

Nevertheless, in actual practice, especially at the hands of the vast bureaucracy that Nehru built, the emphasis on rebuilding the economy of the newly independent India fell more on public undertakings rather than on private initiatives. There was also hope that along with those twin goals of economic development and individual participation, India would attend to problems of social and economic inequality. Finally, as a unique society among developing countries, India had hoped that its simultaneous emphasis on freedom, participation, and planned economic growth would try to reduce social inequality, create a sense of security, and enhance the intellectual and aesthetic creativity that Indians had never neglected even during the lean periods of their long history. Clearly, then, the Indians had aimed at too much. In their simultaneous emphasis on all those goals, they ended up diluting all of them, at least in the initial years after independence was achieved.

What came instead of economic growth was a monstrous self-serving bureaucracy and a political class, wheeling and dealing with powerful business houses to stay in power and enrich themselves personally by manipulating the democratic process. Together these three groups also started muzzling freedom of initiative and expression. Together they set back not only India's rate of economic growth, but also the social and economic initiatives of individual Indians.

What these three could do, in the final analysis, however, was to cause only a temporary setback. What they could not do was to prevent India's vast pool of human resources, with its enormous potential, from continually building excellence and dedication. This high quality of human resources is both in its middle class and, more particularly, in its professional class, indigenous and expatriate. Rarely would you find such a resource in Asia or elsewhere. Its development is not confined to higher incomes only, but extends to greater freedom of expression and an astounding professional mobility. It has been built and sustained on an intellectual quality and creativity that spill over national boundaries. Wherever segments of this class have gone, they have carried with them a level of personal quality, intellectual preparation, dedication to work, and a many-sided commitment which have evoked praise from almost *all* of the host countries. Before long, hopefully, this class would also hit the national social and economic scene and make the needed difference to its democratic process. When the final product of the Indian development process comes on stream, it will be judged by the international development jury as far more comprehensive than previously seen in other developing nations.

Reaction to the End of the Cold War

From India's perspective, formulation of the question "Has the Western world triumphed?" is a bit puzzling. This is because this non-Western society had assimilated the best of the Western world, together with a contribution of its own, long before the Cold War began. This can be explained as follows:

(a) India has produced a classical civilization with an extraordinarily high intellectual content. During the period of Western dominance, starting in the eighteenth century, Western scholars did not want to face the challenge of India's intellectual and philosophical contribution. Therefore, they had been intellectually insensitive, registering neither its contributions nor challenges. In several respects, however, India was much closer in its highly developed faculty of deductive reasoning, including an extraordinarily well-developed mathematical background and a mind given to dialogue and questioning as well as to an interminable weighing of arguments. In that sense, India was a kindred spirit and senior variant of what the Greeks stood for and to which Western civilization traced much of its ancestry.

This may also show that India is not only of the past but also of the present. India's highly assimilated system of Western laws, independent judiciary, responsible executive, freedom of the press, and liberal political ideals is much much closer to the West than the earlier thinkers of the period of Western dominance had characterized it or found justification for ignoring it.

On top of that India had also added a few more dimensions such as spirituality, religiosity, and a constant search for the deeper meaning of life than in fact the Greeks had ever opted for. Thus, Indians were exploring interminably something much wider and deeper. Western observers, given to stereotyping India, characterized it as mysticism. In fact mysticism was the most useful cliché for those European intellectuals who did not want to face the challenge of India's dual and even multifaceted civilization. But despite their indifference and continual denial of India's contribution, historically it is there for scholars to comment upon in a period of declining Western dominance in intellectual and other fields.

(b) Simultaneously, there is the *bridge character* of India between Asia and Europe which has yet another aspect to it. Historically and culturally, India had far greater influence on Asian countries than has been properly acknowledged. Apart from the cultural influence exercised by Hinduism, Buddhism, and the Indian version of Islam in such countries as Thailand, Malaysia, Singapore, Indonesia, China, Japan, and South Korea, India continues to have a special place in the psyche of the people of these nations. In recent times, however, that sentiment has receded beneath the surface as a result of India's poor development since it achieved independence. But since liberalization, there has been, once again, a feeling in those countries that India has not been given due recognition for what it has achieved. This will continue as long as the Indian growth rate remains much lower than theirs and until the time that they begin to make the difficult switch to liberal political institutions and look at India's experience of having already achieved it by giving a priority to public participation.

In that sense India has been a bridge both for Western countries looking into Asia, and Asian countries looking to the West. Western countries that have been hosts to India's educated emigrant professionals have also noticed this bridge character. The way that Indian professionals carry themselves and their increasing contributions to many scientific and technological fields have earned them the respect of their hosts. This will increase and, with it, the interest in India's bridge role.

In keeping with its assimilative disposition since the dawn of its civilization, India is continually absorbing Western and, of late, Asian ideas on economic development. Looking to Asia has also injected the much needed pragmatic approaches toward its own public policies. Asian influence is heavily weighted in favor of results rather than the theoretical models that came through Western social sciences. Simultaneously, the built-in propensity of Asian countries towards striking and renewing normative-pragmatic balances is likely to serve the India yearning to remain anchored in its own commitments and political ideals while devising pragmatic policies based on those commitments to produce desired results. Chances are, therefore, that India may look to three different sources: itself for moral commitments arising in part from its traditional values and in part from its exposure to what it has learned from its encounters with the Western world; the West for constant innovations in science, technology, and education; and the countries of Asia for devising ways of accelerating their economic growth. The extent to which Asian countries of more or less parallel if not similar cultural backgrounds have come out with their own successful policies means that Western ways and policies will have to compete to regain their influence. Chances are that in such a competition the Western influence in Asia will wane. Asian countries would want Western technology, educational facilities, and marketing and management skills but not social values.

Implications for Theory Construction

Regional Theorizing to Precede Global Theorizing

India's development and democratic experience over half a century has implications for theory construction. This is because, despite the total acceptance of political liberalism and a gradual opening up of the economy for trade and investment, it has remained, for a variety of cultural and historical reasons, a distinct society. The same may be said of other societies in the region. This means that, instead of creating clones of Western societies, globalization will more realistically represent a federal structure composed of different societies of different regions that have come through different social and historical experiences and that have, in turn, shaped their own development and democratic processes. This may be true despite the increasing acceptance of the twin canons of globalization: political liberalism and open economies. While global change, by definition, is occurring in different parts of the world, we tend to view it as following the route traversed by industrialized societies of the West. In such an approach, we are influenced by what I have called the "fallacy of parallels and actuals."

The urge to look at vital phenomena of social and economic change in universal terms runs throughout the history of social sciences. The first warning against it came at the hands of Max Weber in his final and posthumously published work, *General Economic History*.[10] He argued that we should look for different kinds of capitalism and not just the kind in Western Europe. For him countries that developed on the basis of agriculture, mining, plantation, or other types of economies will have different kinds of capitalism. Then in the 1960s we had the equally universalistic concept of modernization. This concept tried to see the countries of the non-Western world as replications of the Western world. And now we have the concept of globalization. This concept may also miss the actual phenomenon of development pluralism. Plurality is often considered a theoretical nuisance. A similar indifference often prevails against internal diversity in society. They are both considered obstacles in the way of neat global theories. The point to be made here is that one cannot meaningfully include non-Western societies in a broader notion of global (universal) change, at least not initially, unless, to begin with, one conceptualizes about their particular problems and development strategies, and then pieces together these fragments for an overall view of global change. The route to global-change theorizing will first be through understanding and theorizing of regional peculiarities.

Development Pluralism

The development and democratic experience of India, as well as those in the Indian subcontinent, suggests that societies are not influenced merely by social and historical experiences but also by the vision of their leaders. These visions include the goals that they put forward, strategies they devise, the sequencing and resequencing of priorities, international economic forces, and, above all, responses they generate either in support of what they do or in being pushed toward what other leaders want.

All these together make a difference to development processes in various societies. They make a difference to societies that only a few decades ago were exposed to common historical conditions and experiences. For example, one has only to look at the countries of south Asia, most of which, historically speaking, were a part of a single regime or empire and now are so very different in their development processes.

The Problem of the Growth of Human Political Capacity

In the democratic development of emerging societies, as India's experience clearly indicates, there had been a unique problem that was not faced by Western European and North American countries. India's people were given constitutional rights, including the right to vote, but these rights were used unequally, often leading to greater social and political inequality because those rights were granted before Indians could develop enough political capacity to use them effectively and in a balanced fashion.

The problem of what I have called "ethnopolitical development"[11] did not arise in Western democracies. Since they took two to three hundred years to develop their liberal political institutions, often in response to agitation from various emerging classes, such groups had developed enough political capacity to use what they had fought for. We need to theorize on the particular problem that each developing country faced in establishing the effective use of constitutional provisions for political participation.

The Variety of Normative-Pragmatic Balances

In their development processes, different societies have tried to strike a balance between what they think is normatively desirable and realistically or politically possible. To the Indians, the first normative commitment is to liberal political ideals. But in Singapore, for example, that is not the case so far. The latter has emphasized economic growth, high standards of education, housing, medical care, and environmental conditions under the leadership of elected technocrats or distinguished professionals. There are evaluations to be made of, and judgments to be passed on, these priorities, sequences, and achievements. Then there are tougher questions related to making democracy produce results. For developing societies, these are living issues that require comparative theorization.

Taking a Hard Look at the Corpus of Theoretical Knowledge

Theoretical knowledge in development studies has come largely from the social sciences. And the social sciences themselves were developed in order to understand social and historical problems of societies of Western Europe and North America during the last two hundred years. Such a body of knowledge, unlike theories of the natural sciences, contains certain accretions of the time and place where it was developed. The social science knowledge, often used in development studies without qualifications, does not always show enough sensitivity to peculiar problems of developing societies nor does it easily admit the need for the refinement, refomulations, and replacements of some of its major concepts when we examine development problems of emerging societies. Such a reluctance had worked during the period of Western economic and intellectual dominance. Now the time has come to look at the efficacy of such a body of knowledge and refine and reformulate it wherever necessary.

Endnotes

1. For a detailed discussion of this topic, see A. H. Somjee, *Development Theory: Critiques and Explorations* (London: Macmillan, 1991).

2. A. H. Somjee and G. Somjee, *Development Success in Asia Pacific: An Exercise in Normative-Pragmatic Balance* (New York: St. Martin's Press, 1995).

3. I am grateful to the editor of Macmillan, London, for his kind permission to summarize some of the passages from A. H. Somjee's *Parallels and Actuals of Political Development* (London: Macmillan, 1986): 62–78.

4. Reinhard Bendix, *Embattled Reason: Essays in the Sociology of Knowledge* (New York: Oxford University Press, 1970).

5. A. H. Somjee, *Democracy and Political Change in Village India* (New Delhi: Orient Longman, 1971).

6. Jayaprakash Narayan, *A Plea For the Reconstruction of India Polity* (Rajghat, Kashi: Akhil Bharat Sevasangha Prakashan, 1959).

7. In this connection see A. H. Somjee, "Caste and the Decline of Political Homogeneity," *American Political Science Review* 67, no. 3 (Sept. 1973): 799–816. Also see "India Votes: Alliance Politics and Minority Governments" in Harold Gould and Sumit Ganguly, eds., *Ninth and Tenth General Elections* (Boulder, CO: Westview Press, 1993): 33.

8. *Vohra Committee Report: Nexus between Crime and Politics.* 1995.

9. Barrington Moore, Jr., *Social Origins of Dictatorship and Democracy: Lord and the Peasant in the Making of the Modern World* (Boston: Beacon Press, 1960).

10. Max Weber, *General Economic History* (Glencoe, IL: Free Press, 1950).

11. A. H. Somjee, *Political Capacity in Developing Societies* (London: Macmillan, 1982).

4
—

First World, Third World, Western, Non-Western, What? Latin America's Search for a Model and Theory of Development

—Howard J. Wiarda

Introduction

There are twenty countries in Latin America—thirty-four if one counts the smaller island countries of the Caribbean. The area has never been entirely clear about its political heritage and future directions, let alone which development model it should follow.[1] Nor has the field of comparative politics ever felt entirely comfortable in classifying or categorizing Latin America.[2] After approximately 175 years of independent history (since the 1820s), for example, Latin America should not be put in the same category as the "new states" or "new nations" (since the 1950s) of Africa and Asia.[3] Is Latin America part of the First World of modern, industrial, democratic countries or part of the Third World of developing nations? The answer is both: some parts of Latin America are modern and First World, some are poor and Third World, while most are intermediary between these two.

What about the Western–non-Western distinction? Here again the going gets tricky. Historically, most of Latin America has identified with the West and thought of itself as Western. But as we see below, Latin America is a product of a particular time and set of circumstances in the West; established as colonies of Spain and Portugal in the sixteenth century, Latin America is a product of the Middle Ages, of feudalism, and of the Counter Reformation, not of the modern world of the Enlightenment, the Protestant Reformation, the scientific revolution of Galileo and Newton, the capitalist and industrial revolution, or the seventeenth-century movement toward limited, representative government in England and its North American colonies.

Moreover, while the Latin American *elites* were oriented toward Europe and the West, the indigenous masses in Latin America often retained their traditional cultures and were only incompletely Westernized. In some Latin American countries—Mexico, Guatemala, Ecuador, Peru, Bolivia, Paraguay—the indigenous elements constituted a majority of the population, not a small minority as in the United States—and to this day they are not fully assimilated into prevailing Western (Hispanic, Catholic, Spanish-speaking) ways and continue to assert their rights as indigenous peoples. And when the indigenous and *mestizo* (mixed Indian and European) elements are a majority, there are real, serious problems of national integration. Then, too, there are the large African and mulatto populations of the Caribbean islands, the Caribbean mainland rim stretching from Mexico to Venezuela, and Brazil, which add a third racial-social-cultural ingredient to the Latin American melting pot.

Latin America is thus predominantly Western but incompletely and ambiguously so.[4] Moreover, it represents a special semifeudal and Hispanic fragment of the West, composed historically more of the Middle Ages than of the modern era. Furthermore, this Western identity of Latin America, given the class, racial, and political differences already mentioned, is a *contested* identification, with different groups vying and competing in a dynamic, changing process to assert their particular values and visions as the dominant ones.

The Western Impact

When Columbus discovered America in 1492, it marked the beginning of a period of worldwide, centuries-long domination by European countries and of the extension of Western culture and ways of doing things to the non-Western world. Latin America was the first of these areas to feel the full brunt of Westernization. Spain had conquered and colonized the main islands of the Caribbean within the first two decades of the sixteenth century, Mexico in the 1520s, and all Central America and much of South America by the 1530s. Meanwhile Portugal had claimed and settled the territory now known as Brazil. By the 1560s Spain had largely completed its conquest of the rest of South America, a remarkable accomplishment in seventy years especially if one considers that it took nearly three *centuries* for the North American colonists to complete their conquest of that continent.

At the time of the Spanish conquest, it is estimated that there were thirty million indigenous persons living in the area we now call Latin America, versus only three million in North America. Moreover in Latin America there were large-scale and relatively advanced Indian *civilizations*, as compared with the small-size and often nomadic tribes of North America. The Aztec, Mayan, and Inca civilizations in Latin America each numbered between five and seven million persons. Rather than kill the Indians wholesale or place them on reservations as in the British colonies and the United States, the Spaniards, always outnumbered, substituted themselves for the indigenous leadership as overlords of the Indian populations. They ruled as feudal "lords" over a "peasant" population that happened to be Indian. The mental image one should have is that of a pyramid with steep sides, with a small group of Spaniards and Portuguese at the top and huge numbers of native Indians and imported African slaves at the bottom. Spain and Portugal sought to civilize and assimilate the Indians into Hispano-Western ways, but that process always remained incomplete. In many countries the Western influence and Western institutions constituted a thin veneer resting atop an indigenous population that was only thinly and incompletely Westernized.[5]

In 1492, moreover, there were few "models" of empire that Spain and Portugal could look to for guidance. Spain and Portugal were the first colonial-imperial powers; at this early time in the sixteenth century there were no other examples. One model that Spain looked to for inspiration, therefore, was that of ancient Rome; in many respects Spain's governance of the Americas was similar to Rome's governance of Spain as a colonial outpost over a thousand years earlier. A second source of colonial guidance for Spain and Portugal was their own experiences with islands in the eastern Atlantic that these two emerging powers had colonized earlier: the Canaries, Madeira, the Azores, São Tomé. The system of plantation agriculture established in the Caribbean, for example, was first tried out in the Canaries, as was the system of top-down authoritarian rule emanating from the king in Madrid or Lisbon to his viceroys (literally, "vice kings") or captains general in the colonies.

A third model derived from Spain's own history from the Middle Ages. For nearly seven hundred years Spain and Portugal had been ruled by Moorish invaders from North Africa. Spain's and Portugal's *Reconquista* (Reconquest) of the Iberian Peninsula from the Moors took over five hundred years and gave Iberian feudalism some special features. It was more militant, absolutist, militaristic, authoritarian, intolerant (remember the Moors were also Moslems), and top-down than was feudalism elsewhere in Europe. All these features and institutions of the Reconquest were similarly carried over by Spain and Portugal and used by them in the conquest and subjugation of the native peoples and civilizations of the Americas.

The main institutions brought over by Spain and Portugal to the New World were as follows: (1) In the *political sphere* a top-down, authoritarian, absolutist, and pyramidal structure that went from king to viceroy to captain general to local *conquistador* or landowner, with each official in this hierarchy having absolute power within his sphere of influence. (2) *Economically*, an exploitive, milk-cow, semifeudal or slave-plantation system designed to benefit the mother countries of Spain and Portugal and not necessarily to help develop the colonies. (3) *Socially*, a rigid, hierarchical, elitist, and two-class system that was both social and racial, with a small group of Spanish and Portuguese at the top and a huge mass of Indians and Africans at the bottom. (4) *Religiously*, a similarly hierarchical, closed, absolutist, neoscholastic authoritarian, counter-reformationary, and intolerant belief system (medieval Roman Catholicism) that paralleled and reinforced the state system. And (5) an *educational system* similarly based on scholasticism, rote memorization, revealed truth, and deductive reasoning that retarded Latin American development. We may call this system the "Hapsburg Model" (after the authoritarian monarchy then governing Spain itself) of social and political organization.

Now, in the early sixteenth century, with Spain and Portugal still locked in feudalism and the Middle Ages, it should not be surprising that they would also found their colonies on this basis. What *is* surprising is that this *system* (for it was a system with the political, economic, social, religious, and educational aspects all interlocked) lasted so long. It lasted largely intact for fully three centuries of colonial rule, from the sixteenth through the eighteenth century. In the latter part of the eighteenth century, some Enlightenment and more republican and liberal ideas began to seep into the Spanish and Portuguese empires, serving as a partial inspiration for independence, but these remained a minor crosscurrent within the dominant authoritarianism. Strikingly, and very much unlike the United States, the colonial legacy of Spanish-Portuguese institutions also survived the independence movements of the Latin American territories in the early nineteenth century, the initial stirrings of modernization, and on into the early twentieth century, often referred to as the "twilight of the Middle Ages" in Latin America. Indeed in many respects the legacy of the early Hispanic past is still present in Latin America today, providing several major ingredients in what might be called a distinctively Latin American model of development.[6]

Independent Latin America and the Assertion of New Developmental Models

Independence and After

Unlike the liberal or liberalizing revolutions in the United States in 1776 and France in 1789, the Latin American separations from Spain and Portugal in the early nineteenth century were conservative revolutions. Because of the Napoleonic conquest and occupation of the Iberian Peninsula and the exile or "captivity" of the Spanish and Portuguese monarchies, the revolts in Latin America were meant to hold power and legitimacy *on behalf of* the monarchy and all it stood for. Indeed, in the Spanish case, when the monarchy in Spain was eventually restored after Napoleon's ouster but obliged to accept a liberal constitution, that was when the colonies in the New World rebelled. In the Brazilian case the Portuguese monarchy, fleeing Napoleon's troops, had moved to Rio de Janeiro in 1807; in 1822 Brazil declared itself independent, but as a monarchy rather than a republic until 1889.

Immediately after independence and continuing through much of the nineteenth century, Latin America had a major problem.[7] The Spanish (and Portuguese) colonial system, exploitive and authoritarian, had provided absolutely no training in self-government and certainly not in democracy. There were in the newly independent states of Latin America almost no institutions, little of what we now call "civil society," none of what that early-nineteenth-century French observer of North American society Alexis de Tocqueville termed a "web of associability" capable of holding society together and of mediating between government and governed.[8] In the absence of such infrastructure, Latin America would for a long time be condemned to instability, chaos, and frequent disintegration.

The impression held by many in the United States is that since independence Latin America has been governed by beautiful democratic ideals and constitutions but that actual practice has lagged far behind. The actual situation is more complicated—and interesting. There are in Latin American laws and constitutions elaborate provisions for U.S.-style separation of powers, checks and balances, and human and civil rights. These provisions make Latin American constitutions appear to be imitations of the U.S. basic law, with some French provisions added in. In the Latin American conception, these provisions represent ideals to strive for rather than actual operating reality.

But that is only part of the story. Also incorporated in Latin American basic laws and constitutions are provisions that are, given the problems and institutional vacuum already referred to, quite realistic.[9] For example, recognizing the need for strong leadership in these often disorganized, chaotic societies, the Latin American founding fathers entrusted the executive with broad powers while weakening the influence of the congress and courts. The president was also given vast emergency powers frequently needed in these fractured, disorganized polities to declare a state of emergency, suspend the constitution, and rule by decree. Since it was one of the few institutions capable of teaching civic consciousness and of holding society together, the Catholic Church was often established as the official church, Catholicism as the official religion, and Catholic hospitals, schools, charitable institutions, etc., given public support.

Similarly with the army. Immediately after independence, the armies that had earlier fought against Spain stepped into the void left by the departure of the crown and of royal authority. Like the church, the military was one of the few national organizations existing in society. In many countries the army alone was capable of providing at least a semblance of order and stability. So in these new constitutions—a tradition that continues in modified form today—the army was given special "moderating" powers as almost a fourth branch of government. If disorder broke out, the army was *constitutionally obliged* to step in and correct the situation. There were, of course, abuses of these responsibilities. But to recognize that the military had a constitutional obligation to step into politics under certain circumstances is a far cry from the usual American conception that Latin American armies regularly abuse and usurp constitutional precepts.[10]

The third leg of this power triumvirate (beside the church and the army) was the oligarchy or landowning class. As the only element in the new republics educated, skilled, and capable of generating economic activity, the oligarchy also received special treatment in these new constitutions—not all that different from what the Virginia squirarchy enjoyed in the U.S. Constitution—including property and literacy requirements for voting and a virtual monopoly on political office.

These provisions make the Latin American constitutions and fundamental laws look quite realistic, not the products of idealistic dreamers as they are often portrayed. Grounded in Latin American actualities, they reflected the need for strong, executive-centered leadership to hold society together. At the same time they incorporated the liberal and democratic aspirations that had first surfaced in Latin America in the late eighteenth century and that now and far into the future (even today!) would continue to reflect a basic split in the Latin American "soul." On the one hand Latin America valued order, centralism, hierarchy, authority, corporatism, and discipline; on the other it also valued liberalism and democracy. But, recall, the *form* of democracy tended also to be different from the U.S. model, Rousseauian (organic, centralized, top-down) rather than Lockean-Madisonian.[11]

The first decades of independence in Latin America were often chaotic and disorganized. The democratic regimes that came to power were usually short-lived; authoritarian regimes—both military- and civilian-oligarchic—tended to last longer but to accomplish little. In the absence of any basic societal consensus on the ends or means of politics, power tended to oscillate between conservative and liberal regimes. There was little institutionalization, stability, or development, and almost no agreed-upon national goals or ideology.

New Currents: Positivism, *Hispanismo,* Corporatism, Marxism

By the middle of the nineteenth century, most Latin American countries had begun to settle down. They solved earlier border disputes, the church-state issue proved less contentious, the earlier trends toward disintegration ended or slowed. At the same time, population increased, new lands came under cultivation, and foreign investment began to flow in.[12] New economic institutions (banks, financial houses, others) opened, armies and bureaucracies were modernized and professionalized, and governments slowly acquired effective control over their own national territories. As Latin America began to develop really for the first time, new ideologies and ways of organizing national social and political life crept in. Some of these challenged the existing order and ways of doing things, others were adapted to traditional Latin American practices. The dilemma was, of course, that while authoritarianism was no longer viewed as acceptable, liberalism didn't seem to work very well in the Latin American context. So the hemisphere began to look for new alternatives.

The first of these new philosophies in Latin America, having its major impact from the 1870s until the end of the century, and thus corresponding to Latin America's first spurt of development, was positivism.[13] Positivism was a social and political philosophy imported from France; its founding guru was French philosopher Auguste Comte. Positivism had far more impact in Latin America than it ever had in the United States; it is even embedded to this day in the Brazilian national flag in the form of the motto "Order and Progress." Briefly, positivism advocated the "scientific" organization and rationalization of society and politics to achieve national development goals. It sought to harness all the energies of society to achieve modernization. Society would be orderly and hierarchical; it would be guided in the right directions by educated elites. Positivism stood for change and evolutionary progress but in a controlled, orderly way.

One can easily comprehend why positivism would be so attractive to Latin American intellectual and political elites. It advocated change and progress but not through revolutions. It was change led by the educated elites, devolving little power upon the masses. It stood for development but not genuine democratization or popular participation. It was not divisively individualistic in the U.S. sense but was centralized, organic, top-down, and corporatist in accord with long-standing Latin American traditions. Positivism favored modernization but modernization under the existing social and power structure. For the elites and nascent middle class in Latin America, all these were very attractive features.

The next ideology to make its impact felt in Latin America was *Hispanismo*, or admiration for things Spanish.[14] For most of the nineteenth century, Latin America had hated and reviled the former colonial master Spain, blaming Spain for sucking out its wealth, imposing feudal and backward institutions on the area, and failing to prepare Latin America for independence. But after Spain's withdrawal from Latin America, and particularly after Spain's defeat by the "upstart" United States in the war of 1898, Latin America began to look with greater sympathy and admiration on its former colonial master.

This included newfound admiration for Spanish art, dance, literature, religion, law, language, and even social and political institutions. One of the purest (and best-selling) expressions of *Hispanismo* was the book *Ariel* by Uruguayan writer José Enrique Rodó, in which he contrasted the spiritual, cultured, refined, artistic, Hispanic world with the supposedly crass, materialistic, grasping, uncultured United States.[15] *Hispanismo* also emphasized Spain's Catholic and conservative traditions.

One of the ingredients in the *Hispanismo* "package" was a new political philosophy called corporatism. Modern corporatism had emerged in mid-nineteenth-century Europe particularly in the Catholic countries. By the 1880s it was growing into a mass movement, and by 1892 it had received the blessing of the pope in his famous encyclical *Rerum Novarum*. Like positivism, corporatism was much more popular in the Hispanic countries (Spain and Portugal as well as Latin America) than it ever was in the United States. In contrast to the Marxian class-conflict ideology then also gaining new adherents, corporatism advocated the unity and harmony of capital and labor. It was opposed also to liberalism and individualism; instead, corporatism advocated the reorganization of society and politics in terms of "organic," supposedly "natural" functional (or corporate) units: the family, the parish, the neighborhood; groups of entrepreneurs, workers, farmers, fishermen, soldiers; religious orders, etc. It favored a strong state, an ordered and integrated society, and tripartite cooperation between business, unions, and government. Corporatism thus presented itself as "the third way," between Marxism and liberalism, because of its emphasis on religion and historical continuity, and as an alternative ideology especially well suited to the countries of Iberia and Latin America.[16] Corporatism grew slowly in the first decade of the twentieth century but after World War I and the Bolshevik revolution in Russia it gained new adherents and was probably the most popular political philosophy in Latin America in the 1920s and 1930s.

As with positivism, one can readily understand why corporatism would be so popular in Latin America especially among the elites. Again, it stood for change but controlled and regulated change. It incorporated business and labor into the political process but under state and elite direction. Through its organic, top-down, centralized, and integral features, it was congruent with many Latin American values and institutions stretching into the distant past. It brought labor and capital together, thus avoiding Marxism, while its corporate or group-oriented approach avoided the hated features of individualism and liberalism. Perhaps most important from the elite's point of view, it provided for adjustment to change but under elite auspices and control. Corporatism was so popular in some areas of Europe and Latin America during this period that it was touted as the wave of the future: corporatism was to be the dominant philosophy of the twentieth century just as liberalism had been dominant in the nineteenth.

Corporatism also claimed, with its organic, integral, and statist features, to be uniquely attuned to Latin American society: a new political philosophy for Latin America to serve as a counterpart to the dominant liberalism of North America. Even though corporatism had originated in Europe, the claim was made that it fit Iberia and Latin America better. Here at last was the long-sought indigenous or home-grown (at least home-adapted) political philosophy for which Latin America had been searching. One that seemed to reflect, not the U.S. model, but its own Hispanic realities. However, because of the identification of corporatism during World War II with fascism, corporatism as a political philosophy was discredited and the term thereafter seldom used. Nevertheless in practice (Perón in Argentina, Vargas in Brazil, and many others) much of Latin America continued to follow one form of corporatism or another until long into the postwar era. It is a theme to which we later return.

Corporatism's great rival and "threat" in Latin America in the 1920s and 1930s had been Marxism.[17] Indeed one can view the emergence of corporatism as a more conservative and, in the context of southern Europe and Latin America, a more Catholic response to what was called "the social question": how to deal with the rise of an organized, politicized working class. Corporatism provided one answer to this question, liberal-pluralism a second answer, and Marxism a third. Marxism came in many different varieties in Latin America: socialism, communism, anarcho-syndicalism, Trotskyism, agrarian radicalism, eventually guerrilla movements and Marxian dependency theory. The very diversity of Marxism in Latin America served to divide and weaken the movement; the weakness of labor organizations, peasant associations, and working-class consciousness constituted other debilitating factors. Marxism seldom was strong enough to seize or hold power in Latin America; where it threatened existing institutions it was usually brutally suppressed by the armed forces.

Especially interesting for our purposes in this book were the several efforts to adapt Marxism to Latin American realities and thus to fashion an indigenous Marxism. For example, since industrialization lagged in Latin America and the working class was small, there was little hope for a real proletarian revolution; however, there were many peasants, marginals, and indigenous peoples. So, for instance, the Peruvian Marxist José Carlos Mariátegui (1895–1930) sought to rewrite Marx to make the peasants and Indians rather than the working class the cutting edge of the revolution.[18] Also in Peru, Victor Raúl Haya de la Torre began a mass-based, democratic-socialist party (the *Apristas*), with offshoots in other countries, that similarly offered a theory of change and of "historical time-space" (whatever that means) based more on the Inca than on a European-type proletariat.[19] In Mexico, too, emerging from the revolution of 1910–1920, came a renewed focus on the country's Indian heritage and, in some writers, a glorification of the Indian and of *mestizos* (people of mixed Indian and Caucasian heritage) as constituting a new "cosmic race."[20] But few of these movements achieved political success and certainly not in the countries with minority Indian populations; where they did succeed, they did so more on the basis of their social-democratic platforms than on their indigenous appeals.

Bureaucratic-Authoritarianism and Transitions to New Forms of Democracy

After World War II Latin America still had within its ideological pantheon virtually every political philosophy and form of sociopolitical organization since the dawn of recorded history. These included feudalism, mercantilism, organicism, republicanism, positivism, corporatism, Marxism, capitalism, liberalism, indigenism, socialism, and democracy. In Charles W. Anderson's apt phrase, Latin America resembled a "living museum" of shopworn ideas and ideologies with old ones never discarded and new ones constantly being added.[21] Anderson even constructed a full-blown theory of the Latin American political process out of these disparate elements, thus bringing "system" to a continent that to most outsiders looked chaotic.

Within these Latin American systems, according to Anderson, there were many legitimate routes to power, including revolutions, guerrilla movements, violence, and power demonstrations as well as elections. Politics was more fluid, tentative, and informal than in the United States, with a variety of "power contenders" (church, army, oligarchy, students, trade unions, farmers, etc.) vying for political power and influence in a constantly shifting political kaleidoscope where legitimacy for any kind of regime was usually weak and fleeting. It is no wonder that encompassed in this "system" in the 1940s and 1950s one could find military regimes, more-or-less democratic regimes, authoritarian regimes (both civilian and military), populist regimes, socialist regimes, and corporatist regimes, as well as many crazy quilts of all or several of these.

During the 1950s and culminating in the early 1960s, as a result of both change within Latin America and pressure from the outside (mainly the United States) Latin America began to move—temporarily as it turned out—in a more democratic direction. The period was referred to as the "twilight of the tyrants," as a number of Latin America's most notorious tyrants—Perón, Batista, Trujillo—fell from power. Within the United States at least, there was great optimism that democracy had finally arrived in Latin America. Remember, this was the era of John F. Kennedy, Camelot, and the naive belief among Americans that economic development would produce political systems that looked just like America, or as we imagine America to be: liberal, pluralist, democratic, socially just.[22] This experiment in democratization failed for several reasons but one of them was surely the U.S.-inspired effort to erect individualistic, inorganic, liberal, pluralist democracy in a continent that had always been group- and/or community-based, organic, illiberal, and minimally pluralist. In other words, many U.S. policy makers sought to create a model of democracy in Latin America that had little basis in the area's own realities or history, that lacked indigenous roots, and therefore was doomed to failure. U.S. policy makers today may be repeating the same mistakes in a renewed effort to democratize Latin America.

In part because of the inappropriate use of the wrong democratic model, Latin America began to experience a wave of coups in the 1960s that soon became a flood returning military-authoritarian government to power. By the mid-1970s fourteen of the twenty countries were under military rule; in three others the military constituted the power behind the throne. That left only three countries out of twenty as democracies and even these were referred to as elite-directed democracies. Quite a number of these authoritarian regimes were vicious human rights abusers and were often censured by U.S. and international human rights groups and governments. These regimes were different from numerous Latin American tyrannies of the past in that they were dominated not so much by one man as by an institutionalized military or by a similarly authoritarian civilian-military coalition. For this reason they were referred to as "bureaucratic-authoritarian" regimes, and a considerable literature grew up about this new phenomenon.[23]

We could say much about these bureaucratic-authoritarian regimes but our purpose here is to focus on their use—and manipulation—of the "indigenous model" theme. First, like Francisco Franco in Spain or Salazar in Portugal, the rulers of these regimes sought to discredit or even snuff out liberalism and pluralism as inappropriate and foreign ideologies ill-suited to their countries' unique traditions. At the same time, they sought to elevate to a position of sole importance the other and more traditional facet of their countries' tradition which was authoritarian, closed, top-down, and statist. But in the more complex and socially differentiated Latin America of the 1970s that was too simple a formula; the more traditional Latin America could not rule entirely without and against the other, more liberal Latin America, unless it was willing to use such force and repression as to verge on totalitarianism.

Few efforts were made by the bureaucratic-authoritarians then in power to build bridges or reach across to accommodate the democratic elements. In this respect the bureaucratic-authoritarians repeated the same mistake that the more triumphalist democrats had made in the 1960s: thinking they could rule alone, without, and often against, such traditional forces as the military and the economic elites. This is a formula not for democratic compromise and stability but for endemic civil war. Like Spain in the 1930s, Latin America in the 1960s and 1970s had degenerated into fragmentation, discord, and conflict— "invertebrate societies" as philosopher José Ortega y Gassett called them.[24]

By the late 1970s the bureaucratic-authoritarian (B-A) model was discredited and in the 1980s it was in full retreat. The several reasons for the B-A model's failure are familiar: human rights abuses, economic mismanagement, suppression of opposition groups, inefficiency, corruption, international stigmatization—even (in the Argentine case) failure in waging the Falklands war, presumably what military regimes should do best. But perhaps the main reason, encompassing these others, was that the military regimes sought to rule for and by only one part of the population—the more traditional sectors—while ignoring or suppressing the others. This was an untenable arrangement because of both domestic pressures and international human rights activities. As a result, from the late 1970s on the B-A regimes were, in country after country, replaced by democracy.

One of the notable features of the B-A regimes had been their attraction to and revival of corporatism—and for the same reasons that corporatism had been popular earlier in the century. Corporatism promised a way of organizing disorganized societies, of structuring both business and labor under state control, of providing for change that was guided and controlled, and of avoiding both the class conflict of Marxism and the unfettered pluralism of liberalism. A right-wing version of corporatism was also presented as a distinct, unique, indigenous, Latin American way of organizing social and political life, thus (these B-A regimes hoped) increasing their appeal and popularity.[25]

Opposed to the corporatist paradigm and largely written and advocated by the "other" Latin America that was now in exile or suppressed was dependency theory, or *dependencia*. There are distinct versions of dependency theory ranging from the analytic assessment of scholars such as Theodore Moran[26] to the more overtly political and ideological writings of Andre Gunder Frank and Fernando Henrique Cardoso.[27] *Dependencia* tended to view the world in Marxian, class-conflict terms and particularly saw the United States as the cause of Latin America's underdevelopment. It portrayed the United States as allied with the Latin American militaries and bourgeoisie and thus as a supporter of the B-A model. Dependency theory was presented as a uniquely Latin American creation and, like its rival corporatism, laid claim to being an indigenous ideology for the entire continent. In fact, as a political ideology it represented a much narrower spectrum than that, limited largely to university professors and their students, some clerics ("liberation theology" was one expression of dependency theory), and exiled intellectuals. Dependency theory in other words represented a part of the "other" Latin America which the bureaucratic-authoritarians had suppressed.

Given the close association of corporatism with the B-A regimes, when these regimes were discredited and removed from power, corporatism as a political paradigm was also discredited. That meant denial of and shame for the area's heritage, or at least part of that heritage—not a good basis on which to build an indigenous, home-grown theory of change. In fact corporatism can take centrist, Christian-democratic, and even left-wing directions as well as right-wing ones; but the identification with bureaucratic-authoritarianism was such that *all* of the corporatist philosophy had to be suppressed. The same thing had happened in Spain following Franco's death in 1975 and in Portugal following the revolution against the Salazar-Caetano regime in 1974. The result was that a political belief system that *did* have indigenous roots and *could* have, in modernized, updated form (neocorporatism), served as a basis of consensus and held fractured Iberian and Latin American societies together, was sacrificed.[28]

Interestingly, much the same thing happened to dependency theory. The transition to democracy in Latin America (now encompassing nineteen of the twenty republics), the collapse of the Soviet Union, and the failures of other Marxist regimes (Cuba, Nicaragua) meant that dependency theory went into eclipse as well. Of course there *is* dependency in Latin America just as there is a tradition of monism and corporatism, but for political reasons both of these alternatives have been discredited. Now democracy is the only political ideology and form of government left with any legitimacy. But democracy, as we see in the next section, remains a fragile basket for Latin America to put all of its eggs into; on the other hand, there is no synthesis yet that would usefully tie corporatism and the historic Latin American tradition, dependency, and democracy together. The combination of these facts and omissions may not augur well for the future of Latin America, and certainly not for a genuinely Latin American model of development.

The End of the Cold War and the Present Situation

Democracy of a sort has now been established in every Latin American country except Cuba. Both of the other main alternatives—authoritarian-corporatism and Marxism-Leninism—have been repudiated; democracy remains the only option and enjoys widespread legitimacy. Public opinion surveys throughout Latin America indicate that, depending on the country, democracy is viewed as the best form of government by more than 80, 85, or 90 percent of the population.

But not all is well with Latin American democracy. The problems in many countries still include grinding poverty, vast social gaps, inefficient governments, corruption, drug traffickers, governments that can't deliver on their electoral promises, restive militaries, etc.

Seldom mentioned in this list of problems, however, but crucial for our understanding, are numerous problems with democracy itself. For example, Latin Americans do not always share the U.S. understanding of what democracy means. Americans usually define democracy in terms of fair and honest elections, but for Uruguayans democracy means welfarism, for Brazilians it means patronage. When asked what they mean by democracy, Venezuelans and Dominicans say "strong government," a government that is nationalistic, unified, that takes care of its people. But those, to North American ears, are very strange definitions of democracy and smack of the statist, mercantilist, top-down, and paternalistic regimes of the past. Moreover, when 60 percent or more define democracy as "strong government," that seems to imply the possibility of an authoritarian solution, which in fact has long been the other fork in the road, the *alternative* to democracy.[29]

These same public opinion surveys indicate similarly weak support for what are usually thought of as democracy's essential supporting institutions. Latin American legislatures, courts, and bureaucracies enjoy the backing of less than 25 percent of the population, lagging far behind the Catholic Church and the armed forces in popularity. Nor do political parties (any party!) or labor unions have much legitimacy, their public support ranging in the 15–20 percent level. These numbers indicate that the main institutions of democracy have very low legitimacy and that democratic pluralism is not well institutionalized. Recent polls show that support for democracy itself may be declining, down from 80 percent to 60 percent in Venezuela, for instance. These are the realities and they are not entirely encouraging for supporters of democracy.[30]

What is going on here? If we examine these poll results carefully, the answer becomes clear. On the one hand, democracy as an ideal, as an abstract principle, still enjoys—as it has since the early nineteenth century—widespread support in Latin America. But in the often disorganized and under-institutionalized conditions of Latin America, people realize that democracy may not work or work very well in their context. Hence, their preference for strong government, executive leadership, a nationalistic regime, top-down paternalism, a mercantilist state that also provides abundant opportunities for employment.

The regimes that bridge these two conceptions—Alberto Fujimori in Peru, Rafael Caldera in Venezuela, Joaquín Balaguer in the Dominican Republic, Carlos Saúl Menem in Argentina—are often criticized in the United States for their statist ways; but they may be closer to the mainstreams of public opinion in their own countries than are the American embassy officials or World Bank missions that presume to advise them. This is democracy with adjectives—partial democracy, guided democracy, tutelary democracy, delegated democracy, Rousseauian democracy—and it may well represent a workable compromise between the two main political and ideological currents, liberalism and authoritarianism, that still run side by side in Latin America. Without such compromise, Latin America may continue to splinter and fall apart.[31]

While democracy of a certain kind triumphed *politically* in Latin America in the 1980s, in the 1990s the free-market philosophy of neoliberalism also triumphed, at least superficially, in the economic sphere. The reasons for this triumph include the manifest failures of the socialist economies, the undoubted accomplishments of the east Asian capitalist economies, and the bankruptcy of Latin America's own statist import-substitution industrialization (ISI) model. For some people, democracy in the political sphere goes hand in hand ideologically with a free market in the economic realm, but in Latin America this assumption has not worked out particularly well either. While some countries have undoubtedly been stimulated economically by state downsizing, privatization, and neoliberalism, the results overall have been less than spectacular and often downright disastrous.

In Mexico the neoliberal reforms of the Carlos Salinas administration are seen (for the most part, wrongly) as triggering the peso crisis of 1994 and the subsequent downturn of the Mexican economy resulting in job loss, bank failures, high unemployment, and the impoverishment of its middle and lower classes. Because of the Mexican crisis, politicians in other Latin American countries are loathe to introduce the same neoliberal reforms as Mexico did, fearing the wrath of the voters and even food riots, disintegration, and coups against democracy itself, as occurred recently in Venezuela. In addition, advocates of the earlier statist approach, who could never admit that their formula was wrong and who often occupy comfortable positions at international lending agencies such as the World Bank and Inter-American Development Bank, are using the Mexican crisis as a way to discredit free markets and to stage a comeback for themselves. Although neoliberal economics is often seen as the counterpart to democratic politics, in Latin America so far neoliberalism enjoys much less acceptance and legitimacy than democracy.

Nor has corporatism in its newer ("neo"), modern, European, social-democratic form been re-elevated to a position of legitimacy in Latin America. Given Latin America's centuries-long history of corporatism—corporatism that is so embedded in the political culture and social structure that one author calls it "natural corporatism"—one might expect corporatism to be included among the clustering of traits associated with the area. But it is not. Two factors are involved. The first is corporatism's earlier association in the public mind with fascism, which makes it unfashionable and unacceptable in Latin America. The second is corporatism's association with the now-defunct bureaucratic-authoritarian regimes of the 1970s, which similarly renders it politically unacceptable in the present political context. The term is in such opprobrium that even in its "neo," Christian-democratic, or social-democratic forms it cannot be spoken of in Latin American polite company. Latin America is in denial with regard to some of the most important ingredients in its own political-cultural tradition (others, besides corporatism, include organicism, patrimonialism, top-down authority). It is hard to envision an indigenous theory of politics and society emerging if Latin America continues to deny some of the major strands of its history and society that would go to make up such a home-grown theory.

In the meantime another new complicating factor has been added: the reemergence of indigenous groups in Latin America and the assertion of their own political agendas.[32] In such countries as Mexico, Guatemala, Colombia, Ecuador, Peru, Bolivia, and Brazil, indigenous groups are staking out stronger claims to land and territory, to autonomy, to political association that crosses presently sovereign national boundaries, and to their own religions, beliefs, and cultures. Many of these beliefs and cultural assertions are non-Western. So as we wrestle with the issue of an "indigenous" Latin American theory of development, we have to ask anew, what precisely do we now mean by that term. Do we mean (as primarily employed in this chapter) a theory of development that is predominantly Hispanic and modified and modernized over time in the Latin American context? Or a theory of development that is primarily reflective of the native peoples of the Americas? Or do we mean some hodge-podge, ill-defined, not-yet-worked-out (like the earlier notion of a "cosmic race") combination of the two?

Adding to the confusion are the recent cracks in what has come to be called "the Washington consensus,"the agreed-upon desirability of three factors: democracy, free trade, and open markets or neoliberalism. The third of these is presently under strong attack, the first is looking shaky in several countries, and the second continues (for now) to enjoy considerable popularity at least in elite circles.[33] But note all of these are *Western* concepts— although, as emphasized here, frequently with specifically Hispanic and Latin American features. So the problem for Latin America is thus compounded: not only are the Western foundations of its civilization shaky, open to different definitions, and not necessarily reflective of its own diverse and special tradition; but now the very "Westernness" of some Latin American countries and even their sovereign borders are being challenged by rising nativist movements.

Conclusions

Latin America has long been considered predominantly Western, but beyond that the agreement ends. Is it but a less-developed, pale imitation of the West, fated eventually to "catch up" in terms of social change, economic development, and political institutions? If this is the accepted interpretation (few serious students of the area accept this view), then there can be no such thing as a separate, distinct, Latin American theory and model of development. All that is required is for economic takeoff to occur and presumably Latin America will develop along the same lines as the United States or Western Europe: liberal, pluralist, democratic. But if one accepts, as most scholars do, that while Latin America is predominantly Western, it is at least in part a particular Hispanic, neoscholastic, counter-reformationary, Thomistic, organicist, semifeudal, corporatist, patrimonialist, precapitalist, pre-Enlightenment, pre-industrial-revolution, quasimedieval, pre-limited-government *version* of the West (now obviously updated), then some special theoretical and conceptual interpretations would seem to be called for.

The trouble is, Latin America does not like very much this latter set of characteristics, thinks of them as unfashionable, and does not wish to be seen or interpreted in that light. It *much* prefers to be seen as fully democratic, pluralist, and like Western Europe or the United States. But while these features are also present in Latin America, to emphasize them alone while wholly ignoring or denying the other, less attractive part of its history and tradition is to exist in a make-believe world that would artificially and arbitrarily blot out whole areas of Latin American life. The only way to make that argument tenable is to say that Latin America is *inevitably* and *universally* fated by developmental dynamics to go in the same direction and with the same institutional paraphernalia and developmental outcome as the rest of the West. But that is impossible to conceive for anyone even partly conversant with Latin American history, culture, institutions, and realities. These arguments about a genuinely Hispanic versus a predominantly U.S.-based model for Latin America have now been infinitely complicated by the recent strong reassertion of a nativist or indigenous claim to certain rights, territory, and cultural if not political autonomy.

At present, Latin America has all the formal accoutrements of Western-style democracy and institutions: political parties, regular elections, free markets, separation of powers, and the like. On the surface—and actually somewhat more than that—Latin America looks more or less like the Western democracies. But appearances disguise a wide range of sociocultural differences and problems. First, the Western-style institutions often imported from the United States or Western Europe are not working very well and some of the problems, as in Mexico, Guatemala, Peru, Colombia, Venezuela, etc., are quite fundamental. Second, it is hard to believe that the Latin American countries can be viable for very long if they emphasize only the attractive and liberal aspects of their tradition while ignoring or denying the less attractive (corporatist, elitist, authoritarian) features. And third are the renewed challenges of the indigenous groups, who may to elites represent either a revolutionary challenge to the status quo or a force to be coopted through some further Western-style or specifically liberal-democratic compromise.

Clearly Latin America is going through a period of confusion and contestation over its political culture, dominant traditions, and future directions. It favors democracy and Western ways, and yet all the poll data indicate that Latin America often means something different by certain key political terms than the United States does, or has different emphases and priorities. Most of these differences, over the definition of democracy, for example, relate to the "other Latin America" (Rousseauian, corporatist, organicist, etc.) that is currently being suppressed or denied. Moreover those regimes that seek to bridge these gaps, to maintain democracy while also accommodating to Latin America's own traditions—Caldera, Balaguer, Menem, Fujimori, and others—are often criticized mainly by the outside world for their undemocratic ways or departures from the neoliberal orthodoxy, even though they often enjoy widespread popularity in their own countries. Meanwhile the new aggressiveness of Latin America's indigenous movements in Peru, Bolivia, Mexico, or Guatemala threatens to throw all previous calculations of balancing already diverse cultural currents into a tizzy.

The prognosis therefore is not a very happy one. On the one hand the "Western model" (itself open to diverse interpretations) is not working very satisfactorily in Latin America. On the other, one whole part of the Latin American tradition that is Western but "Hispanic" (in the older sense: patrimonialist, organicist, etc.) is being suppressed and denied, a strategy that cannot be maintained indefinitely. And, third, those who have shown creativity and even political genius in fusing these traditions are roundly criticized from the outside for not being sufficiently "democratic" and often by all the polls in their own societies. If Latin Americans themselves, therefore, cannot yet reach minimum consensus on their basic values, culture, identity, and developmental model, it certainly will not be possible for outsiders to define that consensus for them.

Endnotes

1. For the competing paradigms see Martin Needler, *Political Development in Latin America* (New York: Random House, 1968); Enzo Faletto and Fernando Henrique Cardoso, *Dependency and Development in Latin America* (Berkeley: University of California Press, 1978); Guillermo O'Donnell, *Modernization and Bureaucratic-Authoritarianism in Latin America* (Berkeley: Institute of International Studies, University of California, 1973); and Howard J. Wiarda, *Corporatism and National Development in Latin America* (Boulder, CO: Westview Press, 1981).

2. John Martz, "The Place of Latin America in the Study of Comparative Politics," *Journal of Politics* 28 (Feb. 1966): 57–81.

3. By "Latin America" we here mean the former colonies of Spain and Portugal.

4. Latin America is considered a distinct "civilization" in Huntington's terms, but his well-known book on the subject devotes little follow-up analysis to the area. See Samuel P. Huntington, *The Clash of Civilizations and the Remaking of World Order* (New York: Simon and Schuster, 1996).

5. On the Spanish colonial system see Charles Gibson, *Spain in America* (New York: Harper and Row, 1966); and Lyle N. McAlister, *Spain and Portugal in the New World, 1492–1700* (Minneapolis: University of Minnesota Press, 1984).

6. For elaboration of these themes as well as individual country variations see Howard J. Wiarda and Harvey F. Kline, eds., *Latin American Politics and Development*, 4th ed. (Boulder, CO: Westview Press, 1996).

7. Tulio Halperin Donghi, *The Aftermath of Revolution in Latin America* (New York: Harper and Row, 1973).

8. Alexis de Tocqueville, *Democracy in America*.

9. Glen Dealy, "Prolegomena on the Spanish American Political Tradition," *Hispanic American Historical Review* 48 (Feb. 1968).

10. See Brian Loveman, *The Constitution of Tyranny: Regimes of Exception in Latin America* (Pittsburgh: University of Pittsburgh Press, 1993).

11. Claudio Veliz, *The Centralist Tradition in Latin America* (Princeton, NJ: Princeton University Press, 1980).

12. Roberto Cortes Conde, *The First Stages of Modernization in Latin America* (New York: Harper and Row, 1974).

13. W. Rex Crawford, *A Century of Latin American Thought* (New York: Praeger, 1966); and John Martz and Miguel Jorrín, *Latin American Political Thought and Ideology* (Chapel Hill, NC: University of North Carolina Press, 1970).

14. Frederick B. Pike, *Hispanismo 1898–1936: Spanish Conservatives and Liberals and Their Relations with Spanish America* (Notre Dame, IN: Notre Dame University Press, 1971).

15. José Enrique Rodó, *Ariel* (Austin: University of Texas Press, 1988).

16. Howard J. Wiarda, *Corporatism and Comparative Politics: The Other Great "Ism"* (New York: M. E. Sharpe, 1996).

17. Luís Aguilar, ed., *Marxism in Latin America* (New York: Knopf, 1971).

18. Harry Vanden, *National Marxism in Latin America: José Carlos Mariátegui's Thought and Politics* (Boulder, CO: Lynne Rienner, 1986).

19. Harry Kantor, *The Ideology and Program of the Peruvian Aprista Movement* (New York: Cotagon Books, 1966).

20. José Vasoncelos, *La Raza Cósmica*.

21. Charles W. Anderson, *Politics and Economic Change in Latin America* (Princeton, NJ: Van Nostrand, 1967).

22. Walt W. Rostow, *The Stages of Economic Growth* (New York: Cambridge University Press, 1960).

23. Guillermo O'Donnell, *Modernization and Bureaucratic-Authoritarianism*; also see Howard J. Wiarda, ed., *The Continuing Struggle for Democracy in Latin America* (Boulder, CO: Westview Press, 1977).

24. José Ortega y Gassett, *Invertebrate Spain* (New York: H. Fertig, 1974).

25. Howard J. Wiarda, *The Democratic Revolution in Latin America* (New York: A Twentieth Century Book, Holmes and Meier, 1992); and Guillermo O'Donnell, Philippe Schmitter, and Laurence Whitehead, eds., *Transitions from Authoritarian Rule: Prospects for Democracy* (Baltimore: Johns Hopkins University Press, 1986).

26. Theodore Moran, *Multinational Corporations and the Politics of Dependence* (Cambridge, MA: Center for International Affairs, Harvard University, 1975).

27. F. H. Cardoso and Enzo Faletto, *Dependency and Development* (Berkeley: University of California Press, 1978); A. G. Frank, *Capitalism and Underdevelopment in Latin America* (New York: Monthly Review Press, 1969).

28. Howard J. Wiarda, *Corporatism and Development: The Portuguese Experience* (Amherst: University of Massachusetts Press, 1977).

29. Consultores 21, *Cultura Democrática en Venezuela* (Caracas, Venezuela: Consultores 21, 1996); Isis Duarte et al., *Cultura Política y Democracía en República Dominicana* (Santo Domingo, Dominican Republic: Pontificía Universidad Católica Madre y Maestra, 1996).

30. See the author's companion volumes, *Democracy and Its Discontents: Development, Interdependence, and U.S. Policy in Latin America*, and *Iberia and Latin America: New Democracies, New Policies, New Models* (Lanham, MD: Rowman and Littlefield, 1995, 1996, respectively).

31. Anibal Romero, "Condemned to Democracy (with Adjectives): Latin America in the 1990s," in *Constructing Democracy and Markets: East Asia and Latin America* (Washington, DC: National Endowment for Democracy and the Pacific Council on International Policy, 1996): 84–92.

32. Donna Lee Van Cott, ed., *Indigenous Peoples and Democracy in Latin America* (New York: St. Martin's Press, 1994).

33. See the special issue of the *Journal of Inter-American Studies and World Affairs* focused on "U.S.-Latin American Relations," 39 (Spring 1997).

5

Sub-Saharan Africa: Western Influence and Indigenous Realities

Lana Wylie, a Ph.D. candidate in political science at the University of Massachusetts at Amherst and a recipient of the Leonard J. Horwitz Fellowship, has written articles about political development and has been employed as a researcher for international development projects.

From Angola to Zimbabwe and from Somalia to South Africa, political and economic development efforts have failed to alleviate the African continent's enormous problems. The people of Africa have endured one putative development panacea after another. Democracy and market economics are once again being offered as solutions.

Immediately after independence, most of the new states of Africa adopted constitutions and patterned their political systems after Western examples. However, these institutions were seldom adapted to African culture and traditions, and rarely worked as well as anticipated. More recently the idea (and model) of an indigenous route to development has been put forward, based on native, African institutions. Obviously the idea of African-based models, particularly given the many failures of imported institutions (both Marxist and non-Marxist), is very attractive. But the exclusively indigenous model is also problematic and may not offer Africa the hoped-for solution that its advocates claim.

This chapter wrestles with the issue of Western influences and indigenous realities in Africa. It examines the possibility of a hybrid model, a middle way in which the appropriate Western institutions are combined with indigenous African practices.

Background

Sub-Saharan Africa is home to more than 550 million people who are distributed unevenly among the fifty-one states of the region. While many countries have less than one million inhabitants, Nigeria, the largest, has a population of almost ninety million or one-sixth of the continent's total population. Natural resources are also unevenly distributed due to the wide variety of endowments, climates, and terrains.

Just as diverse as topography are sub-Saharan Africa's social, economic, and cultural conditions. Life expectancy for the continent is a relatively low fifty-two years, yet in Guinea-Bissau it is only thirty-nine years. Education and literacy rates are also low but varied. Only 2 percent of Rwanda's secondary-school-aged children attend school and, although by Western standards the numbers are still dismal in Mauritius, they are much higher—there, 54 percent of children are receiving an education. At 80 percent, Mauritius also has the region's highest literacy rate. By comparison, only one-third of the people in some neighboring states can read or write. Moreover, hundreds of different languages and ethnic groups are indigenous to Africa. Many combinations of peoples speaking several different languages exist within individual state boundaries, not to mention throughout the continent as a whole.

Despite this diversity, African peoples have much in common. Colonialism was experienced throughout the continent. Many post-independence experiences have also been shared. A recent article in *The Economist* began, "On go the killings, the fear, the flight of refugees, the hunger, the disease."[1] This article chronicled the recent chaos in central Africa, but it could have been describing situations that have existed in many areas of the continent over the past several decades. Much of sub-Saharan Africa has been, and continues to be, in political and economic turmoil.

Economically, the situation appears to have worsened since the 1980s. Populations continue to grow while gross national product (GNP) remains stagnant. Today, nearly 40 percent of Africans are under sixteen years old. Meanwhile Africa captures a paltry 3 percent of foreign direct investment. In comparison, east Asia and the Pacific Rim account for 59 percent and Latin America manages to capture a solid 20 percent of foreign direct investment.

A 1996 survey revealed that Africa's political statistics have also remained grim. Since independence, more than twenty countries in sub-Saharan Africa have undergone more than one violent transfer of leadership. Some countries, such as Nigeria, Sudan, and Burundi, have experienced at least five violent changes of government since the late 1950s.[2]

However, during the early 1990s, leaders tended to come to power, not through military coups, but by being elected. For many Westerners, this was extremely encouraging. They believed that liberal democracy was finally taking hold on the continent. They asserted that traditional institutions like the tribe are withering while other Western influences such as consumerism and capitalism have penetrated Africa. However, by the mid-1990s the democratic trend seemed to have stalled as military authoritarians learned to perpetuate themselves in power.

From colonial times to the present day, power in Africa has largely remained in the hands of those adopting a Western approach. The developmental or modernization paradigm, so widely touted in the first decades after independence, contributed to the "Westernization" of Africa. This approach assumed that African countries would progress through stages of development similar to the stages experienced by Western "developed" countries. Eventually, the economies, societies, and polities of Africa would resemble their Western counterparts. The proponents of modernization theory presumed that traditional African practices and institutions were dysfunctional.

However, Westernism has not completely penetrated the continent, in that many indigenous institutions and practices continue to survive. While not all native institutions are beneficial, many have persisted because they are effective. Furthermore, as the failure of the earlier modernization approach demonstrated, the Western approach to development in Africa may not only be inappropriate but has often been harmful.[3] Nevertheless, not all Western influences can be discarded, nor should they be. There are many Western institutions that have been shown to be appropriate to the African context. It may be that successful African development requires both viable indigenous institutions and appropriate non-African models.

Colonial Rule

While parts of Africa were affected by Europeans and Europeanism prior to the colonial period, impact became widespread only in the nineteenth century. By 1900 the African continent had been divided primarily among the British, Italian, German, French, Belgian, Spanish, and Portuguese governments. Every African country save Liberia experienced colonial rule. The amount of time each country spent under colonial tutelage varied widely. Ethiopia experienced five years of Italian rule while Angola was considered Portuguese territory for four centuries.

The style of colonial rule differed among the European colonizers and even among different territories held by the same power. However, two main forms of control can be distinguished. The first, represented by the French, attempted to eliminate most of the traditional structures and institutions. Their goal was to assimilate the Africans into the society of the home country. In contrast, the Germans and the British coopted the native structures in their governance of the colonies and thus, in many ways, did less harm to traditional culture.[4]

While the degree of resistance varied, most African rulers opposed colonialism. The Africans sought alliances with the Europeans only when they faced defeat in an intra-African conflict. Each colonizing country encountered native resistance. For example, the Ethiopians opposed their Italian rulers in 1896; the Asante people of Ghana resisted the British in 1891; and the Ovambo people of Angola fought their Portuguese rulers in the early 1900s. Hundreds of thousands died in the fight against colonialism.

The military superiority of the Europeans eventually overcame these attempts. However, resistance in a variety of forms continued in most areas. For example, guerrilla warfare was adopted by the Bauole in Ivory Coast. Opposition to the colonial order came to a head after World War II with the growth of nationalism.

While colonialism had serious repercussions, various factors influenced the *degree* to which European domination affected indigenous institutions. The differing approaches of the European colonizers to their African territories affected the persistence of traditional structures. For example, the French policies of assimilation and association had severe consequences in some areas. The French commonly removed chiefs and kings from power and replaced them with other Africans more willing to cooperate. In many cases, because these new rulers were illegitimate in the eyes of their subjects, the traditional political structures decayed.

Traditional ways of governance and indigenous structures suffered under all colonizers. One of the most devastating consequences of colonialism was the arbitrary division of peoples. Borders drawn by colonial powers did not correspond to the realities of ethnic groups. In the initial European scramble for territory, African kinship groups were broken up. Somalis were among those who suffered most from this colonial effect. Colonizers divided them between present-day Somalia, Ethiopia, Djibouti, and Kenya.

European conquest also generated new hostilities among Africans. While disputes between different ethnic groups were not uncommon in precolonial Africa, colonialism has often been blamed for exacerbating these tensions. Christian Potholm asserts that "European penetrations also reinforced and, in some cases, created tribal, linguistic, and ethnic divisiveness."[5] For example, divisions between Anglophone and Francophone countries were fostered by their European leaders. Some scholars even argue that tribalism was a product of colonialism. Basil Davidson explains that the Europeans gathered related ethnic groups into tribes to facilitate colonial administration.[6] Furthermore, the colonial legacy has been directly blamed for apartheid in South Africa and the war of liberation in Southern Rhodesia (present-day Zimbabwe) because control was transferred to the white settlers.

The rise of a money economy was devastating to traditional structures in parts of Africa. A labor force was required, export crops developed, trade expanded, and towns created in production and port areas. For example, in the mineral-rich regions of central and southern Africa large numbers of indigenous people were forced to work in mines. This distorted the traditional social and economic system.

While the colonial impact was severe, much of traditional African culture and many indigenous institutions survived. Numerous African leaders managed to preserve their societies—including the Mossi kingdom in Burkina Faso, the Ganda of Uganda, and the Fanti in Rwanda, Ghana, and Burundi—through careful cooperation with Europeans. For example, in Burkina Faso the Mossi kingdom was able to survive by cooperating with colonial powers.

Even in those regions where traditional political structures collapsed under colonialism political culture often persisted. In French colonies where colonial rulers actively strived to destroy the existing political culture, significant cultural elements were preserved. The immense land area posed a serious impediment to the ability of French and other colonizers to destroy the traditional cultures. In most cases direct European influence was felt only in the ports or other areas of interest to colonizers.

The indigenous economy was similarly influenced. The introduction of cash crops had an effect on indigenous societies and agriculture. However, many aspects of the native economy remained intact as the cash crop economy was dominated by men. Women continued to farm food crops in traditional ways. George Ayittey argues that because colonizers were concerned only with cash crops they did not interfere with production or distribution of traditional agriculture.[7] Furthermore, traditional markets and systems of exchange persisted. Thus, while regions suited to production or transport of cash crops were greatly affected by colonialism, other areas felt only minimal effects. This dual economy existed throughout most of Africa during colonial times.

The Post-Independence Period

After formal independence was achieved, many "Western" ideas or institutions remained, and other, newer ones were introduced. The modernization paradigm was accepted by both Western and African scholars and officials as *the* model. African elites sought to "modernize" their countries and, consequently, damaged many traditional African institutions in the process. Many newly independent African states sought to emulate the West politically, economically, and socially. Thus, the influence of the West did not cease with the independence of the African states.

Elites who succeeded colonial rulers were highly Westernized. They were often educated in European or colonial universities established by Europeans and spoke fluent English, French, or Portuguese. Some of these new countries officially adopted European languages after independence. It was also natural for many of these leaders to fashion European-modeled governments.

Nigeria, for example, designed its governance structure on the British model. The Nigerian elite set up a parliament, held elections, and created an independent judiciary and civil service. In Ghana and other countries, European-style political parties were created to help hold often divided societies together. The core institutions of these countries frequently grew more Westernized after independence.

Yet, in most cases Western political structures proved superficial and unworkable. These institutions were often utterly alien to the majority of the populace and thus crumbled, sometimes within months. For example, Nigeria's parliamentary democracy lasted until 1966. Nigeria then adopted the American model of government. That system also disintegrated.

The new leaders of African states also formed authoritarian and other single-party systems, often after brief flirtations with democracy. Some rulers claimed that adoption of an authoritarian model of government was consistent with indigenous ways since many traditional African societies emphasized community and consensus decision making under the leadership of a single chief. For example, Julius Nyerere of Tanzania and Robert Mugabe of Zimbabwe claimed that a one-party state best represented the traditional practice of governance through consensus. Yet, with the exception of a handful of states such as Nyerere's Tanzania, most of these governments lacked any connection to rural populations, drawing their support almost solely from urban elites.[8] Furthermore, as Ali A. Mazrui points out, traditional consensus government usually represented the population as if it formed a single ethnic group. Yet most African states encompass many different ethnic groups. Forced to live together in one state, these groups often compete for meager available resources. Ethnic tension is common. For example, hostility between the Igbo, the Yoruba, and the Hausa of Nigeria was a major cause of that country's brutal civil war. A single-party state would not likely be feasible in states such as Nigeria where ethnic identities permeate society.[9] Thus, the single-party solution was, in many cases, just as alien to African circumstances as parliamentary democracy.

The acceptance of the modernization approach in the first few decades after independence had consequences for traditional institutions. Traditional African political structures continued to decay after independence. New leaders removed even more authority from Africa's traditional chiefs and kings who were seen as relics of a backward Africa and were even accused of collaborating with colonial leaders. In Ghana the traditional authority of chiefs gradually eroded. They became so impotent that the government could effectively remove a chief from authority with a simple newspaper notice. Eventually chiefs' power became totally dependent on the government. According to Ayittey, the role of indigenous leaders in virtually all African governments diminished with independence.[10]

Independence also led to further decay of traditional economic and cultural institutions. Many leaders of newly independent Africa believed that native African ways and institutions were backward and consequently that the masses should adopt modern ways. Traditional African industries and culture suffered because of this attitude. Ayittey explains that African "elites did not understand how the indigenous system operated" and thus "they could not improve its performance and productivity."[11] Examples of the negative effects of these attempts abound. For example, the Ghanaian government attempted to impose new methods of fishing on their coastal fishermen. As a result, many people went without food because the government refused to accept "primitive" methods of fishing in dug-out canoes or traditional methods of preserving fish.[12] Other industries suffered a similar fate as "modern" methods were imposed with often disastrous results.

Another force that has Westernized Africa in the postcolonial period is foreign aid. While external assistance has without doubt brought relief to many parts of the continent, it has also in many cases deepened Africa's reliance on the West. Aid often encouraged the importation of inappropriate technology or luxury goods. Throughout Africa, modern tractors, air conditioners, and other items that governments purchased with foreign aid funds collected dust because either people were not skilled in their operation or repair parts were unavailable. Furthermore, the elites and growing numbers of the masses have been developing tastes for Western consumer goods that were initially imported as part of a tied-aid package. Moreover, African economies became dependent on industrialized states for the technology and finance needed for their development. To this day, most African countries continue to depend on the production of those few commodities that they were forced to produce during colonialism. In many countries these raw materials account for the majority of foreign exchange earnings. The African people have become increasingly reliant upon foreign aid and trade.

Thus, in most African countries independence did not eliminate Western influence. In fact, the new African leaders often accepted the developmental model touted by their Western counterparts or by the professors under whom they had studied in Western universities. Westernism was equated with modernity. Consequently, significant areas of Africa became firmly enmeshed in the Western-dominated capitalist system, and, after independence, experimented with Western-style political institutions. After the collapse of multiparty democracy, single-party, authoritarian regimes became the norm. Yet neither model successfully integrated traditional African practices. Indigenous structures suffered under both forms of state organization.

Resistance to Neocolonialism

By the 1970s, however, it was clear that Western institutions could not be easily transplanted in Africa. Resistance to the West and Westernization grew widespread. Marxism enjoyed renewed support in the mid-1970s and early

1980s. Dependency theory gained prominence throughout former colonial territories. Regimes such as those in Mozambique, Zimbabwe, and Ethiopia voiced Marxist or Marxist-Leninist opposition to capitalism.

A renewed sense of political and economic nationalism permeated the continent. Economic nationalism and the assertion of the new international economic order (NIEO) were attempts by the former colonies to evade some of the negative aspects of the Western-dominated international economy. Nationalist regimes also developed. However, some of these governments, ruled by dictators such as Idi Amin of Uganda, often used nationalism to justify oppression.

Opposition to the West was demonstrated by African leadership of the nonaligned movement (NAM) and the Group of 77. African states viewed nonalignment as a strategy to avoid domination by either side during the Cold War. They permitted and even encouraged competition between East and West in Africa. Governments accepted aid from both blocs while remaining officially neutral in the Cold War. However, opposition to former colonial powers and the West, generally, was an important goal. Africa's leaders believed that neutrality in the Cold War would finally separate them from their colonial past.

The nonaligned movement was initially a vehicle for political resistance. However, demands for change in the international economic order became an equally important goal expressed through this movement. OPEC's ability to exert pressure on the industrialized world through the creation of an oil oligopoly gave the nonaligned countries hope that they could similarly influence the developed states through collective action. African states such as Algeria were among the most vocal advocates of the creation of commodity-exporting associations.

The Organization for African Unity (OAU) also developed in opposition to Western influence on the continent. Its leaders believed that a united Africa would serve as a bulwark to external pressures. African governments hoped that collective action in the NAM, the OAU, and the Group of 77 would advance Africa's political and economic goals. Independence from the West was seen as both a means to these goals and as an end in itself.

Yet, keeping the West at bay through pan-Africanism or Third World collusion was a daunting and often unattainable task. The effort to force the industrialized world to reverse Africa's negative position in the world economy through the NIEO was similarly unsuccessful. The leverage that the Africans had hoped to attain by forming commodity-exporting organizations never materialized. Lack of internal cohesion, the power of the industrialized countries, the international recession in the mid-1970s, and the election of conservative governments in a number of prominent Western countries destroyed these aspirations.[13] African countries continued to rely heavily on Western assistance. Loans and grants from the World Bank and the International Monetary Fund (IMF) strengthened the West's influence over the continent.

Under IMF and World Bank pressure in the 1980s, African leaders agreed to implement structural adjustment and stabilization policies. The stabilization approach, particularly, has entailed a renewed emphasis on market solutions. Government involvement was curtailed, wages frozen, interest rates increased, and trade liberalized during the 1980s, often wreaking havoc in these countries. The implementation of economic reforms increased borrowing from the IMF and the World Bank throughout the 1980s. The rising debts of African states amplified their dependence on these institutions and industrialized states. This increased dependence on external institutions and the neoliberal emphasis of economic policy prescriptions has further entangled Africa in the Western-led global economy.

Post-Cold War Africa

The conclusion of the Cold War ended Africa's ability to play one superpower off the other. African states could no longer rely on support from the communist bloc. The West, in many respects, had become the only game in town. Just as the Bretton Woods institutions had imposed economic conditions on Africa in the 1980s, so the end of the Cold War brought *political* conditionality as well. The West now assumes that economic and political conditionality is necessary for African development. Western aid agencies and international institutions now "encourage" democratization or political liberalization.

In the post-Cold War era Western governments have employed their aid in Africa to promote political changes. In 1990 the U.S. ambassador to Kenya warned that:

> There is a strong tide flowing in our Congress, which controls the purse strings, to concentrate our economic assistance on those of the world's nations that nourish democratic institutions, defend human rights, and practice multi-party politics.[14]

Other aid donors had similar warnings for Kenya's leaders. The Kenyan government bowed to this pressure, causing Kenya's President Moi to declare that Western coercion was behind his government's acquiescence to democratic elections. Other regimes throughout Africa were also encouraged to liberalize by the industrialized world.[15]

As a result of external pressure and internal opposition to authoritarian rule, some countries of Africa joined democracy's third wave in the early 1990s. A 1995 report by the African Institute of South Africa named thirty-three African countries that possessed political parties, elective institutions, or elections.[16] For example, free elections were held in Benin and Zambia in 1991, in Malawi in 1994, and in Sierra Leone in 1996.

Especially encouraging were the end of apartheid and the installation of democracy in South Africa. The 1994 elections that brought the first black leader to power in South Africa were declared free and fair. Furthermore, the South African economy is by far the strongest on the continent. South Africa has become the model to emulate for other African states that are attempting to enact political and economic liberalization.

Yet many scholars believe that the type of democracy currently prevalent in Africa only masks authoritarian practices. In these virtual democracies, the leaders have discovered how to control elections and other features of democracy both to maintain their power base and to obtain the approval of Western aid agencies. Richard Joseph has applied Robert Bates' schema to democratization in Africa. Bates suggested that tyrants "convert" and become champions of liberal democracy in order to protect themselves. Joseph argues most of the conversions to democracy in sub-Saharan Africa "were made reluctantly as tactical moves to retain power."[17] Joseph argues that the conversion of Compaore in Burkina Faso, Babangida in Nigeria, and many others fall into this category.

Furthermore, some scholars warn that the current Western emphasis on economic and political liberalization in Africa is reminiscent of the earlier modernization approach. While the more recent version emphasizes civil society and the creation of an accountable state, its calls for democratization and market economics echo 1960s modernization theory. John Harbeson points out that the difference today is that "parallel political and economic transitions are billed as necessary rather than inevitable, and retrogression is characterized as unacceptable rather than implausible."[18] While the recent version of modernization theory is less ethnocentric than its predecessor, it also often fails to take account of the political, economic, social, and cultural realities of Africa.

This failure raises doubts about the future success of ongoing political and economic changes in Africa. Even in South Africa, the West's current champion, problems are beginning to surface. Rising unemployment, the collapsing rand, growing lawlessness, and a political opposition divided by ethnic tensions have raised doubts about the future of South Africa. These problems have caused some to muse whether "they represent the first skid down the slippery African slope, one which has oiled the failure of so many other countries to build a prosperous democracy after winning political liberation?" [19]

The viability of South Africa's democracy after the retirement of Mandela in 1999 is also being questioned. Then, people ask: "What is to stop South Africa slipping the way of Zimbabwe, a supposed multiparty democracy ruled as a de facto one-party state, with a government that rides in limousines, periodically clamps down on the press, and blames white ownership of the economy for the country's ills?"[20] There are real questions as to whether the imposition of Western-style democracy will take hold in Africa.

Many authors argue that while democracy has a precolonial history in Africa the Western version is inherently alien to Africans. Claude Ake asserts that "in order for African democracy to be relevant and sustainable it will have to be radically different from liberal democracy."[21] The polity must reflect African community-oriented culture. Ake asserts: "The familiar political assumptions and political arrangements of liberal democracy make little sense in Africa. Liberal democracy assumes individualism, but there is little individualism in Africa: it assumes the abstract universalism of legal subjects, but in Africa that would apply only in the urban environment; the political parties of liberal democracy do not make sense in societies where associational life is rudimentary and interests groups remain essentially primary groups . . ."[22]

Thus, if scholars such as Ake are correct, Western institutions like liberal democracy are likely to eventually fail in Africa. It is widely argued, however, that a democracy reflective of African realities would be more sustainable. Although the actual shape of this proposed African model remains unclear and would likely vary according to political histories, African societies have successfully molded many Western practices and institutions to their particular contexts.

The Hybrid Option: The Mingling of Indigenous and Western Ways

Over the decades since independence, many African leaders have learned that Western institutions and practices cannot be easily transplanted into their societies. The various histories, cultures, institutions, economies, and societies of Africa not only are very diverse but also very different from the West. So, they have begun to search for solutions to their manifold problems in indigenous rather than imported institutions. Home-grown institutions would presumably be more viable and functional than have been the artificially imposed Western ones. Despite the massive onslaught of Westernization and the failure of leadership efforts such as the NIEO and the nonaligned movement, much of African tradition has survived. For example, while many large kinship groups were splintered by the arbitrary colonial boundaries, the importance of kinship has survived both the colonial and independence periods. Kinship ties, in rural Africa especially, have remained strong. Though urbanites place more emphasis on the nuclear family, the wider kinship connections still play a significant role in their lives. Naomi Chazan, Robert Mortimer, John Ravenhill, and Donald Rothchild assert: "There is rarely a bureaucrat, university lecturer, or migrant worker who does not feel the need to meet the expectations of his or her relatives."[23]

Furthermore, the strength of kinship helped many traditional political structures survive. Ethnic connections often formed the basis of political systems. Traditional political systems are fairly common locally in many African countries. Chazan explains: "Chiefs, paramount chiefs, or other traditional officeholders still control much land and have access to communal labor. These authorities allocate shares of jointly owned lands to kin groups and define community holdings. They may still levy taxes, collect other forms of revenue, and serve as judges and arbiters of local disputes."[24] Precolonial political structures have been altered but often remain otherwise intact throughout Africa.

Economic and cultural elements of traditional Africa have also persisted. Despite the availability of Western cultural garb in the urban centers, it has not penetrated deeply into society, particularly the rural areas. Although Levi's, Coca-Cola, and Michael Jackson tapes are sold on the streets of Gambia's capital city, only the wealthiest of the younger urbanites are in the market for these Western items. The rest of the country remains traditional.

Frequently, however, these indigenous political, economic, and cultural structures have survived by accommodating Western practices or institutions. Indigenous elements have sometimes combined with Western institutions to produce a modern, but truly African, alternative. For example, an indigenous language in east Africa, Kiswahili, adopted the Roman alphabet but has since remained the primary language. It is used by the people and government of Tanzania. At the same time, the percentage of educated people fluent in English has declined. The use of Kiswahili is also strong in neighboring states such as Kenya.[25]

Western communications media have similarly been altered by traditional culture. In addition to transmitting in the native language, African radio broadcasts and newspapers are frequently altered in other ways that reflect the indigenous cultures. For example, newspapers in east Africa have adopted the Swahili tradition of communication through poems. It is commonplace to see a section of the paper devoted to poems to the editor.[26] This mixture of Western and indigenous cultures may help produce a late-twentieth-century African alternative.

Botswana demonstrates this practice at the state level. Botswana's postcolonial history of economic growth and political stability has its basis in the incorporation of indigenous traditions into the political system. Tribal or ethnic chiefs and consensus politics have been incorporated into the country's political structure. The chiefs continue to be respected members of the polity. They have authority, especially at the grassroots level. The traditional court system and the role of the chiefs as arbiters of disputes remain respected and legitimate. These traditional leaders are also involved with development efforts and meet regularly with cabinet ministers.

Thus, scholars and political leaders have discovered that the institution of the tribe or ethnic group often performs many useful services. It may provide police and justice functions, offer social services, and serve as a means of conveying ethnic interests to central governments and to implement public policies. Hence, the negative and "traditional" image that the institution of the tribe had in the past is being revised. In some countries, similarly, the institution of the chief is being incorporated into constitutions and the governmental system. Reassessing the roles of tribalism and chiefs has also stimulated a reexamination of state structure, leading to considerations of different forms of federalism as distinct from unitary centralism. The new and more positive view of traditional institutions has also been used to stimulate pride in native cultures and practices.

These new currents in Africa are controversial, however. While some countries are searching for an indigenous model to replace or modify the discredited imported ones, other countries continue to suppress traditional ethnic loyalties. The debate continues over whether to build on and modernize indigenous practices or to eliminate them to make way for "real" modernization. At the same time, it is not at all clear that the African people value their indigenous institutions in the same way that their own intellectuals do or that there is any agreement on which institutions should be preserved or enhanced or that these are more viable or functional for modernization than imported Western ones.

Conclusion

Western influence during the colonial period was concentrated in those areas brought into the international economy by Europeans. In port and mineral or export-crop areas European political, economic, social, or cultural practices were dominant. A Westernized African elite developed in these areas. However, the impact was far from pervasive because "Europeanization" was muted elsewhere on the continent. Western influence was also held at bay by Africans and their institutions, which proved adept at protecting their heritage.

Post-independence Africa under African, albeit often Westernized, leaders continued the spread of Western practices usually to the detriment of indigenous ways. Now part of the Western-states system, Africa began to superficially resemble the industrialized states. Parliaments were formed, and for a brief period in the 1960s, multiparty democracy existed. Civil war, government collapse, and chaos often resulted from the top-down imposition of Western institutions and ways because they did not reflect or address the indigenous cultural, social, economic, and political realities.

The post-independence African elite attempted to protect Africa from the West in the Group of 77 or the OAU. While some minor accommodations were made by developed countries, these institutions have been unable to overcome the overwhelming influence wielded by the West.

Yet, much of traditional African politics, economics, culture, and society have, thus far, withstood the Western onslaught. African practices managed to survive by blocking out or else adapting to Western institutions. Many African states have taken Western institutions and altered them to fit the African context.

While African states in the twenty-first century are likely to be as diverse as they are today, Rwanda, South Africa, and Botswana embody three possible and alternative paths for the continent. Will the countries of Africa be overwhelmed by the chaos and anarchy that are so prevalent in Rwanda and central Africa today? Or, as in South Africa, will Western-style democracy and economic reforms be pushed forward, further challenging the social, political, and economic realities of indigenous Africa, and possibly failing to take hold, turning the inchoate multiparty democracies into de facto, corrupt, one-party states? Or lastly will some combination of indigenous and Western elements as in Botswana pave the way for development in the twenty-first century? Africa's future lies in its ability to select those beneficial non-African institutions and adapt them to African realities.

If our goal and that of African leaders is to expand democracy in Africa, then that means that Western-style democracy will have to be adapted to African practices and culture. But we have also seen that there is resistance in Africa to the continuing influence of indigenous institutions and that there are ongoing efforts to eliminate them. Hence it may be that Africa's manifold troubles will continue, since not only is there little consensus on Western and imported institutions but there is no solid agreement on home-grown ones either.

Endnotes

1. "Behind the Zairian Shambles," *The Economist* 341: 39.
2. "A New Beginning," *The Economist* 341: 17–18.
3. For a summary of the critiques of the modernization approach see Howard Wiarda, ed., *New Directions in Comparative Politics* (Boulder, CO: Westview Press, 1991), or Vicky Randall and Robin Theobald, *Political Change and Underdevelopment* (Durham, NC: Duke University Press, 1985).
4. For comparisons of colonial policies in Africa see Christian Potholm, *Theory and Practice of African Politics* (Englewood Cliffs, NJ: Prentice-Hall,

1973), and George Ayittey, *Indigenous Institutions* (Ardsley-on-Hudson, NY: Transnational Publishers, 1991).

5. Potholm, 1973.

6. Basil Davidson, *The Black Man's Burden: Africa and the Curse of the Nation-State* (New York: Times Books, 1992).

7. Ayittey, *Indigenous Institutions*, 402.

8. Ali A. Mazrui, *The Africans: A Triple Heritage* (London: BBC Publications, 1986): 180.

9. See Okwudiba Nnoli, *Ethnicity and Development in Nigeria* (Aldershot: Avebury, 1995).

10. Ayittey, 1991, 443.

11. Ayittey, 1991, 424

12. Ayittey, 1991, 425.

13. For further discussion of Africa's involvement in the international economy see Naomi Chazan, et al., "Africa and the World Economy," *Politics and Society in Contemporary Africa* (Boulder, CO: Lynne Rienner Publishers, 2nd ed., 1992), and Thomas Callaghy, "Africa and the World Political Economy: Still Caught between a Rock and a Hard Place," in J. Harbeson and D. Rothchild, eds., *Africa in World Politics: Post–Cold War Challenges* (Boulder, CO: Westview Press, 1995): 41–68.

14. Larry Diamond, "Promoting Democracy in Africa," in *Africa in World Politics*, 258.

15. Diamond, "Promoting Democracy in Africa," 258.

16. "A New Beginning," *The Economist* 341: 17–18.

17. Richard Joseph, "Democratization in Africa after 1989: Comparative and Theoretical Perspectives," *Comparative Politics* 29, no. 3 (April 1997): 375.

18. John Harbeson, "Africa in World Politics: Amid Renewal, Deepening Crisis," *Africa in World Politics*, 3–22.

19. "South Africa: How Wrong Is It Going?" *The Economist* 341: 21–23.

20. Ibid.

21. Claude Ake, "The Unique Case of African Democracy," *International Affairs* 69, no. 2 (1993): 241.

22. Ake, "The Unique Case of African Democracy," 243.

23. Chazan, et al., *Politics and Society in Contemporary Africa*, 78.

24. Chazan, et al., *Politics and Society in Contemporary Africa*, 80.

25. Mazrui, *The Africans*, 244.

26. Mazrui, *The Africans*, 245.

6

Islamic Models of Development

—Anwar H. Syed

Anwar H. Syed, professor of political science at the University of Massachusetts, has written extensively about political theory, international relations, American politics, and comparative politics. His book, Pakistan: Islam, Politics and National Solidarity, *integrates political theory and comparative politics.*

The world of Islam includes more than a billion people who call themselves Muslim and profess and practice their faith in various ways and degrees. While they are found in almost all parts of the world, they are a significant majority in more than forty countries. Muslims established great empires during successive periods in history: the Umayyads (661–750), Abbasids (750–1258), Ottomans (1453–1920), Safvids (1501–1742), and Mughals (1526–1857).[1] Often a ruler was progressive, receptive to innovation, a patron of arts and sciences, and tolerant of differences in thought and practice. But according to some versions by the tenth century and certainly by the twelfth, the springs of innovative thinking had begun to dry up in the Muslim world. The dominant educational establishment (consisting of the *ulema*, Islamic theologians and jurists) insisted that knowlege, properly called, was that concerned with the scriptures, and since it had already been perfected, further thinking on the subject was not only unnecessary but disruptive and subversive of the believers' cohesion and unity. When Europe emerged from medieval modes of thinking and initiated a new way of generating knowledge, called the "scientific method," the Muslim world, settled in a sense of self-sufficiency, took no notice. Armed with modern science and technology, which gave them unsurpassed capabilities, European powers went out and established systems of dominance and control over virtually all of the Muslim world.

The patterns of dominance and control were not uniform. The French directly ruled Algeria and Tunisia, the Dutch Indonesia, and the British the areas now constituting Pakistan for extended periods of time. The French ruled Lebanon and Syria, and the British ruled Iraq, only briefly. But the British established protectorates or spheres of influence in Egypt, Saudi Arabia, the emirates of the Persian Gulf, Iran, and Afghanistan. In many of the same areas American power and influence have succeeded those of the British since the early 1950s. Thus, the impact of Western ways on the Muslim world has been uneven. During the nineteenth and the early twentieth centuries, Egypt and Turkey chose to adopt aspects of Westernization. Pakistanis retained English as their working language in the higher bureaucracy, the judiciary, the universities, and in much of their public discourse. No other Muslim country kept a Western language, except the ones in North Africa that had adopted French as their second language. Unlike the Dutch in Indonesia, where the number of natives who had attended a modern high school did not exceed a few dozen in the 1920s,[2] the British established many schools and colleges in the areas now composing Pakistan, where education in modern arts and sciences was imparted. But even the British were niggardly when it came to professional and technical education. At the time of independence in 1947, West Pakistan (now Pakistan), with a population of more than thirty million, had only two medical schools, one engineering college, and one agricultural college.

Except in Saudi Arabia and the Persian Gulf emirates, Muslims were attracted to Western forms of political and economic organization. They began their post-independence careers with free market economies, political parties, and parliaments. But the people concerned, and even many of the emerging elites, had little experience in operating democratic forms and institutions, and these soon gave way to authoritarian regimes. The military intervened and seized power through coups in Egypt, Pakistan, Iraq, Libya, Turkey, and Indonesia and, in some cases (notably Pakistan, Iraq, and Turkey), it did so more than once. A substantial part of the economy in some of them (Egypt, Iraq, Syria, Iran, and Pakistan, among others) was placed in the public sector.

But neither the public sector nor military rule nor other kinds of authoritarianism did much to improve ordinary people's quality of life. The oil-exporting countries (Saudi Arabia and the Persian Gulf emirates) are prosperous, but they are a class by themselves: they are *"rentier"* states, with very small populations and enormous revenues. Many other Muslim countries are downright poor, lacking access even to such basic amenities as potable water, health care, primary education, and transportation. In some of them (Pakistan, Egypt, Afghanistan, and Iran), many people become sick because of malnutrition. On the other hand, the elites are said to be wealthy and uncaring, governments both corrupt and incompetent, and the states heavily in debt to both foreign and domestic lenders and dominated by foreign governments (especially the United States), lending institutions (notably the World Bank and the International Monetary Fund), and multinational corporations. No Muslim country comes anywhere near any of the industrially advanced countries in understanding and using modern science and technology. None has a university that compares with any of the more notable institutions of higher learning in the United States, Great Britain, or Western Europe.

Not unexpectedly, Muslim thinkers and opinion-makers have been pondering the reasons for their decline, degradation, poverty, and the general disorder in their political and social affairs. How did it happen that they, who once ruled much of the known world and excelled in arts and sciences, have now become downtrodden? They blame it partly on the West's intrusion into their lands, but primarily upon the Muslims' own abandonment of the true Islamic way of organizing and conducting their lives. Muslims will fail to improve their affairs, not to speak of recapturing their former glory, unless they return to the path of Islam. This is the position taken in more recent times by Hasan al-Banna (1906–1949) and Sayyid Qutb (1906–1966), the founder and the ideologue respectively of the Muslim Brotherhood in Egypt, Ali Shariati (1933–1977) and Ruhollah Khomeini (1900–1989) in Iran, and Abual ala Maududi (1903–1979) in Pakistan.[3] Some differences of emphasis notwithstanding, the traditional ulema make essentially the same argument.

On occasion, intellectuals and/or politicians have appealed to their nativity in searching for models of political and economic organization. But, as a result of interaction over many hundreds of years, the native tradition in each Muslim country has become inextricably mixed with Islamic influences. Even if the two could be separated and a purely native tradition identified, it might not be applauded by the people concerned. The attempts of Reza Shah and his son, Muhammad Reza Shah, in Iran, and those of Mustafa Kemal in Turkey and Anwar Sadat in Egypt to glorify their respective native traditions do not appear to have been successful.[4]

Will Islamic models of development work? There is first the question of whether such a model will gain general acceptance in a given Muslim country. This acceptance cannot be taken for granted, for Muslims are divided into sects and Islam does not mean the same thing to all of them. Witness the case of Afghanistan where the Islamic *mujahideen*, after cooperating for ten years to expel the Soviet army from their country in 1989, have been fighting among themselves now for more than eight years. The government of Saudi Arabia claims that it is already Islamic, but there are rumblings of dissent and even revolt within the country, partly because the government is regarded as corrupt but partly, too, because some Saudis and many outsiders maintain that monarchy is an institution repugnant to Islam. Consider also that in many Muslim countries a part of the population holds a secular outlook. Though a minority, the group is influential and simply rejects an Islamic model. But suppose that such a model were adopted: could it be implemented, and would it more effectively meet the issues and problems facing Muslims? Saudi Arabia has been rich but extravagant and incompetent. The case of the Islamic Republic in Iran is no more reassuring. It may have made the Iranian people a trifle more "pious," but almost undoubtedly it has made them considerably poorer than they were under the shah. In terms of political freedoms they are just as much deprived as before.[5] Thus, the efficacy of Islamic models is problematic, to say the least. But before coming to any firmer conclusion, let us see what they are like.

The Original Islamic Model

Islam is not only worship but polity and society the essentials of which, including a body of law, God is believed to have revealed to the prophet Muhammad (570–632). God's law and injunctions are contained in the Quran, and together with the Prophet's own sayings and practice, known as his *sunnah*, they are called the *shariah*. In Muslim belief, sovereignty belongs to God; in functional terms, this means that his law is supreme. Since law serves no purpose unless it is implemented, Muslims have the inescapable obligation to enforce the Islamic law. A state that does so is an Islamic state, and it is Muslims' obligation to establish such a state. It existed in its true and ideal form during the Prophet's rule in Medina for about ten years (622–632) and, by consensus of the Sunni Muslims (who are the great majority of Muslims), it existed also during the rule of the first four of his immediate successors, called the pious or the rightly guided caliphs (632–661).[6] A few issues should be addressed if we are to have an adequate picture of this system of rule beyond rulers' faithful implementation of God's law and injunctions. First is the issue of legitimacy involving the question of how the ruler comes to his position. Then there is the issue of popular participation in settling the affairs of state. Lastly, there are the twin issues of political obligation and accountability, referring to the people's duty to obey rulers and their right to remove them if their conduct is unlawful.

We see no uniformity of procedure by which the following people referred to here became rulers. Muhammad, being the Prophet and the founder of his community, ruled, as it were, by divine right; the Muslims in Medina fully expected him to be their ruler. According to the Sunni belief, he left no specific advice as to how his successor should be chosen. Abu Bakr, the first pious caliph (632–634), was elected to his position by a small number of the town notables, and was later accorded a more general acceptance. As he was dying, he *appointed* Umar bin Khattab to succeed him. The latter ruled for ten years (634–644) and, before his death, he named a committee of six notables to choose the next caliph. They chose Uthman bin Affan. In 656 a group of rebels killed Uthman in an incident I shall say more of shortly. They and a large crowd of other people then appeared at the door of Ali ibne Abu Talib (the Prophet's son-in-law) and persuaded him to become the new caliph. The pious caliphate ended with Ali's assassination in 661 after which a very long period of kingship began. It is noteworthy that during neither the time of the Prophet nor that of the pious caliphs was succession to rule institutionalized.

The Quran asks Muslims to settle their common affairs through mutual consultation. This injunction is the source of the claim that Muslims are entitled to political participation. In this regard also, the practice during the pious caliphate was uneven. The Prophet's mosque in Medina often served as the caliph's workplace. Most of the notables in the town had been the Prophet's companions, and they came to the mosque fairly regularly. The caliph, thus, had plenty of opportunity to consult the notables. Umar, the second pious caliph, would appear to have done the most consulting. Abu Bakr and Uthman did so more selectively. Ali shifted his capital to Kufa in Iraq and consulted the notables who had accompanied him, but it seems he did not think much of their advice. In any case, it should be understood that the obligation to consult, like succession to rule, was not institutionalized. The people at large were not credited with the right to participate in deciding issues of public policy. No approved list of the consultees existed. It was open to the caliph to choose the persons whom he would consult. Above all, he was under no obligation to accept the advice he had received. He was to listen and then make up his mind according to his own lights.

Abu Bakr and Umar, the first two pious caliphs, considered themselves and other public officials answerable to the community for their conduct. The people in Medina, and those who happened to be visiting the town, often questioned Umar about his decisions. He listened to them patiently and tried to satisfy them, without penalizing them in any way for their questioning and criticism. The issue of accountability came to a head during the rule of Uthman, the third pious caliph. Some accounts have it that he was unduly generous in giving jobs and other allowances to his kinsmen. This nepotism caused a group of Muslims to agitate against him. Its leaders broke into his house, made their accusations, and asked him to step down from his post. He refused, saying that God had given him his office, and that only God could take it away. Upon hearing this, they killed him. Some of the Prophet's companions, along with one of his wives, Ayesha, accused Ali (the fourth pious caliph) of neglect in identifying and punishing Uthman's killers and made war upon him (in which Ali's accusers were defeated). On the same ground, or pretext, Muawiya, who had been governor of Syria for more than twenty years, declined to accept Ali as a legitimate caliph. The ensuing war, however, ended in a stalemate. The process of accountability and the related issue of political obligation were left unsettled.

Before we leave this original Islamic model, to which Muslim revivalists and the ulema generally want to return, a few additional observations may be in order. First, note that there was no division or separation of powers in the pious caliphate. The caliph was the head of all branches of government. He made regulations on subjects about which the Quran and the Prophet's sunnah were silent. He could hear cases as the empire's chief judge. He decided how public funds were spent. He appointed and dismissed military commanders, provincial governors, judges, tax collectors, and other important functionaries. In spite of having this vast authority, each one of the pious caliphs lived modestly, drawing an allowance from the treasury that barely maintained his family and him in a lifestyle comparable to that of most other Muslims. It would not be wrong to say that in each case the caliph suffered a loss of personal income as a result of accepting public office. After meeting the expenses of operating the state, he distributed the surplus revenue among Muslims almost equally (with minor variations according to their service to Islam during the Prophet's time). He envisaged a good society as one whose members were pious, egalitarian, frugal, even austere, in personal spending, but forthcoming and giving "in the way of the Lord," meaning for societal purposes. He viewed the community as a brotherhood in which the wealthy should help the poor and the gap between them would be narrowed as much as possible.

The Shia Persuasion

A word should now be said about the Shia (also called the Shi'i or the Shiites). They form about 95 percent of the population in Iran, 55 percent in Iraq, 70 percent in Bahrain, and 20 percent in Pakistan. They are present in significant numbers in Saudi Arabia, Kuwait, the emirates, and in most of the other Muslim countries.[7] They believe that the authority to rule properly belonged (and still does) to the house of the Prophet, represented by Ali and his descendants through Fatima, his wife and the Prophet's daughter. Ali should have been the first caliph and those who assumed that office before him were simply usurpers. He was the first *imam* (legitimate ruler, leader, or guide), and the line of his descendants, for purposes of rulership, included eleven others. The last of them, the twelfth imam, known as Mehdi, is believed to have ascended to heaven where he remains, and Mehdi is, therefore, called the "hidden imam." He will return to earth and set the world right shortly before the "day of judgment." He alone is entitled to rule, and in his absence, all governments are more or less illegitimate. Muslims may remain aloof from them, obey them if they must, but if a government's practice is un-Islamic, resistance and revolt may also be appropriate.[8] In a more recent version declared by Ayatollah Khomeini and his associates in Iran, a government is legitimate if it is supervised and directed by the higher-ranking Shia clergy, who presumably know the mind of the "hidden imam" and can, therefore, represent him. Needless to say, the rest of the Muslim world does not accept this formulation.

The Medieval Islamic Model

As mentioned earlier, kingship replaced the "pious" caliphate after 661. An individual reached the throne either because a king had named him as his successor or, in the case of a disputed succession, because he had been able to defeat his challengers. In the final analysis, military force became the arbiter of the title to rule.

During the eighth century, the ulema began to emerge as a self-conscious group. They defined legitimacy in terms of a Muslim ruler's acceptance of the obligation to enforce the Islamic law (the shariah). They and the kings reached an informal understanding. The king would appoint them as judges, jurists, declarers of the law in disputed cases, arbitrators, and administrators of endowments. They would enforce the shariah upon the ordinary Muslims, but they would not question the king's personal lifestyle or his pursuit of po-litical power, his ways of dealing with friends and foes, issues of war and peace, or his conduct of the administration in general. Islam and government were thus joined, but Islam and politics were separated.[9]

As a result of this understanding, the issues of legitimacy, accountability, and political obligation were muted or reinterpreted. Without the means of influencing politics, the ulema, including political thinkers, dropped the issue of legitimacy. They recognized military force as the giver and preserver of ruling authority and declared that they were on the side of the victor.

That the shariah was implemented throughout the world of Islam—that Muslims from Morocco to central Asia and even India read the same books, said the same prayer, and followed the same law—was no small accomplish-ment. The shariah signified a kind of unity and cohesion within a global Mus-lim community. Since the ulema had played a large role in building this community, they valued it highly and were loathe to approve of anything that might disrupt it. They feared "chaos," called *fitna*, resulting from the civil strife that resistance and revolt against any current ruler might generate. Consequently, they counseled obedience, or at least acquiescence, even if the ruler was "impious" in his personal and/or official conduct. But note also that the community owed the ruler no loyalty. If a general from within or without overthrew him, then he, the winner, would be accepted as the new ruler. The more notable among the medieval Muslim jurists and politi-cal thinkers, who adopted the position described above, were Al-Baqillani

(d. 1012), Al-Mawardi (974–1058), Al-Ghazali (1058–1111), and Ibn Jama' (1241–1333).

Between 661 and about the end of the nineteenth century, kings in the Muslim world were absolute rulers, and none of them acknowledged accountability to anyone other than God or his own conscience, such as it might have been. The related issue of participation, as we understand it today or even as it was understood during the pious caliphate, did not arise. The king consulted his ministers and other notables, and on occasion the ulema, as he deemed fit but not as an obligation. The ordinary citizen (or the "subject" as he was then regarded) did not expect or even hope to be heard except when he had a personal grievance. On the whole, he longed only to remain aloof from the government whose agents (the police and the tax collector) were more likely to be oppressive than helpful. Of the medieval jurists and thinkers, Ibne Taymiyyah (d. 1328) should be mentioned as a notable exception inasmuch as he advocated resistance to impious and unjust rulers.

The More Recent Models

I have referred above to Hasan al-Banna, Sayyid Qutb, Maududi, and Khomeini, who wanted to recreate the original Islamic model of the Prophet's Medina and the pious caliphate. They were willing to modify some of its details to meet contemporary needs. They did not regard the work of the medieval jurists as authoritative or final and felt free to revise it. They were, for instance, not afraid of *fitna*, and they urged resistance and even revolt against impious and unjust rulers in the Muslim world. But they were ambivalent, or one might say open-minded, with regard to the issues of legitimacy, accountability, and participation. On the one hand, they would accept a ruler if he were a good and pious Muslim and if he sincerely strove to enforce the shariah in his country. They would then not ask how he had come to power. On the other hand, they would not object if the community chose to standardize the process of reaching power through elections. They would not object to the use of force to remove an impious or unjust ruler, but neither would they object to the institutionalization of such a ruler's removal through parliamentary impeachment. These considerations raise the larger issue of whether Islam and democracy, as understood in the West, are compatible.

Islam and Democracy

Let me first deal with an issue which many Muslim commentators regard as critical but which may actually be minor. Whereas in Western democracies the people are said to be sovereign, in Islam sovereignty belongs to God. This means that a Muslim legislature cannot pass laws repugnant to God's law. It cannot, for instance, legalize sex out of wedlock, homosexuality, drinking of alcoholic beverages, or gambling. But even while remaining within God's law, a Muslim legislature can have plenty to do. Decisions about raising and spending revenues, providing education and health care, promoting arts and sciences, building infrastructure, maintaining public order and tranquility, and administering justice can keep a modern government and its legislature busy. Consider also the medieval Islamic jurists' conclusion, even if regretful, that "necessity" makes lawful that which may otherwise be forbidden. For example, Islam forbids interest on loans. But because of the contemporary world's interconnectedness, no economy anywhere in the Muslim world can function without giving and taking interest. Even Saudi Arabia and the Islamic Republic in Iran tolerate interest. Pakistan does the same and calls it "profit" or a "service charge."

What about some of the institutions, forms, and practices associated with democracy? The ulema are likely to hold that a Muslim polity really needs no legislature because the law already exists in the form of the shariah. This is an exaggeration. Of more than six thousand verses in the Quran, less than one hundred contain the law, and of these a substantial number relate to personal matters such as marriage, divorce, custody of children, and inheritance. The penal law covers less than a dozen acts (adultery, fornication, murder, assault, theft and robbery, giving false testimony and making false accusations against another person, and waging war against a legitimate Muslim government). Thus, much is left uncovered and, as I have said above, a Muslim legislature can have its hands full. Ruling authorities in Saudi Arabia and most of the emirates (except Kuwait) maintain that all power, including that of making laws or regulations, belongs to the executive, and that an assembly, elected or appointed and called the *shura*, can have only an advisory role. But this is not a generally accepted position in the Muslim world today.

Spokesmen for Islam—whether traditionalists or revivalists—are flexible about elections and political parties. Ideally, and perhaps even logically, they would like to limit the franchise to the pious, but for pragmatic reasons they have been willing to accept a universal adult franchise that also includes women in Pakistan, Indonesia, Iran, Egypt, Turkey, and some other countries. The ulema in Pakistan and Iran are organized into political parties, and Islamic parties have contested elections in Turkey, Jordan, Egypt, and Algeria. According to Maulana Maududi, whose work is widely read and appreciated in the Muslim world, parties may contest elections in order to highlight issues before the electorate, but officeholders should forego their party affiliations once they reach the legislature and debate and vote according to their conscience and not according to a party line.[10]

In the models under discussion, democratic freedoms and rights are subject to an overall framework of Islamic beliefs and values. Muslims may criticize the government of the day, as they did during the pious caliphate. But no one may stand on a street corner and deliver a speech denouncing the

Prophet; that would be "blasphemy" and punishable. Guilds, trade associations, professional organizations, and political parties may be formed but may not advocate measures repugnant to Islam. Non-Muslim minorities are to be tolerated, allowed to worship and follow their own religious law in personal affairs. They may be subject to a poll tax in return for exemption from military duty, and they are excluded from holding certain high public offices (head of state and head of government among others). Non-Muslim minorities do not have the status of "first-class" citizens in an Islamic state. But this is not a critical issue in assessing Islam's compatibility with democracy, which is to be judged on the basis of how a regime deals with the people that it regards as its own. Surely, it cannot be said that in the nineteenth and early twentieth centuries America failed to be a democracy because American society and government discriminated against Jews, Catholics, African Americans, Asians, and native Americans. Consider also that, outside of Lebanon, Egypt, and Indonesia, the number of non-Muslims in the great majority of Muslim countries is very small indeed.

If democracy is not functioning in much of the Muslim world, is this the case because Islam is in the way? Bernard Lewis, one of the better-known Western specialists on Islam and Muslim history, has recently concluded that Muslims may take the democratic or the authoritarian road, depending upon how they reinterpret Islam and their tradition. Both courses of action are open. In some ways, "of all the non-Western civilizations, Islam offers the best prospects for Western-style democracy," inasmuch as it shares with the West much of the Judeo-Christian and Greco-Roman heritage "that helped to form our modern civilization." But in terms of its political experience, Islam offers a poor prospect for liberal democracy. Lewis thinks that Islamic peoples' historical, cultural, and religious traditions are likely to inhibit democracy. Unlike Westerners, Muslims did not develop consultative assemblies or councils underlaid by corporate entities. As a result, Muslim governments have been "intensely personal." There were rulers, but no state; judges, but no court; neighborhoods, but no city. In actual Muslim practice, the right to private property has been insecure even though Islamic law says it is inviolable; rulers felt free to confiscate the property of those with whom they happened to be displeased.[11]

These considerations are not irrelevant to an understanding of the Muslim historical experience. But the revivalists, and many educated Muslims, will set them aside on the ground that Mr. Lewis is using the terms *Islamic* and *Muslim* synonymously. They may say that the Muslim political tradition since 661 has not been Islamic, and that they reject it. They may even claim, as Maulana Maududi did, that Muslim art, architecture, music, and poetry are no more "Islamic" than gambling and prostitution on the part of some Muslims. The authentic source of guidance for determining whether Islam and democracy are compatible is not Muslim history but the shariah and the practice of the pious caliphate. The latter appear to leave the choice open. As Mr. Lewis points out, the Islamic caliphate is in no sense a despotism; the elective principle is central to the Sunni jurisprudence; the relationship between the caliph and the people is contractual; and the ruler is under, not above, the law. He concludes that Muslims are, thus, free to reinterpret Islam so as to open the way for democracy. The prospects of their being able to do so may not be good, "but they are better than they have ever been before."

I am inclined to agree with Mr. Lewis that the Muslim historical experience since 661 impedes democracy. But I will submit also that this experience has little to do with Islam as doctrine, or with the way it was implemented during the pious caliphate. If Muslims are able to rise above the post-661 tradition and rely on the earlier sources of guidance, the door to democracy is open.

But will the Islamic "fundamentalists" let the Muslim democrats have their way? There may be some confusion as to who a "fundamentalist" is. It should be noted that this was originally a Christian (Protestant) term, not an Islamic or Muslim one; but, of late, it has entered Muslim usage also. In one manner of speaking, any Muslim who takes his religion seriously and believes that the state in which he lives must adopt and enforce the Islamic law and injunctions is a fundamentalist. In this sense the term denotes those who want to revive Islam in its original purity. This persuasion may or may not have a political dimension. The followers of Abd al-Wahhab (1703–1792), who are predominant in Saudi Arabia, want to remove the crust of local and native influences that Islam has gathered in various places during its journey through history. But Abd al-Wahhab made an alliance with the ancestors of the present Saudi rulers and did not object to their modes of governance. The Wahhabis are doctrinal fundamentalists; they do not, for instance, recognize saints or other intermediaries between man and God; they demolish, instead of building, tombs and mausoleums. The Wahhabi government in Saudi Arabia enforces the shariah, and in that sense also, it is a fundamentalist regime. It is, however, amenable to American advice and influence and, therefore, its fundamentalism is of no great concern to the West. The Islamic Republic in Iran, too, is a fundamentalist regime, but it denounces some Western values and, more importantly, American domination of the Muslim world. One may then say that there are two types of Islamic fundamentalism: one domestically "Islamic" and internationally pro-Western; the other "Islamic" at home and assertive, even defiant, in its foreign relations. It is to this latter variety that the United States and others in the Western world object.

Fundamentalist organizations, dedicated to the Islamization of their polities and societies, operate in a number of Muslim countries. They do not approve of the regimes and systems now in place, and they would like to replace them by force, if necessary and possible. They have succeeded in Iran and, to an extent, in Afghanistan but, as we will see later, it does not follow that they will succeed everywhere. Moreover, it is possible that in time they will mellow, as all revolutionaries do, or that they will be overthrown in places where they have captured power.

Economic and Social Concerns

The Quran and the sunna have little to say about how production of goods and services is to be organized. The Meccans were traders, and the Muslims in Medina (where the Prophet went to live in 622) also engaged in commerce when they were not fighting. A small amount of farming was done in the vicinity of Medina but most Arab tribes in the larger neighborhood raised goats, sheep, and camels. Beyond the forbidding of interest (or usury), which was considered exploitative, Islam would appear to have accepted the ongoing, free enterprise system of production. It placed greater emphasis on issues of distribution. It discouraged accumulation and concentration of wealth, and it asked the wealthy to spend in the way of the Lord (that is, for societal purposes) whatever they possessed beyond the requirements of a moderately comfortable living. Thus, in the Islamic way, it is not wrong to make a great deal of money, but it is wrong to keep it. It is, then, open to question whether Islam approves of individual or even corporate ownership of huge industrial and commercial or banking establishments dedicated mainly to making the maximum possible profit for their owners.[12] In this connection, it may be mentioned in passing that Hasan al-Banna and his Muslim Brotherhood favored small cottage industries and cooperatives.

Considering that the penalty for theft is the amputation of the thief's hand, one might think that the right to private property was sacred in Islam. But we hear also that the land and all wealth belong to God (meaning the community). Many ulema hold a Muslim government's nationalization of industrial and commercial property and its forcible acquisition of land for the purpose of effecting land reforms to be un-Islamic. But some Muslim intellectuals and political leaders have advocated Arab and/or Islamic socialism. Notable among them are Muhammad Iqbal, M. A. Jinnah, and Zulfikar Ali Bhutto in Pakistan; Ali Shariati in Iran; Rashid Rida, Sayyid Qutb, Mustafa al-Sibai, Abdel Moghny Said, and Gamal Abdel Nasser in the Arab world. Arab and Islamic varieties of socialism are said to be related, for as Said observed, Arab socialism is rooted deep in the soil of Islam.[13]

In functional terms Islamic and Arab socialisms have meant the nationalization of large industrial and commercial enterprises, banks, and insurance companies, and their placement in the public sector. But as elsewhere in the world, the public sector in Muslim countries—Pakistan, Iran, Turkey, Iraq, Syria, and Egypt—turned out to be incompetent and wasteful. Nor can we say that it redistributed enough wealth and earnings to realize Islam's egalitarian ideal. In many Muslim countries, a tiny percentage of the population is enormously wealthy, but the great majority is unspeakably poor, and the gulf between rich and poor grows. In Egypt Anwar al-Sadat rolled back the public sector which Nasser had created, and it is now being dismantled and "privatized" in much of the rest of the Muslim world.

Tribal and caste (now called "ethnic") distinctions have always existed in Muslim societies and in some of them (Pakistan, Afghanistan, Iran, Iraq, and Turkey) continue to cause conflict and disorder. A more vital, and possibly enduring, issue relates to the status of women. Before the advent of Islam, women in much of the Middle East had virtually no rights at all; they were regarded as the property of their fathers or husbands. Islam made marriage a contract between husband and wife, gave the woman the freedom to choose the man she would marry, enabled her to own and inherit property, permitted her to get education and operate a business. But it should not be surprising that fourteen hundred years ago Islam stopped short of bringing the woman to a position of full equality with man. Daughters inherited half as much as did the sons upon their father's death. The testimony of two women equaled that of one man in certain types of court proceedings. It was considerably more difficult for a woman to divorce her husband than it was for him to divorce her; she could have no compensation in the event of a divorce other than that which had been stipulated in the marriage contract, and she could not have the custody of children for more than a few months.

Women were asked to dress modestly, not to flaunt their bodies, and not to do anything to attract the romantic attention of men. Islam emphasized the chastity of both man and woman but, in this connection, it placed heavier burdens upon the woman than upon the man. The great majority of the Muslim ulema recommend women's segregation from men: they believe that women should not participate in workplaces, schools, assemblies, or any other forums where men are present. If they must appear in these places, they should be properly covered. I should hasten to add that while the ulema's view in this regard is followed in Iran (the Islamic Republic), Saudi Arabia, and some of the Gulf emirates, women are much more free to do what they want elsewhere in the Muslim world.[14] But the status of full equality with men is still a distant goal for them as it is even for women in Western societies.

The Prospect of an Islamic State

Is any of the Islamic models, referred to above, likely to be implemented in the Muslim world in the foreseeable future? The pious caliphate can hardly be called a model, since it did not regularize the procedures for succession to rule, accountability, and participation. The caliphs acted in an ad hoc fashion. The common element among them is that they were all "pious," meaning that they were all dedicated to the public interest and did not covet personal gain. Any number of Muslims today will tell you that the likes of the first four pious caliphs are not likely to be found in our time. The model of the pious caliphate, to the extent that it is a model at all, is therefore unavailable.

The medieval model, in which the ulema enforced the shariah upon the ordinary people while the ruling kings lived and pursued politics as they wanted, is no longer accepted as a genuine Islamic model. Saudi Arabia and the Gulf emirates follow it, but their claim to being Islamic is disputed. The Islamic credentials of the present regime in Iran are suspect in the rest of the Muslim world and, eighteen years after the revolution, perhaps even in Iran itself. In other words, since 661, the Islamic state has been absent from the Muslim political scene, and claims of its reemergence in our time are not to be taken seriously. Pakistan calls itself an "Islamic republic" but, in the country itself, this designation is dismissed as a bad joke by the ulema and others.

Through much of Muslim history, the ulema occupied lucrative positions. They were a prosperous and influential class. But in much of the Muslim world (outside of Saudi Arabia and the emirates), they suffered a substantial loss of income and influence during the West's domination of their societies. Other elites emerged and took positions of power and influence. Now the ulema would like to recapture the role they once had, but the newer elites (industrialists, merchants, bankers, landed aristocrats, lawyers, journalists, and professors, among others) are in the way. The ulema may accept democratic forms and procedures, universal adult franchise, even the presence of women in a parliament while they struggle for power. But it is by no means certain as to what they will do if they ever come to power. The *Taliban* in Afghanistan (a group of people trained in Islamic seminaries in northwestern Pakistan) have ordered women out of schools and workplaces, and told them to hide themselves from top to toe if they must come out of their homes. They are also enforcing the Islamic penal law (beheading the adulterer and the adulteress and amputating the thief's hand). The Islamic Republic in Iran has held several elections for president and parliament since 1979, but it is essentially a one-party regime. Recently, groups other than the ruling Islamic Republican Party have been allowed to contest elections, provided that they do not oppose the regime's basic "Islamic" character.

Barring a short period in Muslim Spain and the recent turn of events in Iran, the ulema have never been rulers at any time in Muslim history. The prospect of an Islamic state of their description, meaning essentially a state which they will operate or at least direct, depends upon whether the people and the influential elites in Muslim countries accept their advocacy. This is not likely to happen. All of the Islamic parties combined have never won more than twenty seats in the 217-member National Assembly of Pakistan in any of the five elections held since 1970. Islamic parties in Jordan and Turkey have done better in recent elections but they have not won legislative majorities. The Islamic party in Algeria, poised to win a majority, has been thwarted and denied political authority by the country's military establishment. The Muslim Brotherhood is hounded in Egypt, Syria, Iraq, and elsewhere, and so are other Islamic "fundamentalist" groups. The ulema seized power in Iran through a very special set of circumstances and developments, and then many of the other elites fled. Should the ulema attempt similar takeovers in other Muslim countries, these other elites may not yield without a fight in which the ulema may not have popular support.

In sum, none of the known Islamic models (espoused either by the traditional ulema or even by the lay fundamentalists) is likely to materialize in the larger Muslim world in the foreseeable future. One might distinguish a state committed to implementing Islamic law from one that, while setting aside the law, wants to honor broader Islamic principles and values. These include, according to "modernized" Muslims (such as M. A. Jinnah, the founder of Pakistan), democracy, equality, social justice, tolerance, brotherhood of man, precedence of the public interest over personal interest, orderliness and self-discipline, dedication to duty, security of life and property, emancipation of women, a certain leveling of wealth, help to the needy, advancement of learning, and Muslims' capacity to solve their problems. Muslims may be "enabled" but not forced to pray and fast and do the other things that will bring them bliss in the hereafter. The ulema will say, perhaps correctly, that this model is not particularly Islamic. Even so, Muslims are more likely to unite behind a model like this than any the ulema will enforce.

If the Islamic models are not likely to be adopted in the near future, which way is the Muslim world going? Socialism is almost universally in retreat and the same is true of its Arab and Islamic versions. The free market economy, deregulation, privatization of public enterprises, downsizing of the bureaucracy, reduced subsidies, and higher taxation (often mandated by the International Monetary Fund as a condition of its assistance) proceed, albeit at different speeds, in the Muslim world as elsewhere. No Islamic model of economic organization is anywhere in sight. In this area the West appears dominant.

But the same is not true of politics. Here neither Islam nor the West holds sway. Most of the governments in the region under study are essentially authoritarian even when they have parties, elections, and parliaments. Among ruling elites many are not sure that democracy suits the "genius" or the political culture of their people. The counterelites and the people at large, on the other hand, want participation through democratic institutions. A more vexing problem is that nowhere in the Muslim world, with the possible exception of Turkey, have either the elites or the people yet learned the art of operating a democracy. They will learn it only if they have the opportunity to practice it, even if imperfectly, over an extended period of time. In Pakistan, for instance, the people have repeatedly taken to the streets and rioted during periods of military rule because they wanted democracy restored. The country has had five general elections during the last twelve years, but four times during this period the president has dismissed the National Assembly and the government based upon it because they were allegedly corrupt and incompetent. Military rule is no longer in fashion. Party dictatorships, such as the ones in Iraq and Syria, are extremely oppressive and potentially unstable. The West professes to favor democracy but values its own interests in the area even more. It does not want to pressure Egypt, Saudi Arabia, and the emirates, for instance, to democratize their political systems. Western policy makers are apprehensive that the resulting governments might be less stable and less amenable to Western dominance than the present authoritarian regimes are. The likelihood, then, is that Muslim polities will remain in a state of flux, and that they will just "muddle through" in the foreseeable future.

Endnotes

1. For an account of the beginnings of Islam and the succeeding empires, see Sidney N. Fisher, *The Middle East: A History* (New York: Alfred A. Knopf, 1979). For the Mughals, see J. Allan, et al., *The Cambridge Shorter History of India* (Cambridge, England: The University Press, 1934); reprint, New Delhi: S. Chand and Company, 1964.

2. George McT. Kahin, *Major Governments of Asia* (Ithaca, NY: Cornell University Press, 1963): 549.

3. John L. Esposito, *Islam and Politics* (Syracuse, NY: Syracuse University Press, 1987): 130–151; and chapters 4–9 in Esposito, ed., *Voices of Resurgent Islam* (New York: Oxford University Press, 1983): 67–217. For Maududi, see also Anwar Syed, *Pakistan: Islam, Politics, and National Solidarity* (Lahore, Pakistan: Vanguard, 1983): 74–80.

4. M. E. Yapp, *The Near East Since the First World War* (New York: Longman, 1991).

5. *Washington Report on Middle East Affairs, April 1996*, 73–77. Published by the American Educational Trust.

6. Esposito, *Islam and Politics*, 5–9; Fisher, *The Middle East*, chapters 3–8.

7. James A. Bill and Robert Springborg, *Politics in the Middle East* (New York: HarperCollins, 1990): 391.

8. For an account of the Shia political doctrine, see David Pinault, *The Shiites: Ritual and Popular Piety in a Muslim Community* (New York: St. Martin's Press, 1992): chapter 1; and Bernard Lewis, *Islam and the West* (New York: Oxford University Press, 1993): chapter 9.

9. Cf. Anwar Syed, *Pakistan: Islam, Politics, and National Solidarity*, 14–27.

10. Abulala Maududi, *Islamic Law and Constitution* (Lahore, Pakistan: Islamic Publications, 1960): 345–46.

11. Bernard Lewis, "Islam and Liberal Democracy," *The Atlantic Monthly*, February 1993.

12. For a discussion of economic issues in Islam and among Muslims, see Charles Issawi, "The Adaptation of Islam to Contemporary Economic Realities," in Yvonne Haddad, ed., *The Islamic Impact* (Syracuse, NY: Syracuse University Press, 1984): chapter 2.

13. For more on Islamic socialism, see Anwar Syed, "The Pakistan People's Party: Phases One and Two," in Ralph Braibanti, et al., eds., *Pakistan: The Long View* (Durham, NC: Duke University Press, 1977): 84–89.

14. Cf. Leila Ahmad, *Women and Gender in Islam: Historical Roots of a Modern Debate* (New Haven, CT: Yale University Press, 1992).

7

Eastern Europe and the Search for a Democratic Political Culture

—Dale R. Herspring

After a career at the Department of State, Dale R. Herspring became professor of political science and department chair at Kansas State University. His publications include The Soviet High Command, Civil-Military Relations in Communist Systems, *and* Russian Civil-Military Relations.

Introduction

One misleading assumption held by some outside observers is that the countries of Eastern Europe bear a striking resemblance to one another. These observers often speak of the region as a semi-homogeneous entity, primarily because of the Cold War experience. During this high point of Soviet domination, individuality and/or national peculiarities were often repressed in favor of the Soviet model. In short, if it was good for Moscow, it was good for Eastern Europe.

This unitary view of Eastern Europe was reinforced first by the heavy-handed approach the Kremlin took in dealing with the desire of some of these countries for greater national independence—for example, the use of Soviet troops against Hungarians in 1956 or the Czechoslovaks in 1968. This "unitary" perception was further reinforced by Moscow's creation of the Warsaw Pact and the Council for Mutual Economic Association. These two organizations tied these member countries together (and to Moscow) both militarily and economically, so that many Western observers, especially those concerned about the military threat from the East during the height of the Cold War, tended to view them as a unitary whole dominated by the Kremlin. "The Polish or East German or Hungarian army is a tool in the hands of the Kremlin" was a phrase often heard in governmental meetings set up to discuss the military threat presented by the Warsaw Pact.

There is no question that Moscow exerted considerable control over the countries of Eastern Europe (and especially in the military sphere). However, it would be wrong to assume the existence of a homogeneous social, political, or economic relationship between Moscow and its "allies." Deep differences between Moscow and its allies preceded the establishment of communism, and despite the Kremlin's efforts to enforce political, social, and economic uniformity, significant differences between the USSR and its satellites remained—even during the Soviet period. Similarly, it would be equally fallacious to assume that the Soviets were able to enforce cultural, political, economic, or social homogeneity *among* the countries of Eastern Europe. Just as deep differences persisted between Moscow and its allies, there were important differences between each of the East European states during the Soviet period.

The thesis of this chapter is that the primary defining characteristic of the polities of Eastern Europe is heterogeneity. This characteristic is a result of the very different political cultures that have existed for centuries and continue to exist in these countries. In some, like Poland, there is a highly individualistic orientation; in others, like Serbia, there is an equally strong collectivistic approach to political issues. As a result, some of these countries are closer to the Western model than others—not because of attempts to import the "Western model," but because some political structures are more compatible with some pre-existing political cultures than they are with others. Or, to put it another way, the chances of developing democratic political institutions are much higher in some countries than in others. For example, countries like the Czech Republic appear to be well on their way toward adopting a Western democratic political system, while others, such as Serbia and Bulgaria, have a long way to go primarily because their indigenous political culture is less hospitable to democracy than that of the Czech Republic.

The primary impact of the collapse of communism on Eastern Europe was to permit this heterogeneity in political culture to reemerge as an active political force. Long pent-up pressures for a multifaceted approach to dealing with the problems facing these countries again became part of the political landscape.

The key point is that the approach each polity will take in the future toward the creation of a stable political system will be heavily influenced by its own political culture. And the nature of the political culture in each polity will be a result not only of the Soviet period, but of its own historical experience.

The Western Impact on Eastern Europe

Before discussing Western impact on Eastern Europe, let us take a look at the concept of political culture because it plays a key role in our discussion. "Political culture refers to the values, ideas, norms, belief systems, and patterns of behavior of a particular people or country."[1] History plays an important role in transmitting these values and beliefs, but so do other factors such as religion, language, economic development, political socialization, attitudes toward authority, etc. What is important about political culture is that each polity develops its own, often unique political culture. For example, for cultural and religious reasons women are excluded from political life in a country like Saudi Arabia, while they play a vital role in a country such as Sweden. Indeed, one of the underlying assumptions of this chapter is "that autonomous and reasonably enduring cross-cultural differences exist and that they can have important political consequences."[2] Political culture changes, but generally only gradually. From a political standpoint this gradual change means that despite the major changes that have occurred in Eastern Europe over the past hundred or so years, important differences remain among these countries—differences that continue to influence the way political decisions are made as well as the prospects for democracy in these countries.

With the foregoing in mind, permit me to note that the extent of Western influence on the countries of Eastern Europe varies country by country. In some cases, such as Serbia and Albania, it is minimal. In others, such as the Czech Republic or Poland, it is considerable. Since this is largely due to their differing political cultures, let us now turn to a discussion of the major reason for this variation: factors influencing the various differing political cultures of the countries of Eastern Europe.[3]

Language

Languages are important in Eastern Europe not only because they emphasize the diversity of the region but also because some are more Western oriented than others. Languages in Eastern Europe are split between four different language families: Slavic, Ural-Baltic, Romance, and Albanian. Within the Slavic language group, there are the Western Slavic languages (Polish, Slovak, Czech) and the South Slavic group (Bulgarian, Serbo-Croatian, Macedonian, and Slovenian). The South Slavs (with the exception of the Croats and the Slovenes) use the Cyrillic alphabet, the same one used by the Russians. The only Ural-Baltic language in the area is Hungarian. Romanian is a Romance language much closer to Latin in many ways than it is to the other languages in the region. It also includes a number (about 15 percent) of Slavic words. Finally, there are the Albanians. The Albanian language is part of an Indo-European language group, but it differs markedly from any other Indo-European languages in that group. These language differences have important cultural implications for the countries of the region.

In the north we find the Poles, who although they are able to understand the Slovaks, find it difficult to communicate with the Czechs, not to mention the Russians. Meanwhile, the Slovaks, Czechs, and Poles are separated from the other Slavic-speaking peoples of Eastern Europe by the Hungarians. The latter language has almost nothing in common with any of the others in the region. The only other languages remotely related to Hungarian are Estonian and Finnish. Indeed, Hungarian is a language with almost no English or Slavic cognates.

East of Hungary is Romania. Rumanians can neither understand Hungarians nor easily communicate with any of their other neighbors—with the exception of the Moldovans, who also speak Romanian. South of Romania is Bulgaria, a country speaking a Slavic language that closely resembles Russian. To the west of Bulgaria is Macedonia. Whether or not Macedonian is a separate language is a hotly debated issue. For political reasons (i.e., all have at one time or another claimed this area as their own), Bulgarians, Greeks, and Serbs maintain that it is not a separate language. Needless to say, Macedonians look at the matter differently.

Next we come to the former Yugoslavia. Most observers consider Serbo-Croatian to be a single language, in spite of the battles and wars that have been fought between these two ethnic groups. Slovenian is fairly close to Slovak and includes a number of German words. Albanian is believed by some to be a distant cousin of Hindi. There are also some other languages spoken in the region: Romani by Gypsies, Yiddish by Jews, German in parts of Romania, Greek by a minority in Albania, and Turkish by a minority in Bulgaria.

Linguistic factors affect political culture in Eastern Europe in two significant ways. First and most obvious, there are tremendous linguistic differences between the various countries themselves. If language is a key to how one interprets political phenomena, then each of these people will tend to view reality somewhat differently.

The second and more important implication is that some of these language groups tend to be Western oriented, while others are more focused on the East. For example, the Western Slavs all use the Latin alphabet and tend to see themselves as Westerners speaking a Slavic language. As a Polish commentator put it, "Poles consider themselves to be Westerners who should be speaking English or French." The same Western orientation is evident among Czechs, Slovenes, and Croats.

The situation with regard to Hungarians is similar in spite of the unique nature of their language. German is the second most common language in Hungary and Hungarians resent any suggestion that their Ural-Baltic language does not make them un-Western. On the other hand, Albanians see little relationship between their language and the West, while the Rumanians often romanticize themselves as descendants of the Roman legions.

The situation is very different with regard to the Serbs and the Bulgarians. Relying on the Cyrillic alphabet, they tend to identify linguistically with the Russians. In fact, the languages are so similar that for many years Bulgarian students were not permitted to claim Russian as a foreign language.

The bottom line is that when it comes to languages, the Poles, Czechs, Slovaks, Hungarians, Slovenes, Rumanians, and Croats tend to see themselves as Western, while the Serbs and Bulgarians find their linguistic identity in the East. The Albanians identify linguistically with neither the East nor the West.

Religion

As with languages, there are significant religious differences among the countries of Eastern Europe. Poles, for example, are almost all Roman Catholics. Indeed, many Poles find it hard to accept someone as a Pole who is not Roman Catholic. Protestants were generally presumed to be Germans, while the Eastern Orthodox were believed by many Poles to be Russians. Indeed, for many years when the country was under external domination, the Catholic Church served as the heart of Polish national identity, and the Poles had a saying, "To be Polish is to be Roman Catholic."

In many ways, the Czech lands are the home of the Protestant Reformation—the place where Jan Hus was burned at the stake for his heresies. Slovakia, meanwhile, is almost entirely Roman Catholic. Hungary is split sixty-forty between Roman Catholics and Protestants, while except for a Hungarian minority, Romania is primarily Orthodox. Bulgaria is also Orthodox, as are Serbia and Macedonia. In addition, Slovenia and Croatia are Roman Catholic, while a large number of Bosnian Serbs are Muslim, as are the majority of Albanians.

What is important about this breakdown is that it parallels the situation in language. Poles, Czechs, Slovaks, Hungarians, Croats, and Slovenes tend to be Western oriented. Poles, for example, look to Rome for religious inspiration, while Czechs are tied closely to the Protestant world. The Bulgarians, Serbs, and Rumanians, who have close ties to the Russian Orthodox Church, tend to be Eastern oriented. Macedonia is somewhat distinct, with strong ties split between the Greek Orthodox Church to the south and the Macedonian Orthodox Church.

Economic Development

While I do not intend to go into the debate over the relationship between a democratic political culture and the level of economic development, I will postulate that there clearly seems to be at least an associational relationship, that is, the higher the level of the economic development, the greater the probability of a democratic polity.

Of all of the countries of Eastern Europe, the Czech Republic is the most developed. In fact, prior to World War II, the Czech lands were among the most developed in all of Europe. Unfortunately, the communist system did much to undermine the vitality and efficiency of the Czech economy. However, it remains ahead of most of its neighbors in the region. The same is not true of Slovakia, however, which continues to lag far behind Prague in economic development. Poland, by contrast, has taken major strides toward the creation of a modern economy and is well on the road toward industrialization. However, it too maintains a large farm economy.

Romania is even more underdeveloped than Poland or the Czech and Slovak lands. Indeed, it is one of the most underdeveloped countries in the region. Hungary has made significant progress, especially in mechanizing agriculture, but it too lags far behind its Western neighbors. Bulgaria was the one country of Eastern Europe to benefit from Soviet domination, and is far better off today economically than it was in 1945. For its part, Yugoslavia appeared to be making important progress until the country collapsed. The civil war in former Yugoslavia, together with Western sanctions imposed on Serbia, have almost totally destroyed the country's economy. While an end to hostilities would contribute significantly to improving the economic situation, so much has been destroyed and some areas were so underdeveloped even *prior* to the fall of Yugoslavia that rebuilding the economies of Croatia, Serbia, and Bosnia would take a long time. Finally, when it comes to economic development Albania is Europe's "basket case." The end of communism served only to intensify economic chaos in a country that was already far behind the rest of Eastern Europe.

Ethnic Minorities

Another factor affecting the political culture of many Eastern European states is the presence of ethnic minorities in many of them. These minorities not only lead to irredentism; in some cases their agitation makes the central government more authoritarian in its attempt to check them than might otherwise be the case. The existence of two different cultural entities within the boundaries of the same country can also frustrate the creation of a mutually acceptable, single, broadly accepted political culture. This in turn can exacerbate the problems involved in creating a democratic political culture.

When it comes to irredentism, it is important to realize that borders in the region have shifted back and forth over the centuries. In truth, almost everyone in Eastern Europe can make the claim that land somewhere else in the region rightfully belongs to them. Poles, for example, are quick to point out that at one time in history they occupied all of Germany up to the Elbe. In fact, the name Berlin is not German, but Old Slavic (meaning place of the nets). Often, the movement of these boundaries leads to intensified feelings of nationalism, or a national sense that one or another country has of having been wronged by history. This is especially true of Hungary. Almost a third of Hungarians found themselves outside of Hungary as a result of what many consider to have been unequal treaties during the early part of this century (e.g., in the Slovak Republic, Romania, and Serbia). Meanwhile, Turks have been upset at their treatment in Bulgaria, Albanians fret under what they consider Serbian and Macedonian repression, and Greeks object to Albanian dominance.

The Poles are among the few populations of Eastern Europe whose ethnic makeup and political boundaries coincide. They inhabit a territory that is almost 100 percent Polish. At the same time, it is important to remember that Poland's borders have been moved back and forth over the past several centuries—indeed, at times Poland ceased to exist as a state. It was only as a result of World War II (when the borders were moved once again) that Poland became almost ethnically pure. The "purification" of Poland did not come without a price, however. Millions of Jews were exterminated, and large numbers of Germans were expelled from what had been traditionally considered German territory. The Russians—and the Polish communist government—were able to use this border change as an effective tool in tying Poland to the former USSR. The idea was simple: the Germans had not recognized the annexation of their former territories by Warsaw. West Germany was an American ally; the only guarantor of Polish sovereignty, therefore, was the USSR.

World War II also did much to remove the German minority from the Czech lands—and in Poland, they were expelled. Indeed, with the exception of some Slovaks, the Czech Republic now has almost no non-Czech minorities. The same cannot be said for Slovakia. The latter has a Hungarian population numbering some six hundred thousand individuals. The treatment accorded to this minority was a source of bilateral tension with Budapest under the communists and has not significantly improved since then. With the exception of the Gypsies and Jews, Hungary itself is relatively pure ethnically. Meanwhile, Romania is home to some two million Hungarians, primarily in Transylvania. Fearful of Hungarian pretensions on the country, Bucharest has taken a number of actions over the years in an effort to "Romanianize" the Hungarian populace. Hungarian schools have been closed, the use of the Hungarian language prohibited, and efforts made to cut back on ties between Budapest and the local Hungarian population.

Bulgaria has had its own problems with its Turkish minority. Toward the end of the communist regime, for example, Sofia attempted forcefully to assimilate the Turks into mainstream Bulgarian life. A campaign to end the teaching of Turkish in schools was launched, and all Turkish Bulgarians were ordered to Bulgarize their names. These policies led to a number of disturbances and the immigration of thousands of Bulgarian Turks to Turkey.

Macedonia also has an ethnic minority problem: about 25 percent of the population is Albanian. So far, the Albanians have not presented a problem for the government, which has been making a strong effort to pacify them. Meanwhile, Albania has a small Greek minority, a situation that has given rise to conflict between Athens and Tirana over the years.

If the former Yugoslavia is nothing else, it is a model of what can happen when the minority problem gets out of hand. Except for Slovenia, all of the remaining republics have until very recently contained significant numbers of minorities. Serbia, for example, includes the Kosovo, the ancestral and emotional Serbian homeland that is now populated almost entirely by Albanians. Croatia used to contain a very large Serbian minority, but one of the results of the recent war has been to drive most of them out of Croatia into either Serbia or Serbian sections of Bosnia. Meanwhile, the various parts of Bosnia are probably more ethnically pure now than at any time in that country's history—a clear result of the policy of "ethnic cleansing."

History

To most Americans, history helps integrate their society. But this is definitely not the case in Eastern Europe. Here it contributes to separateness. The primary reason is that divisive events that happened many years ago remain fresh in the minds of the populace through such things as poems, legends, or even textbooks. Serbian devotion to the Kosovo, for example, derives from the fact that it contains Serbia's ancestral capital as well as Serbia's most holy church. In addition, Serbian children—regardless of whether they have ever seen the Kosovo—are raised reciting poems that stress its critical importance to Serbian national identity. Given this background, it is no surprise that Belgrade is unwilling to make any concessions over the future of this area—even if it is primarily populated by Albanians. Indeed, one of the justifications used by Serbs for their repressive regime is the need to keep rebellious minorities such as the Albanians in line.

The situation is similar in other parts of Eastern Europe. Serbs continue to hold a grudge against Croats because of the slaughter of hundreds of thousands of Serbs by the Croatian Ustasha during the Second World War. Croats, meanwhile, believe the Serbs have worked overtime in their efforts to dominate every part of Croat life. For their part, Hungarians resent their treatment historically by the Serbs in the Vojvodina, as well as by the Rumanians in Transylvania and by the Slovaks in Slovakia. Poles harbor deep resentments toward Germans as well as Russians for a number of historical reasons, and the Slovaks have long felt that Czechs discriminated against them.

The important thing to keep in mind when dealing with Eastern Europe is that history to these peoples is not something that is merely studied in school, a subject that one reads about and then forgets. For most of Eastern Europe, history is very much alive. Unfortunately, in most cases it either leads to tensions between countries or it frustrates efforts to integrate various ethnic groups within a country.

The Clash of East and West

East European political culture is unique in that it has been a crossroads between the Western tradition of democratic pluralism and the Eastern or Russian absolutist approach. In effect, it shows attributes of both traditions.[4]

Western Europe

In the West, the concept of pluralism is very much a part of political life. A ruler's power should never be absolute. This principle emerged directly from the Western Judeo-Christian tradition which argued in favor of separation of church and state. The idea was that individuals should be provided some private space—space that permitted them to work out their own solutions to moral and political issues. The individual still had a duty to God, but God and the state were not the same thing. A theocratic state was by definition wrong. Theocracy and democracy cannot coexist; Western theorists believed, and still hold, that political leaders have no right to interpret what God wants the rest of the populace to do.

This pluralistically oriented society has permitted the development of many groups independent of the state—for example, in late medieval Europe, cities became independent centers of commerce, and the guilds became important forces within cities. The king often was increasingly dependent on the cities, and the guilds and middle class ran them for money and support—a situation that further limited his power. This tradition of many independent power centers gave rise over the centuries to the concept of a social contract: the idea that a deal was struck between the rulers and the ruled. If rulers violate the contract, then the ruled have the right to replace them. Limited sovereignty also led to the rise of the idea of "rule by law." The key point was that law was autonomous; it was not the tool of the sovereign.

Like law, the West has also seen education as autonomous from both church and state. Emphasis was to be placed on speculation, on the development of critical thinking. At base, this idea assumed that knowledge was not just a question of understanding God's will. Rather, it was a matter of asking difficult questions, many of which might not be answerable by looking only to theology.

When it came to developing political systems, Westerners relied mainly on structures invented to routinize the process of changing political leaders via secret ballots. Everyone has—or should have—an equal right to participate in the political system.

The Russian System

The Russian tradition has been almost 180 degrees different from the Western approach. The Russians considered the idea of a balance of power inherently wrong. To be effective, power should not be fragmented. From a moral standpoint, Russians traditionally believed that absolutism was a moral good. All groups in society should be controlled by the center. Besides, an absolutist government could get more done than a democratic one, which many Russians have dismissed as a debating society.

Politically, this belief in unitary absolutist government meant that the main purpose of political institutions was to carry out the sovereign's will. With this concept in mind, why worry about representative institutions? Participation meant the opportunity to carry out the tsar's orders, not the right to have personal input in decision making.

Along the same line, cities should not be—and were not—autonomous. The tsar took what he wanted from the various cities. This in turn meant that the idea of a social contract made no sense to the Russians. Leaders were not in power because they were chosen by the people. God put them there. Power went from the top down. Besides, the only contract was between God and the tsar.

From the standpoint of church-state relations, the main idea was that the church should be subordinate to the state. After all, the tsar was God's personal representative. Doing what the tsar commanded meant doing God's will. Not surprisingly, this meant that belief in the tsar's divinity prevented the development of an autonomous law. The law was nothing more than the expression of the sovereign's will. Its purpose was twofold: first, to make the system run smoothly; and, second, to help the populace understand how to do the sovereign's will.

Education was closely tied to the church. There was little emphasis on critical thinking. Instead, the primary focus was on rote learning. Education was collectivistic. The main purpose was to learn how to behave in a manner that reinforced the group and strengthened the state.

Eastern Europe

Historically Eastern Europe has represented a transitional stage between Russia and Western Europe. The region shared many of the Western experiences, but these factors were incorporated into Eastern Europe against the backdrop of Russian influence. In this sense, Eastern Europe is halfway between Russia and the West. In some ways it closely resembles the West, while in others it is closer to Russia and the East.

Take, for example, autonomous groups. While most groups were not nearly as controlled in Eastern Europe as they were in Russia, they were less autonomous than their counterparts in Western Europe. Native institutions tended to be weak because societal bonds were weak. This led to the rise of a bureaucratic state run by a relatively small elite. This elite in turn worked to marginalize regime opponents—although bureaucrats recognized that autonomous entities such as independent trade unions had a right to exist (a far cry from the Russian case). Nevertheless, none of these groups were strong enough to deal with the political center in the way similar structures in Western Europe did.

For their part, intellectuals tended to identify with the regime, and much of the opposition to governmental policies tended to take place within the ruling elite itself. This meant that although there was far more governmental opposition than in the Russian case, the majority of the populace did not actively take part in politics. Participation was limited to a small elite.

Limited popular participation yielded a concept called the "discretionary power of the state." Under this idea, the state had the right to act in any area of politics unless expressly prohibited from doing so by law or custom. This formulation very definitely did not mean the same as rule by the will of the majority. Rather it meant that the government could pretty much do what it wanted—with a few exceptions.

The state's discretionary power led to the creation of a "facade" of politics. There was outward respect for constitutional principles, and on many occasions the courts delivered objective decisions. In addition a number of interest groups existed and were active in the political process. The problem, however, was that the efficacy of courts, interest groups, and other actors depended on what concessions the elite was prepared to make.

Education was another area in which Eastern Europe was halfway between the East and the West. Here as in many other areas, there was a strong difference between the Balkans and the rest of the region. Central Europe (Hungary, the Czech lands, and Poland) had a tradition of critical thought much like that which existed in Western Europe. In the case of the Balkans, the rote learning characteristic of Russia was more the rule.

Finally, unlike Russia, most of Eastern Europe accepted the rule of law. The problem, however, was that the concept was not nearly as developed as in Western Europe. In fact, it was very difficult to enforce laws if the country's ruler did not agree. The one exception was if laws covered either a custom or an area in which the sovereign was specifically prohibited from acting—a situation which provided for more individual rights than was the case in Russia.

As far as church-state relations were concerned, they varied by country. In some places (Poland, Slovakia, Slovenia, and Croatia), the Roman Catholic Church was relatively autonomous. In other cases (Romania, Bulgaria, and Serbia), the obedient role played by the Orthodox Church vis-a-vis the state more closely resembled the Russian model. In countries such as the Czech lands and Hungary, there was a mixture of Protestantism and Catholicism, while in Albania Islam was the primary religion.

The End of the Cold War

The major impact of the communist period from 1945 to 1987 was to create a new working class and lead to a massive expansion in urbanization. Peasants did not disappear in Eastern Europe, but their numbers certainly diminished. At the same time, a new elite was created, one that was just as authoritarian as before. Indeed, the postwar communists had disdained the average citizen. After all, the communists had a monopoly of knowledge on how society should be organized and engineered to achieve the best social, economic, and political ends.

One of the biggest problems faced by the communist elite in Eastern Europe was that the people almost always looked upon that elite as an alien institution. There were cases, to be sure, where some believed that communism was a more just system or that it improved the living conditions of the average citizen. But by and large most of the region's population saw the communist period as an opportunity for the Russians to exploit and plunder their countries for Moscow's benefit.

As for the development of a democratic political culture, the major effect of the communist experience was to entrench further many of the attitudes and values which were least conducive to the development of democracy. For example, the entrenchment of a political elite, who had little interest in public opinion, as well as the introduction of voting procedures that had little impact on political decisions, tended only to deepen the cynicism already prevalent in the countries of the region.

The communist period also reinforced the belief in statism—the idea that the state could and should resolve all of society's problems. Statism shifted attention away from individual responsibility and convinced average citizens even more that the government owed them a living. This failure of meaningful citizen involvement in politics meant that almost without exception few East Europeans were ready for the post-communist experiment in democracy. The widespread acceptance of statism led many to look to the new regimes to solve most of their problems.

If the new "capitalist" economy was not working, then it was clearly the regime's fault. Rather than holding themselves responsible as the body politic for resolving issues, the people of some East European states, frustrated with their countries' failure to move immediately from the darkness of Soviet domination to the dawn of post-communist affluence, tended to look to demagogic or xenophobic solutions—whether in the form of attacks on scapegoats or reliance on leaders with simple solutions to complex problems.

Conclusions

As should be evident by this point, to suggest that the West has triumphed in Eastern Europe would be inaccurate. Western influence (or the Western model) is stronger in some sections of the region than in others. But to suggest that the East Europeans are consciously following a Western model only recently introduced would be to assign far too much importance to American ability to influence events in these countries. Indeed, one can divide these countries into at least three categories based both on their political culture as well as the current situation in the region.

The Emerging Democrats

In this category I would place Poland, the Czech Republic, Hungary, and Slovenia.[5] All of these countries—to varying degrees—have embraced what we often call the Western model (i.e., the adoption of a more or less democratic political system together with a mixed economy). While a detailed discussion of these countries is beyond the scope of this chapter, what is especially interesting is that all of them have long-standing cultural ties to the West.

When it comes to religion, for example, the Poles, the Czechs, the Slovenes, and the Hungarians are all Western Christians. Similarly, all four of these polities speak a Western-inspired language that draws its inspiration from the West—the Poles, Czechs, and Slovaks with their Latin script, and the Hungarians with their strong denial that their language is Eastern. These countries also share important economic characteristics: the Czech Republic is the most developed, although the other three are working hard to catch up. None of the four states are faced with significant ethnic minorities. The Hungarians are concerned about the way members of their ethnic group are treated in other parts of Europe, but in all four instances, the lack of an *internal* ethnic problem facilitates the development of a democratic political culture.

Furthermore, in all four cases, there are strong historical ties to the West. Poland is perhaps an exception, having fought for its very existence for the past two hundred years, but even Warsaw sees its history closely bound to the West. Hungary, the Czech Republic, and Slovenia were all closely tied to the Austro-Hungarian Empire—a factor which also helped them identify with the West rather than the East. Finally, Poland, Slovenia, and the Czech Republic are notable for their toleration of autonomous political institutions. The Roman Catholic Church in Poland in particular has been a bulwark against external domination, and Prague has shown willingness to tolerate a variety of dissident groups—including a Communist Party during the interwar period. In this sense, the communist period was an aberration. Hungary's acceptance of religious tolerance was a sign of how far religious pluralism in that country had come.

The Potential Democrats[6]

In this category I place Slovakia, Albania, Macedonia, Romania, and Bulgaria. All give lip service to the Western model, but all have a long way to go to make it a reality. For example, Romania recently took an important step with the election of a democratic leader, but whether or not that will evolve into a stable, democratic polity remains to be seen.

All of these countries tend to be on the opposite end of a continuum when it comes to the characteristics of a democratic political culture as outlined above. In religion, for example, three of them are Orthodox and one is Muslim. Based on the East European experience, they do not provide the kind of background from which one would expect a democratic political culture to emerge naturally. In this case, Slovakia is an exception. Its apparent Western orientation (Western language, Roman Catholicism) is outweighed by other factors. Linguistically, Romania and Slovakia should be on the Western side; Bulgaria and Macedonia on the Eastern side. In fact, language does not seem to be a sufficient condition to give these countries a Western orientation. As far as Albania is concerned, the most one can say is that its language does not give it a Western orientation.

Economically, all of these countries are in the same category—faced with serious problems. Most of them are primarily agricultural and all face the daunting task of trying to put their economies back together. When it comes to history, Slovakia was tied to Hungary, while Romania and Bulgaria have a clear Russian orientation. Albania as usual went its own way, and Macedonia has as much of a Greek orientation as it does Serbian and Bulgarian.

The major exception to what one might expect from a country's history is Slovakia. There are three reasons for this situation. First, the Slovaks were treated like vassals by the Hungarians when the latter ruled them. Second, they received little training in political leadership under the Czechoslovak experiment, and third, they are faced with a serious minority problem. Having said that, should the current authoritarian regime be replaced by a more democratically oriented one, there is a good chance that Slovakia will resume its march toward the West.

The Imponderables

Serbia, Croatia, and Bosnia all fit into this last category. None of the three have given any sign of interest in the development of a meaningful democratic polity. This is not surprising when one considers the nature of Serbian political culture—orthodox, Russian-oriented in speech, historically tied to the East, presented with serious minority problems, and under-developed economically. Belgrade has a long way to go to become a democratic polity.

Croatia, on the other hand, would seem to have all of the necessities for the creation of a democratic polity. The problem, however, is that a democratic political culture does not flourish well during war—which is a state that Croatia has been in for some time. Should the country's leadership decide to move toward the Western model, Croatia would seem to have the prerequisites necessary for the creation of such a system. Meanwhile, there is little one can say about Bosnia. This artificial polity is practically still in a state of war. The fighting may have stopped, but given the continuing bitter ethnic feuds—which were made worse by the recent atrocities—the chances of successfully introducing the Western model into this polity would seem distant at best.

In spite of the uproar that greeted Samuel Huntington's essay cited above, it does contain some truth. One can argue that he may have over-emphasized the importance of ethnicity, although it remains a serious problem, but the fact is that some countries are more predisposed toward democracy than others. This is not to suggest that countries like Serbia have no hope of becoming democratic in the Western sense of the term, only that the road will probably be longer and strewn with more rocks than will be the case for countries like Poland. It is time for Western analysts to dispense with the naive assumption that the rest of the world is waiting breathlessly for the opportunity to adopt the Western model. The reality is that even those countries which do accept the major outlines of this model will produce a system which places the appropriate institutions within the framework of the prevalent political culture. We can bemoan the continued existence of non-democratic—or less than democratic—political cultures, but we have no alternative but to learn to live with them.

Endnotes

1. Howard J. Wiarda, *Introduction to Comparative Politics* (Belmont, CA: Wadsworth Publishing Co., 1993): 22.

2. Ronald Inglehart, "The Renaissance of Political Culture," *American Political Science Review* 82, no. 4 (Dec. 1988): 1205.

3. The following draws on this author's "Eastern Europe: Successful Transitions or Descent into Chaos?" in Howard Wiarda, ed., *U.S. Foreign and Strategic Policy in the Post-Cold War Era* (Westport, CT: Greenwood Press, 1996): 85–105.

4. Much of the material in this section is based on George Schoepflin's excellent "Culture and Identity in Post-Communist Europe," in Stephen White, Judy Batt, and Paul G. Lewis, eds., *Developments in East European Politics* (Durham, NC: Duke University Press, 1993): 16–34.

5. One could legitimately place the former German Democratic Republic in this category, but it has been left out from this analysis because it is now part of Germany.

6. The line between the "Emerging Democrats" and the "Potential Democrats" follows closely along the lines indicated by Samuel Huntington in his classic essay, "The Clash of Civilizations," *Foreign Affairs* (Summer 1993): 30.

8

Russia and Central Asia

—Steve D. Boilard

Steve D. Boilard is assistant professor of government at Western Kentucky University. He is the author of Reinterpreting Russia *(Salem, 1997) and* Russia at the Twenty-First Century, *a previous volume in the Harcourt Brace series,* New Horizons in Comparative Politics.

Introduction

As a geographical concept, Russia has existed for well over a thousand years. Its history has been epochal, often tragic with periodic triumphs. By dint of its length and intensity, Russia's history is said to be deeply etched upon the souls of its people. Even today, as Russia takes its place in the so-called New World Order, many Russians harbor a somewhat fatalistic sense of their country's authoritarian-directed development, which has gained the momentum of a millennium. Others seem to have accepted Francis Fukuyama's thesis that the "end of history" is finally at hand, as the oppression of tsarist absolutism and the nightmare of Soviet totalitarianism give way to Western liberalism.[1] To still others, however, the course of Russia's development is anything but certain since it has been thrown into chaos by the discrediting of official Marxist-Leninist ideology, the collapsing of the state-directed economy, and the fragmenting of the Soviet Union itself. Modern Russia evidently is experiencing an identity crisis: unrepentant communists in the Soviet mold are taking their popularly elected seats alongside laissez-faire liberals in the Russian legislature, and the Russian

Mafiya and the Russian Orthodox Church are proving to be two of the most successful post-Soviet institutions.

The notion of a Russian identity crisis is not new. Since at least the time of Tsar Peter the Great in the late seventeenth and early eighteenth centuries, Russians have been divided over whether they have a place in Western civilization or constitute the larger part of a distinct Slavic civilization. Peter's policies, of course, were informed by the former views: he promoted the emulation of Western dress, values, culture, and arts and sciences. The Russian court adopted the French language; the Russian government employed German advisers. Those who opposed Westernization urged respect for Russia's unique history and culture. They understood Russia's Slavic heritage distinguished the country spiritually, ethnically, and historically from the West to the point that the two cultures were incompatible. The tension between "Westernizers" and "Slavophiles," as advocates of these two positions came to be known, has manifested itself in various ways over the centuries. It underlies questions of Russia's identity and development to this day.

The Westernizer/Slavophile dichotomy arises from Russia's somewhat ambivalent existence on the border of two civilizations: the Western and the Slavic.[2] After Peter the Great's reign, questions about Russia's membership in either or both of these civilizations were especially salient as the Enlightenment spread in the eighteenth century and the Soviet empire arose in the twentieth. Most recently, Gorbachev, Yeltsin, and others seeking to adopt Western political and economic structures and promote Western values resurrected the Westernizer/Slavophile debate.

Although the Westernizer/Slavophile dichotomy historically has received more attention, there is a second cleavage significant to the question of Russia's development. This dimension concerns not so much identity as it does Russia's interests. The debate in this dimension separates "Atlanticists," who understand Russia's interests to lie in Western Europe and North America, from "Eurasianists," who locate Russia's interests in Eastern Europe and central Asia. As with the Westernizer/Slavophile dichotomy, the primary orientations of this theme have roots deep in Russian and Soviet history. Tsarist Russia of course managed to direct its energies, at different times, to various points in Europe, the Middle East, and Asia. The two main schools of thought competing for the tsar's ear advocated a focus on Europe and a focus on Eurasia.

By the time of the Cold War, Atlanticists further split between those who saw the greatest opportunities in (Western) Europe, and those who believed the United States was the more important target—especially given the presumed subordination of Western Europe to its North American patron. Moscow's foreign policy during the Cold War vacillated between these two points, sometimes using its relations with the United States to rein in the

West Europeans, and sometimes using its relations with Western Europe to divide the alliance. Today, although political distinctions are still made between the United States and Western Europe, the Soviet-era divide-and-conquer strategy has largely been laid to rest. In the post-Cold War era, therefore, it makes sense to speak of a "Euro-Atlanticist" approach which focuses on Western Europe and the United States as a collective whole—"the West." This orientation emphasizes the importance of the nuclear arms, markets, financial resources, and technology associated with the Western countries. The alternative view looks to Eastern Europe and central Asia as the more suitable partners for Russian diplomacy, trade, and foreign policy. This Eurasian orientation emphasizes pre-tsarist Russia's domination by the Mongols, the current threat of Muslim fundamentalism in the south, Russia's long and often tense border with China, and other geostrategic concerns in the region.

These two themes—civilization membership and locus of interests—emphasize questions defining Russia's development: Who are the Russians, and where do they belong? After more than one thousand years, Russians themselves are still undecided.

The Impact of the West to 1917

Russia's identity crisis stems in part from ambivalence about the salubriousness of outside influence. From prehistoric times, the Slavic peoples occupying the area of modern Russia were subject to successive waves of invasion. Sometimes these foreign influences worked to the Slavs' long-term benefit, introducing agricultural techniques, administrative mechanisms, and other skills and technologies. But many raids were conducted with a murderous cruelty that became a recurrent theme of Russia's past. Although the Slavs attempted to establish defenses, invaders were largely unimpeded by natural geographic barriers. This helps account for Russians' preoccupation with security.

The early eastern Slavs came under the control of Scandinavian Vikings (Varangians). Rurik, a Varangian leader, seized the city of Novgorod (about 100 miles south of present-day St. Petersburg) in the ninth century. After successive conquests, Rurik's successor, Oleg, established a capital at Kiev (the capital of modern Ukraine). The result was Kievan Rus, the first united Russian state. Subsequent rulers expanded the borders of Rus, adopted a written language based on the Cyrillic alphabet, and established a Russian Orthodox Church—a variant of Christianity linked to Constantinople and intentionally separate from Rome. By the eleventh century the Russian state had developed a distinct identity and boasted considerable commercial, cultural, and religious importance.

After its zenith in the eleventh century Kievan Rus steadily declined and eventually fell victim to a combination of internecine battles, disrupted trade, and periodic raids by marauding armies. Its people began to migrate northward—a trend that would have long-term implications for Russia's future development. In the thirteenth century Kievan Rus fell to the Mongols (Tatars, in Russian parlance). Kiev was destroyed, and the rival city of Moscow steadily became more important. Still, for two centuries the Mongols dominated the Russians and exacted annual tribute. Although the Mongols generally allowed Russians to continue their day-to-day lives, the "Mongol Yoke" was economically and politically oppressive. When Russians would occasionally rise up against the Mongols, they encountered savage counterforce and retribution.

The Russians, led by Ivan III ("the Great"), eventually overthrew their Mongol oppressors, finally terminating the savage Mongol conquest in 1480. Ivan then consolidated Muscovite Russia by conquering the cities of Tver and Novgorod. When Constantinople fell to the Turks in 1453, Moscow assumed itself to be the "Third Rome," at once strengthening the concept of Russia as a united Christian empire and distinguishing it from the Western Christians. Ivan adopted the title "tsar" (a Russian variation on "Caesar"), and Russia's tsarist era began.

The powers of the tsar were consolidated and augmented under Ivan III's grandson, Ivan IV ("The Terrible"). But with Ivan IV's death in 1584, Russia's ruling circle became plagued with conspiratorial regents, foreign intrigue, and a series of false pretenders to the throne. A "Time of Troubles" had descended upon Russia, and embattled corrivals called upon foreign powers, including Sweden and Poland, to intervene. This condition of domestic turmoil and foreign occupation continued until the early seventeenth century. It was a chaotic and humiliating period to which some of today's Russian nationalists, perhaps unfairly, compare post-Soviet times. Finally, in 1612, the Poles were driven from Moscow. A year later the Russian Assembly elevated Mikhail Romanov to tsar, and the house of Romanov would rule Russia for the next three centuries, until the Revolution of 1917.

Under Peter the Great in the early eighteenth century, Russia became a significant European power and took on a more Western identity. Peter's Russia was almost continually at war, and secured a number of impressive victories over other powers. It was Peter who developed Russia's navy and organized its army more effectively. Peter traveled extensively in Europe, and he was eager to transplant large features of European culture to Russia. His interest in the West was perhaps best symbolized by his moving of Russia's capital city from Moscow to St. Petersburg (on the shore of the Baltic Sea) in 1712. Peter developed a reputation as a modernizer and social reformer, which contrasted sharply with many of his predecessors (and not a small number of his successors).

A successor who did share Peter's penchant for Western ways was Catherine II ("the Great"), who ruled Russia from 1762 until her death in 1796. Formerly a German princess, Catherine considered herself a great ruler and a philosopher of the Enlightenment. Despite her familiarity with liberal ideas, however, she did little to attenuate the autocratic nature of the Russian court. Russian and Western historians alike frequently describe her as an "enlightened despot." In fact, Catherine's despotism and her distrust of and ambivalence toward peasants were characteristic of the Russian monarchy. Whatever the particulars of the various "Great," "Terrible," and "Bloody" tsars and emperors, the imperial edifice sat atop an oppressed, sometimes restive, population.

Russia's international position under the tsars swung between strength and weakness. Russia emerged as a Great Power in the eighteenth century, and at one point in the early nineteenth century Russia and France were the only two major powers on the continent. Napoleon's invasion of Russia and occupation of Moscow, followed by Tsar Alexander I's pursuit of Napoleon's retreating army and subsequent occupation of Paris, are illustrative of the shifting balance of power. Russia participated as one of the four Great Powers at the subsequent Congress of Vienna, but its fortunes continued to shift with the dynastic and imperial wars so characteristic of nineteenth-century Europe's international relations and diplomacy.

Domestically, a pattern of alternating reform and repression had taken root in Russia. After a major uprising in the 1770s, almost a century would pass before Alexander II, the tsar at the time, finally removed a significant cause of popular unrest by abolishing serfdom in 1861. By this time, however, even the freeing of the serfs could not appease radical groups opposed to the regime. Intellectuals, nationalists, populists, and revolutionaries advocated a variety of visions for their country. The Westernizer/Slavophile cleavage divided the regime's opponents between those who advocated an ethnically distinct Slavic state grounded in Orthodoxy, and those who sought to resurrect and expand Russia's European identity and politics, which had begun under Peter I.

The discontinuity of the two visions was nevertheless papered over as the radicals found common cause in their disdain for the current regime. The government unwittingly helped to unite its opponents through the imposition of widespread censorship, the practice of religious and political persecution, and its involvement in unpopular (and sometimes disastrous) foreign wars. During this time the Western powers were not especially enamored of the tsarist regime, which they considered politically illiberal and culturally backward. The logic of realpolitik nevertheless drove the Western powers, particularly the United States and Great Britain, to ally with Russia against greater evils—especially imperial Germany during the First World War.

The Bolsheviks' success in the Revolution of 1917 threw Russia's relationship with the West into turmoil. The new regime's ideology fitted the ideas of a German, Karl Marx, to the unique conditions of Russia. Lenin himself was an intellectual well versed in Western ideas, and had spent years living in exile in Europe before the revolution.[3] Although Marxism-Leninism was hostile to the social, economic, and foreign policy foundations of the advanced Western countries, there was nothing inherently anti-Western about the ideology. Marxism-Leninism putatively built upon the legacy of the West, pushing it toward its rendezvous with a utopian destiny, rather than rejecting the West's accomplishments outright.

The Bolshevik leadership's understanding of the role of the West in Russia's development nevertheless was fraught with inconsistency. A major source of controversy was Lenin's separate peace with the German kaiser at Brest-Litovsk. Lenin incurred much opposition from Bolshevik radicals, most famously Leon Trotsky, for his at least temporary abandonment of the world revolution. If Lenin's rationale for Brest-Litovsk is taken at face value, it indicates a certain hubris, perhaps a complacent certainty, that Marx's historical materialism would ultimately carry the day.

The West's unwillingness to allow the Russian front against Germany to go quiet after Brest-Litovsk prompted an Allied invasion of Russia—an event never neglected in official Soviet history. The civil war that followed the revolution was a complicated affair, with no neatly drawn dichotomies. The "White" forces that opposed the new regime comprised a broad range of groups, including monarchists, liberals, moderate socialists, and others. Although the Allied Expeditionary Force was rationalized as part of the fight against Germany, assisting the Whites was certainly one of its goals. In that goal the West failed. For most of the remainder of the twentieth century, the West and the Soviet Union would be implacably opposed, with Moscow eventually directing a development path for a group of countries that came to be known as the "Second World."

Soviet "Development" as a Non-Western Model

Soviet leaders dictated the country's development by employing a variant of Marxism that became known as Marxism-Leninism, or sometimes simply Leninism.[4] Notwithstanding this label, Lenin himself should not be thought of as an architect who laid out a detailed map for the Soviet Union's political and economic development. Instead Lenin improvised and backtracked, as evidenced by Brest-Litovsk and his abrupt shift from War Communism to his New Economic Policy. Lenin died before a reasonably fixed development plan could be formulated, and thus it fell to Stalin to pick up the pieces after the civil war and industrialize and militarize the country to a level adequate to withstand Germany's attack during the Second World War. Less than a detailed plan, Leninism offered theoretical principles on which to base the new system that was ultimately to usher in communism.

Three basic features set this system apart from the prevailing Western model at the time. First, and in accordance with Marx's call for the abolition of private property, factories, shops, housing, and transportation—virtually all property except simple consumer goods—were nationalized and collectivized. This program was consistent with the ideology's raising of the community above the individual. Second, the country's economy was placed under the direction of the central government. More than mere Keynesianism, Leninism called for the placement of all economic decisions, from production choices to prices, under the control of state agencies such as *Gosplan* and *Goskomtsen*. Third, Leninism sought to remake the various peoples living on Soviet territory into a new nation, undivided by class, religious, or ethnic differences. The intended result of this three-pronged strategy was to eventually arrive at a truly communist society. In addition, the Soviet Union would serve as a vanguard, catalyst, or orchestrater (Leninist ideology was ambivalent on this point) of world communism.

As a rough guide for the Soviet Union's development, Leninism was neither wholly Western nor wholly Slavic. To be sure, it was anticapitalist and viewed the Western countries with antipathy. Indeed, it postured as the very antithesis of the values, policies, and institutions that had taken root in the West. But at the same time Leninism's emphasis on transcending ethnic, religious, and national differences put it at odds with the Slavophiles' doctrine. Further, by the time of the Cold War, Moscow's development goals very much paralleled that achieved in the West: industrialization, urbanization, scientific and technological progress. In other words, although the Soviets rejected the capitalistic financial and economic foundations of Western development, they seemed to be pursuing the same materialistic goals. Thus the truly non-Western development models pursued by various Third World countries were equally incompatible with the goals of both superpowers.

On the matter of the geographical locus of Moscow's interests Leninism was similarly ambivalent. On the one hand it purported to be a scientific doctrine that had equal validity for all the world's peoples. And in this regard the Soviets understood themselves to be the leader of the communist movement for the entire world. The bipolar logic of the Cold War had the Soviets constantly calculating the "correlation of forces" which must ultimately (it was believed) turn in favor of world socialism. In this way Leninism assigned to Moscow the world revolutionary role of ushering in the Marxian millennium. Yet until such an opportunity arose Soviet leaders maintained what in many ways was a conservative policy, holding on to domestic power and protecting the international gains of socialism against foreign and indigenous threats.

Thus, Moscow was at once the leader of world socialism (Marxism), the defender of the Second World (especially as justified in the Brezhnev Doctrine), and the geostrategic pole opposite Washington.

But Moscow also had a distinctly Eurasian orientation. The conservative aspect of the Soviet Union's development was to maintain its inner and outer empires: the union itself and its sphere of influence in Eastern Europe. The combination of these two empires covered most of Eurasia, from the Elbe to the Pacific Ocean, and from the Arctic to the Black and Caspian Seas. Despite its globalist rhetoric, Moscow's greatest success in nurturing Leninist development was limited to Eurasia. In summary, Moscow was a Eurasian power with life-and-death interests focused on the Euro-Atlantic region.

Whatever the ideological underpinnings of Moscow's development model, its progress toward the Marxian goal of unalloyed communism was a matter of constant revision and reinterpretation. The regime used Leninism's theoretical precepts to justify its policies and its very hold on power, and so it could not drastically or abruptly alter those precepts without jeopardizing the Communist Party's proclaimed right to lead. At the same time, the Soviet leadership had to explain the fact that the state was becoming stronger, not "withering away," as Marx had predicted. In the mid-1930s Stalin had proclaimed that the Soviet Union had achieved socialism, Marx's "first phase of communist society." Verbal assurance that the Soviet Union would soon achieve Marx's "higher phase of communist society"—genuine communism—became a shibboleth of the leadership until the final years of Gorbachev's rule. Intermediate progress toward this goal was labeled with neologisms such as Khrushchev's "full-scale construction of communism" and Brezhnev's "developed socialism."

Although Marx's radiant future of a stateless, classless society never appeared any closer, by some measures the regime was highly successful in industrial and military development. Impressive gains were achieved under the Five Year Plans (FYPs) initiated by Stalin. Even if the suspect official production figures are discounted, the Soviet Union came close to making good on Stalin's insistence in 1931 that his country compress a century of modernization into a decade. In the span of the first three FYPs (1928–1940), electrical generation increased sevenfold, oil extraction more than doubled, and steel production more than quadrupled. And despite the enormous human costs of the Terror and collectivization, the Soviet Union was able to turn back Hitler's invasion and dominate virtually all of Eastern Europe.

With the Soviet Union's emergence from the Second World War as a military superpower possessing a rapidly industrializing economy and a scientific sector that rivaled even America's, Western analysts became preoccupied with the likely result of Moscow's economic and political development. Some believed that the Soviets would increasingly be faced with the need to develop Western-style institutions. This "modernization" school, led by Walt

Rostow and others, presumed a roughly linear development toward First World modernity. The forces of industrialization and urbanization that accompanied economic growth would create social forces that would demand democracy. Socialism was dismissed as a "disease" of the transitional stages of development, and it surely would be cured as modernization progressed.[5]

Slightly different was the logic behind George Kennan's analysis in his "X" article, which laid out the logic of America's containment policy. By maintaining "long-term, patient but firm and vigilant" pressure against Soviet expansionism, the United States could keep the Stalinist Soviet virus "contained" until the country must surely break up or "mellow."[6] Containment was therefore a rather conservative doctrine, calling for the preservation of the geopolitical balance of power until such a time as the Soviet Union should reform or collapse as a result of its own internal weaknesses and contradictions.

Aside from preventing Soviet expansion into Western Europe, the influence of the West on Soviet development during the Cold War was not immediately evident. The Soviet regime used strict censorship and regulation of travel to limit the penetration of Western ideas and culture. Yet Western influence crept in, particularly among Soviet youth who sought access to Western music, fashions, literature, and magazines. The availability of these increased with the loosening of censorship after Stalin's death and the cultural exchanges made possible by détente.

The onset of détente in the late 1960s prompted another reevaluation of Soviet development by Western analysts. The Soviet regime appeared to be as secure as it ever was, showing no obvious signs of an imminent validation of either the modernization thesis or Kennan's prophesy. With the amelioration of the worst excesses of the Stalinist Terror and with the introduction of limited reforms, a less noxious, but still non-Western, Soviet Union seemed to be developing. Moreover, the correlation of forces appeared to be turning in favor of Moscow. The Soviet Union's attainment of rough nuclear parity with the United States was affirmed in the SALT treaties, and its Warsaw Pact allies in Eastern Europe—most notably East Germany—received international recognition in several treaties in the early 1970s. Not only had the East European regimes based on Leninism been stabilized; additional countries in Asia, Africa, the Middle East, and even Central America moved to the ranks of socialist fraternal allies through the early 1980s.

These apparent successes of Moscow lent a certain respectability to the Soviet Union and a certain grudging acceptance that the Soviet development model might be viable after all. To many, the Soviet system had indeed mutated in response to modernity, but not by embracing Western liberalism. Sovietologists such as Jerry Hough thought they saw a meaningful middle class developing within the Soviet population, as well as a Soviet equivalent of interest groups.[7] In other words, the Soviet Union had modernized, but along a new path that rejected both Stalinism and liberal pluralism. Those who had been seeking such a "third" model of development were encouraged by this perception. Variants of "social democracy" took hold in the Scandinavian and some West European countries. These developments provided strength to the "convergence" theory, which saw both the liberal, individualistic Western systems and the Stalinist communist systems softening towards a middle ground, a "third way." Convergence theory was essentially a form of modernization theory, in that it associated modernity with a logic ("industrialism") that directed a country's developmental path.[8] As Marx might have said of Hegel's dialectic, convergence theorists agreed with modernization theory's understanding of the general process, but not with the process's ultimate destination.

By the 1980s the Soviet Union had reached the height of international respect. Although there were similarities to the goals of Western modernity, its noncapitalist development path was apparently validated. The world was all the more stunned a few years later, therefore, when the Soviet leadership under Mikhail Gorbachev rapidly confessed to the country's numerous economic shortcomings, abandoned the key tenets of Leninism, conceded the Cold War, and ultimately presided over the Soviet Union's collapse.

The Rejection of Leninism and the End of the Cold War

Leninism as an ideology was never fully accepted by the Soviet population, as periodic defections, the presence of underground dissident movements, the circulation of samizdat writings, the survival of the Russian Orthodox Church, and other phenomena attested. Leninism as an economic system similarly failed to capture the population's cooperation and allegiance, fueling a thriving black market (or "second economy") which operated alongside the "official" economy. But politically the regime's ability to rule was virtually unchallenged by the public, and the Party managed to retain power for almost three quarters of a century.

The discrediting and termination of the Soviet experiment were initiated by the highest official of the Communist Party itself, General Secretary Mikhail Gorbachev. Gorbachev, of course, did not make this his goal when he ascended to power in 1985; rather, he sought to "correct" what he viewed as reversible errors made by previous Soviet leaders. Until the very end of the Soviet Union in 1991, and perhaps even afterwards, Gorbachev retained faith in certain core values of Leninism. At the very least, he continued to believe in the quest for the elusive "third way." But in loosening the regime's intolerance of opposition and in surrendering the party's monopoly of political power, Gorbachev unleashed the latent forces of opposition that had remained, and perhaps even grown, since the revolution. These forces quickly launched a revolution—perhaps a counterrevolution—that rejected three fundamental aspects of Leninism. In a sense, three separate revolutions brought Gorbachev's tottering Soviet Union to its grave.

One of the revolutions rejected the nondemocratic nature of the Soviet government. Despite the regime's claim that the scientific nature of the Communist Party's ideology and the homogeneity of the "proletarian" majority made pluralism unnecessary, large segments of the population demanded a voice and genuine representation in political affairs. Despite the regime's claims that the Soviet constitution (the most recent version of which had been adopted in 1977) was a model for all the world, the people demanded genuine constitutional limits on the exercise of state power.

The demands for true democracy linked especially with demands for national self-determination—a second revolution. As a multinational state the Soviet Union comprised well over 100 national groups, with the Great Russians making up only about half of the country's population. The architects of the Soviet state had granted fifteen of these national groups their own "union republics," and the borders of these would serve as the fault lines along which the Soviet Union disintegrated. Official Soviet doctrine had denied that such a thing could happen. Lenin, Stalin, and other early Soviet leaders had sought to create not merely a new state and a new economic system, but also a new nation and a new society—a "New Soviet Man," unencumbered by any politically meaningful awareness of ethnic, religious, racial, or other ascriptive characteristics. The Soviet leadership sought to create a single class identity which would unite all "workers," whatever their ethnic and national backgrounds. At times the Soviet leveling techniques resembled the Russification policies that had been pursued by the tsars. At other times, Soviet leaders attempted to defuse nationalist demands by officially recognizing the different national groups that composed the union, and allowing them their own union republics and autonomous areas. Over time, the Soviet regime's attempts to deal with identity proved ambivalent.

Despite these ambitious objectives, the biases and nationalistic drives of the pre-Soviet cultures kept resurfacing. In the late 1980s the liberation movements of the indigenous peoples of the Soviet Union, including, ironically, the Russians themselves, drew strength from the democratization movements that had been unleashed and even encouraged by Gorbachev. The five central Asian republics were among the least eager to sever their bonds with Moscow, as they were heavily dependent economically and militarily on the all-union structures of the Soviet Union. They had been incorporated into the Russian empire in the eighteenth and nineteenth centuries, and Soviet relocation policies had salted the republics with large numbers of ethnic Russians. In per capita terms the central Asian republics were the poorest of the Soviet Union, and their standard of living was liable to drop still further without assistance from Moscow. But nationalist movements arose nonetheless, making much of their Muslim heritage, the periodic mistreatment of their culture and their religion by the Soviet regime, and their earlier mistreatment under imperial Russian rule.

The third revolution against Leninism in the late 1980s sprang from consumer dissatisfaction. When anti-communist revolutions finally erupted throughout the Soviet bloc in 1989–1991, popular dissatisfaction with living conditions fueled the counterrevolutionary fire. Bolstered by less sanitized economic and social data made available by glasnost, longtime dissatisfaction with the quality and variety of consumer goods, the condition and reliability of transportation, the allocation of living space, and other aspects of living standards ballooned into widespread, increasingly vociferous demands for the introduction of market reforms. Gorbachev gradually responded to some of these demands with programs under the rubric of perestroika. But his reforms encountered opposition throughout the bureaucracy, and their result appeared to be worsening rather than improving of the Soviet standard of living.

Leninism as a system was thus rejected on three fronts: for the Communist Party's monopoly of power, for its suppression of national cultures (and often its oppression of peoples), and for its inability to meet consumer needs. The system was destroyed not because of Western intervention or imperialism, but because of its rejection by the peoples who lived under it.

Yet although the enticements of First World prosperity helped steal the hearts of Soviet citizens away from the more idealistic appeals of Leninist ideology, the Soviet Union's collapse did not result from unfulfilled consumer desires alone. On a structural level, the Soviet Union progressively became weakened by the command economy's inability to meet the demands placed upon it by the state and the military, as well as by the consumer. And the growing perception of unresponsiveness and incompetence that characterized Brezhnev's Soviet Union further weakened the bond between citizen and state. To the extent that each of these contributed to the revolutions of 1989–1991, the new government of post-Soviet Russia was faced with the immediate need to correct the institutional cause, and not merely the individual manifestations, of its social and economic pathologies.

Post-Soviet Russia

After the formal dissolution of the Soviet Union in December 1991, the Russian Federation emerged as a sovereign state whose government and constitution professed a commitment to democracy, market economics, and national self-determination. The new Russian leadership, with Boris Yeltsin at its head, thus pledged to respect the principles of the three revolutions that brought about the Soviet Union's demise. Many in the West welcomed what they saw as Russia's long-awaited turn toward liberal modernity.

Notwithstanding early signs of repentance and conversion in post-Soviet Russia, the final fulfillment of the three revolutions remains stymied by the effects of demographics and political culture. Most critically, even after shedding the Soviet Union's fourteen non-Russian union republics, Moscow continues to rule a multinational empire. Although about 83 percent of the population is ethnically Russian, non-Russians make up substantial portions of the population in many regions. Ethnic Germans, Ukrainians, Tatars, and Chuvashes, for example, predominate in certain enclaves as a result of historic settlement patterns and Stalin's deportation policies. Similarly, although 71 percent of Russia's population identifies itself as Russian Orthodox, many regions are populated by persons of other faiths. Islam, for example, is the predominant religion in the Caucasus, and Muslims collectively constitute about 6 percent of the country's population.[9]

If Russia were a truly pluralistic society, these ethnic and religious cleavages might not be especially relevant to Russia's national cohesion. But as the republic of Chechnya's secession efforts have demonstrated, Russia's ethnonational cleavages can trigger secession and civil war. As a practical matter, the very principle of national self-determination invoked by Russians in leaving the Soviet Union has come back to haunt the Russian Federation. Support for the Federation's territorial integrity, though firm in the abstract, weakens when particular cases are considered. For example, a 1995 survey found over two-thirds of Russians opposing Moscow's military action against Chechnya's secession. The same survey found a majority supporting the notion that a "patriot" must oppose the military operation, while only 19 percent felt patriotism requires support for the forcible retention of Chechnya.[10]

Moscow's efforts to advance the country's political and economic development are further hindered by public attitudes that frequently conflict with the government's goals. This public reluctance became especially apparent with regard to economic reforms. For example, a 1996 survey found that only about a third of the population wanted to live and work within a market-based economy, while over 40 percent favored an economy based on state planning.[11] Despite initial enthusiasm for economic reform, support has diminished as reforms have progressed. For instance, in 1992 only about a third of Russia's citizens believed that personal incomes should be regulated to ensure that "no one earns more than others." In 1995, that figure had risen to over half.[12]

Clearly cynicism about capitalism is spurred by the economic dislocations that have accompanied post-Soviet Russia's economic transition: a sharp drop in per capita real income, widespread unemployment and underemployment, unpaid wages, inflation, and the penetration of business and industry by criminal gangs, syndicates, and corrupt officials. In general, Russians feel frustrated by what they see as the post-Soviet government's inability to meet their material needs; in 1995 three in five Russians believed that the state should be responsible for their standard of living, but over half the population believed that the state was incapable of improving their lives.[13]

Russian citizens' attitudes about political pluralism and representative democracy have also weakened over time. The initial groundswell of support for replacing the party with "democrats" disappeared by the time of parliamentary elections in 1993 and 1995. The percentage of Russians agreeing that the communists have "too much influence in politics" dropped from 47 percent in 1992 to 16 percent in 1995. (Also in 1995 42 percent believed that the "democratic reformers" possessed too much influence in the country.)[14] It appeared that popular support for democracy did not run as deep as that for more prosaic concerns. Surveys in 1994 and 1996 found that if given the choice between democracy and order, almost 80 percent of Russians would choose the latter.[15] Similar priorities are revealed in a 1995 survey offering the choice between democracy and improved living conditions (only 18 percent chose democracy). And a 1996 survey found Russians preferring the pre-1990 Soviet system to Western-style democracy by 41 percent to 27 percent.[16]

By the time of the 1996 presidential election, almost five years after the collapse of the Soviet Union, support for Yeltsin and his policies was as low as that for Gorbachev in the final months of the Soviet regime. For much of the campaign Yeltsin was far behind the communist candidate, Gennady Zyuganov, in opinion polls. It was only with a concerted effort by Yeltsin's allies in the government and media that Zyuganov was ultimately defeated in the runoff election. And once the Zyuganov threat had passed, Yeltsin's popularity promptly sank again. Moreover, regional elections conducted in the months following the 1996 presidential campaign saw the defeat of a large number of "reformist" candidates. With Yeltsin's government repeatedly stymied by parliamentary opposition and regional bureaucrats, the medium-term prospects for Russia's reformist course were a matter of intense speculation.

Conclusions

The decade following the disintegration of the Soviet Union has witnessed the resurfacing of some of the enduring questions about Russia's development. Most salient was the renewed debate between Westernizers and Slavophiles. Gorbachev and especially Boris Yeltsin, Russia's first democratically elected president, pursued a course that largely adopted Western institutions, values, and policies. Far from converging toward some mythical third way, Russia's political and economic systems were rebuilt largely on the

American model, with a constitution that establishes a presidential democracy and guarantees individual rights, an economic system that is rapidly being privatized and decentralized, and a diplomatic stance that seeks partnership with the West. Post-Soviet Russia's rising levels of crime and poverty and the country's falling morale and international prestige have triggered something of a backlash, with Russian nationalists such as Aleksandr Solzhenitsyn labeling the introduction of Western values and culture an unhealthy departure from traditional Russian and Slavic values.[17] Some Russian and Western observers argue that Western institutions and values, though attractive, are not suited to Russia's unique culture and thus Russia should not rush to adopt them. Some Slavophiles, seeking to consolidate Slavic "civilization," have called for reintegration of the Slavic republics of Russia, Ukraine, and Belarus. The tension between Westernizers and Slavophiles has manifested itself in legislative and presidential races, with semireconstructed communist groups gaining a significant share of the anti-Western vote.

Related to this controversy has been a reemergence of the debate between Eurasianists and Euro-Atlanticists. Those who see Russia's future tied with the West emphasize the importance of institutions such as the European Union, the Group of Seven, and the North Atlantic Treaty Organization—none of which the Russian Federation is currently a member, but all of which Moscow has expressed some consideration of joining. On the other hand, Eurasianists look to Russia's south, seeking a strengthening of economic and cultural ties with central Asia and perhaps even a reintegration of some of the central Asian republics with Russia. On this matter Eurasianists and Slavophiles are somewhat incompatible.

As noted earlier, Russia is experiencing an identity crisis, and questions about the applicability of the Western development model remain a matter of some controversy. The question of Russia's development is most succinctly captured in the debate concerning whether the 1917 Revolution represented a break in Russia's natural development toward modernity. Desiring to validate the claim that 1917 brought the proletarian revolution foreseen by Marx, Soviet historians emphasized the industrial and economic development, or "capitalist phase," of tsarist Russia. But despite Stalinist Russia's impressive industrial and military successes, it is now difficult to argue that Brezhnev's "developed socialism" represented a "higher" level of development. It is more appropriate to label the Soviet years as a time of *mis*development, driven by economic and social forces that misallocated resources, wasted labor, destroyed the environment, and dehumanized the population. The political mobilization achieved by the Party nurtured a perverse political culture that rewarded dishonesty and bred cynicism. The misdevelopment carried out under Soviet rule may well take generations to undo.[18] While one still can find reason to disagree with the thesis that the discrediting of fascism and Leninism in this century represents the triumph of Western liberalism, questions regarding the suitability of Leninism as a model for development can finally be laid to rest.

Endnotes

1. Francis Fukuyama, "The End of History?" *The National Interest* 16 (Summer 1989): 3–19.

2. See Samuel Huntington, "A Clash of Civilizations?" *Foreign Affairs* 72, no. 3 (Summer 1993): 22–49.

3. It is telling that a distinction was made in party circles between Bolshevik "Westerners," such as Lenin, who had lived abroad before the 1917 Revolution, and party "natives" who had remained in Russia.

4. See, for example, Ken Jowitt, *New World Disorder: The Leninist Extinction* (Berkeley: University of California Press, 1992).

5. See, for example, W. W. Rostow, *The Stages of Economic Growth: A Non-Communist Manifesto* (New York: Cambridge University Press, 1960).

6. George F. Kennan, "The Sources of Soviet Conduct," *Foreign Affairs* 25, no. 4 (1947): 566–82.

7. See, for example, Jerry F. Hough, *The Soviet Prefects: The Local Party Organs in Industrial Decision-Making* (Cambridge, MA: Harvard University Press, 1969); Harold Gordon Skilling, *Interest Groups in Soviet Politics* (Princeton, NJ: Princeton University Press, 1971); and Susan Gross Solomon, ed., *Pluralism in the Soviet Union: Essays in Honour of H. Gordon Skilling* (New York: St. Martin's Press, 1983).

8. See Clark Kerr, *The Future of Industrial Societies: Convergence or Continuing Diversity?* (Cambridge, MA: Harvard University Press, 1983).

9. Statistics are drawn from the 1994 Russian census and a 1995 survey by the Russian polling firm, *Mneniye*.

10. Dmitry Chubukov, "Democracy Tested in Battle," *Moscow News* (U.S. ed.) 8 (February 24–March 2, 1995): 3.

11. *Open Media Research Institute Daily Digest* 74 (April 15, 1996): 1 (hereafter cited as *OMRI Daily Digest*).

12. Arthur H. Miller, William M. Reisinger, and Vicki L. Hesli, "Understanding Political Change in Post-Soviet Societies: A Further Commentary on Finifter and Mickiewicz," *American Political Science Review* 90, no. 1 (March 1996): 161.

13. Ibid., 158.

14. Ibid., 161.

15. Yuri Levada, "Threat or Bogus?" *Moscow News* (U.S. ed.) 12 (March 31–April 16, 1995): 2; and *OMRI Daily Digest*, 1.

16. *OMRI Daily Digest*, 1.

17. See Aleksandr Solzhenitsyn, *The Russian Question: At the End of the Twentieth Century* (New York: Farrar, Straus and Giroux, 1995).

18. Vladimir Shlapentokh argues that post-Soviet Russian society is now quite similar to the feudal societies of Western Europe in the High Middle Ages. Shlapentokh, "Early Feudalism—The Best Parallel for Contemporary Russia," *Europe-Asia Studies* 48, no. 3 (1996): 393–411.

9

Conclusion: Development in Its Regional and Global Dimensions

—Howard J. Wiarda

The idea of a distinct, Third World model, or series of models, of development is undoubtedly attractive. Who could resist such a notion, particularly after the disappointment and misery brought on by earlier failed models and the often heartfelt demand by Third World peoples and leaders to do it "our way"? Who could stand against the idea of a home-grown, indigenous, grassroots model of development? The idea of an indigenous or non-Western model of development is indeed so attractive that one wonders why so few political leaders and intellectuals failed to think of it earlier.

During the 1970s and 1980s such indigenous theorizing and model construction swept through much of the Third World. It took different forms in different areas: for example, renewed emphasis on the modernizing role of caste associations in India as they converted from traditional institutions into quasipolitical parties or interest groups; the rediscovery of the positive role of ethnicity and tribalism in Africa as providing useful social services, police, and other functions; and the formulation of a distinctive Islamic theory of law and social science finding dramatic if not particularly attractive expression in the Iranian revolution of 1979. In Latin America the

149

emphasis on corporatism by one group of scholars and on dependency theory by another group represented rival efforts to fashion a distinct model appropriate for that area.

In Russia the collapse of the older Soviet system led to a reemphasis among some groups on Slavic and uniquely Russian ways of doing things, while Eastern Europe after the fall of the Berlin Wall and the disintegration of the Warsaw Pact divided between those countries that moved closer to the Western economic and political model and those who, on religious, linguistic, ethnic, cultural, geographic, and socioeconomic grounds, remained divided and uncertain as to their future. In east Asia, the undoubted success economically of that region's countries gave added credence to their assertion of a distinct Asian model of development, but whether the Asian claim included a separate political model as well as an economic one remained open to question. Thus in *every* Third World or non-Western area—although obviously varying from area to area, a theme to which the discussion shortly returns—we have seen the articulation and increasing assertion of local, indigenous, nationalistic, and grassroots models of development to replace or supplement the earlier, often discredited, imports.

In addition to the inherent attractiveness of indigenous approaches to development, there are social and political factors, specific to regional, national, and local circumstances, that help explain why the indigenous approach was so attractive in the 1970s, 1980s, and, in different circumstances, 1990s. First, by the 1970s it had become clear throughout much of the Third World that the imported Western models, whether derived from capitalist or socialist countries, were not working very well in these non-Western contexts; hence, the idea grew of substituting home-grown models for the frequently dysfunctional imported ones. Second, after Vietnam and Watergate, the United States seemed almost to lose its way for a time, lost confidence in its own vision and purpose as a nation and turned self-critical, and failed to push hard for its own developmental model, thus allowing other alternatives to come to the fore. Third, the Cold War parity and apparent standoff between the two great superpowers of the 1970s and 1980s enabled Third World leaders to see the advantages of playing off the two against each other while advancing their own indigenous or nationalistic models.

Fourth—and here we need to jump ahead to the 1990s—after the Soviet Union collapsed, local, ethnic, and nationalistic groups in Russia and Eastern Europe, long bottled up by Soviet totalitarianism, were able to gain greater autonomy and assert their own traditions and practices in ways denied them before. It may prove ironic that indigenous and strongly nationalistic ideas were put forward in Russia and Eastern Europe at a time when the attractiveness of indigenous solutions was already beginning to fade in most other areas of the developing world—although that may be getting ahead of our story. In any case, it needs to be emphasized that the rising popularity for a time of indigenous approaches to development was due not just to their inherent attractiveness but also to larger socioeconomic and political forces in the world.

The Diversity of Indigenous Models

While the popularity of indigenous theories of development was widespread in the Third World, it is striking how diverse the responses were in each of the areas here analyzed. We make a mistake if we believe that the Third World response either to the inadequacies of the imported Western models or to the opportunities for maneuver that the Cold War rivalry between the superpowers afforded was the same everywhere. In fact, this book documents just how diverse the non-Western experience has been as between geographic areas and their social, political, and cultural experiences. Moreover, even *within* these areas there is room for great diversity between countries in terms of the popularity of indigenous solutions, which elements within that experience were emphasized, and the willingness of elites to assert indigenous solutions as opposed to acceptance of Western ways. China is very different in this regard from Japan, Iran's sense of an Islamic state is very different from Saudi Arabia's, Nigeria is very different from Tanzania, and Mexico very different from Brazil.

The east Asian case, for example, is sui generis. First, while there is a common Confucian tradition, it takes different forms and is overlain with different ingredients (Taoism, Shintoism, Maoism) in different countries. Second, the interpretation of Confucianism itself has changed: at one time its self-effacing admonitions were viewed as a barrier to development; now it is seen as providing the self-discipline, order, and emphasis on education necessary for development. Third, while in some cases the assertion of an "Asian model" is seen as a rationalization for authoritarianism and ongoing human rights abuses, in others it represents a widespread sense that the West has lost its way economically, socially, politically, and morally, while Asia has found it. Then too, while some countries and leaders (Lee Kwan Do of Singapore, Mahathir Mohamud of Malaysia) have championed a distinct Asian model, others (Japan, South Korea, Taiwan), wanting to keep close commercial and other ties to the West and especially the United States, have been more muted both in their criticisms of the West and in their assertion of a separate Asian way of doing things. Finally, it is still not entirely clear what an Asian model would entail: is it an economic model of state-led economic growth, a political model of considerable top-down rule, a cultural and social model of clean streets and formalized politeness, or some combination of these?

We next discussed south Asia, primarily India. Like China in a sense, India is a culture, a civilization, a billion people, and virtually an entire continent in itself. The first point that Professor Somjee made is that since its birth as an independent nation in 1946, India has been—and remains—a liberal, representative democracy in the Western (British) mold; so far there is little desire to go in some other direction besides democracy. Second, *within* India and within its various states, there is a great deal of cultural and social diversity, including distinct religious and ethnic movements, and a wide range of opinion about the value of retaining India's current political and intellectual model or substituting or perhaps supplementing it with something else, including indigenous influences; but there is no consensus on what or how or even whether this should occur. Third, when India eventually changed its economic model in the 1990s, it did so not so much because the Soviet model had collapsed (a negative example) but because of the remarkable economic success (a positive influence) of such neighboring countries as Singapore. And fourth, Professor Somjee concludes, not only is India today a vibrant society, a mix of indigenous and imported (Asian *and* Western) influences, but it and other parallel "culture areas" ought to serve as the focus of *regional* theorizing about development before we go on to grand, global models.

The Latin American case is equally fascinating. Here we have a case, first, of an area that is predominantly Western but a fragment of a semifeudal, premodern West (Spain and Portugal) circa 1500. Second, while Latin America has often been confused and/or divided about its destiny, the general trend over the centuries has been gradually increasing approximation to the Western political and economic model. Third, when Latin America did begin to flirt with the possibility of pursuing its own way, there were at least two rival claimants to that honor—corporatism and dependency theory—which in a sense canceled each other out. Fourth, in the present era we have seen in Latin America what might be called "dual indigenization": one model still trying to define the area's uniqueness in Hispanic terms (Catholic, Spanish-speaking, etc.) and the other representing the increasing assertion of nativist or Indian rights. Meanwhile, on both the political (democracy) and economic (neoliberalism) fronts, Latin America has edged closer to global (Western) trends.

Africa is one of the areas where interest in indigenous models of development has been most pronounced. To begin, Africa was the continent where Western colonialism and imperialism were most rapacious, imposing artificial boundaries that divided the continent's natural groupings and subjecting it to unspeakable atrocities. Second, when Africa finally achieved independence in the 1950s and 1960s, the models of political and economic development it used were all imported from abroad, were ill-adapted to African realities, and led to numerous breakdowns and calamities. So, third, it is not unexpected that Africa would subsequently try to rediscover its roots, to fashion new social and political systems based not on ill-fitting imported models but on native, home-grown, usually decentralized or even federal traditions and institutions, including ethnic organizations. Unfortunately these efforts at indigenization have proven no or little more successful at achieving development or improving the lot of the African peoples than did the earlier imported models. Moreover, even the efforts recently at decentralization were largely based on imported models, not necessarily native ones. Meanwhile democratization in Africa has proceeded irregularly and in only a few countries; what may be promising are the efforts at economic privatization and state downsizing, which may reduce corruption and promote economic growth.

The attraction of indigenous theories has also affected the Islamic world—perhaps more so than anywhere else. Part of the reason for this attraction is the manifest failures, again, of the imported models and the powerful sense of frustration, even rage, in countries throughout the Islamic world over their lack of domestic or international success. Then too, in the Quran and the shariah, Islam has a coherent body of beliefs, a legal system, and civic guidelines that could, conceivably, serve as the basis for a distinct, Islamic political, social, and cultural model. However in the Islamic world, as well as within individual Islamic countries, there are deep divisions over these issues. For example, Iran, Iraq, Egypt, Saudi Arabia, Pakistan, and Indonesia are all Islamic states in one form or another, but they are also very different not just in their social, economic, and political directions but in their attitudes toward and relations with the West. Moreover, as Professor Syed's chapter makes clear, both Islamic leaders and the *ulema* have readily used Islam for partisan political purposes. And, in an area where we hear a great deal about Islamic fundamentalism and where the idea of a distinct, indigenous (Islamic) model is perhaps strongest of all Third World areas, we must be stunned by Professor Syed's conclusion that there is "not much to it."

In Eastern Europe and Russia some very different issues arise. The questions here are not so much whether to embrace a full-blown and separate theory of development, but how to deal with strong, often competing nationalisms and rival ethnic and religious loyalties, and where to draw the boundary between "the West" and something else ("the East," the Slavic world, Eastern Orthodoxy, the Islamic world). Using linguistic, religious, ethnic, and nationalistic criteria, Professor Herspring concludes that such countries of Eastern Europe as Poland, the Czech Republic, Slovakia, Hungary, and Slovenia will likely remain anchored to the West and to Western models, both politically (democracy) and economically (modern, mixed economies). However using these same criteria he is far less certain about the prospects for Romania, Bulgaria, Serbia, Bosnia, Croatia, Albania, and Moldavia. While these latter countries are likely to remain politically uncertain, economically laggard, and ethnically divided, there are few serious efforts—unlike in Africa, Asia, and the Islamic world—to develop a distinct *theory* of development.

Much the same could be said for post-Soviet Russia. Once again as in Eastern Europe the problem is deep ethnic, religious, cultural, and national differences. Debate in Russia often rages over whether it belongs, or should belong, to the West or to something else (Slavophile, the East, Asia, Eastern Orthodox). These tensions have been exacerbated by the recent collapse and disintegration of the Soviet Union, the formation of the Commonwealth of Independent States, and the powerful centrifugal forces in Russian society. In my own travels in Russia I have been impressed that Ukraine, Belarus, the Baltic states, and Moscow and its environs are mainly oriented toward Europe and the West, but that east of Moscow the non-West (still not well defined but much more Third World) sets in very quickly. Hence Russia, not unlike southeast Europe, remains divided and even torn apart over its future; but other than nationalism, statism, strains of authoritarianism, and pride in its Slavic distinctiveness there is as yet no serious effort in Russia to construct a full-fledged and uniquely Russian theory of development.

As this brief review suggests, the theme of an indigenous theory or theories of development has elicited mixed reviews in various parts of the world. It has been embraced in some areas, rejected in favor of the Western model in others, and treated with decidedly mixed attitudes in most. The necessity or sense of doing it "our way" has been strongest in Asia, Africa, and the Islamic world, but only in a few countries has there been an effort to eliminate Western influences, trade, and contacts entirely. Despite some reservations and efforts at finding indigenous solutions, northeastern Europe (Poland, Hungary, the Czech Republic, Slovakia) and Latin America have largely joined the West—Europe and North America, respectively—while Russia and southeastern Europe have been all but torn apart over these issues. Not only is there considerable diversity among the world's cultural and geographic regions over these issues, but within regions, within individual countries, and even within individuals there are often conflicting sentiments about continuing local ways versus integration into global trends (capitalism, democracy, free markets).

What's Wrong with an Indigenous Model?

In the 1970s and 1980s the idea of indigenous theories of development seemed to offer much hope and promise. The idea was eagerly embraced by those who had become disillusioned with earlier development models, all Western and imported, that failed to work very well in non-Western contexts. Indigenous models of change were thus born out of both a certain despair with the earlier and often unsuccessful experiments with development, and a passion, almost a romance, often naivete, that doing things "our way" would be better. But now we need to subject the idea of indigenous theories of development to the same kind of careful critique that we used earlier, in the introduction, on Western developmentalist models.

In practice indigenous models of development have not, for the most part, worked out very well. Attractive in theory (who, having spent time in the Third World, could not be sympathetic to the idea of a local, home-grown theory of development?), indigenous models have often been subject to the same problems as other well-meaning development plans. Following is a list of some of the major problems associated with indigenous models of development:

Who Decides?

Who should decide what an indigenous theory consists of, what are its main ingredients, how it should be defined? This issue is actually very controversial. Should it be the Iranian mullahs, the priesthood, or the people? Should it be intellectuals and political leaders or voters? The fact is that different groups and individuals in a society often have very different ideas on this subject, and advocates of an indigenous theory have provided no mechanism for deciding between them.

Political Manipulation and Bias

Generalissimo Francisco Franco in Spain stressed what he called "authentic" Spanish values: discipline, order, authority, traditional Catholicism. But he used these values to justify suppressing dissent and keeping himself in power; others disagreed that these were the only or even main Spanish values. In like manner Asian autocrats like Lee Kwan Do of Singapore and Mahathir Mohamud of Malaysia have used the veil of "Asian models" to disguise and rationalize their own authoritarianism. African leaders have talked eloquently of "authenticity" and local models, but frequently these have been smokescreens for corruption, favoritism for one group over others, and authoritarianism.

Class or Ethnic Favoritism

It is not just individual rulers who have used the smokescreen of indigenous values to disguise self-seeking motives but often whole classes or ethnic groups. Latin American elites tend to emphasize their authoritarian, corporatist, and patrimonial roots as a way of justifying their continuation in power; but lower-class elements often have a different, more democratic view. In Africa one ethnic group's values have often been set forth as the values for the entire society but that seldom sits well with other ethnic groups; nor does the distribution of government jobs and favors on the basis of ethnicity rather than merit.

Elites versus Masses

Elites in the Third World have often favored aristocratic, top-down, and hierarchical social structures—and the indigenous theories that favor them. But for the common people this usually means their interests are repressed or forgotten. Elites and intellectuals may favor an indigenous theory of development because it protects their interests, but what if the masses prefer Coca-Cola, rock music, *Melrose Place*, and all the goods associated with Western consumerism?

Contested Beliefs

In *every* country and culture surveyed in this book, the idea of an indigenous theory of development was hotly contested. Attractive as an abstract idea, it is in practice very controversial. Does acceptance of an indigenous development theory imply acceptance of the murderous Pol Pot regime in Cambodia? Does it mean in Islamic society acquiescence in the subordinate place of women, a theocratic society, or excessive harshness ("cruel and unusual punishment") against criminals? In other words, an indigenous theory of development does not emerge full-blown, instantaneously, or with automatic acceptance; instead it is often contested—often violently—by diverse groups and classes in society.

Functionality

Does it work? An indigenous theory or model sounds nice—especially to outsiders—but does it deliver in the way of goods and services? And by this we mean not just Coca-Cola and other consumer goods but such fundamentals as jobs, education, health care, social services—a higher standard of living. If these are not forthcoming, then people may simply prefer the Western models which *do* have a track record in providing such goods and services. In fact, indigenous models do not so far have a proven history of providing what people want.

Conflicting Theories

In Latin America we could probably arrive at an agreed-upon definition of Hispanic culture, but what about the indigenous Indian or African groups that not only have different cultures but may also assert claims to autonomy that cross national boundaries? In southern Africa blacks may have one kind of political and social model in mind while whites have another—or else the different African ethnic groups may have several distinct models: who then is to decide and on what basis? Should followers of Islam adhere to the Sunni or Shiite versions? As we can see, this idea of an indigenous model gets very complicated.

Cultural Relativism

If each global region has a distinct model and social science of development, then how do we make judgments among them? Are we really ready to say that all solutions and models—even the most abusive ones—are equally valid (cultural relativism) or that the United States has *nothing* to offer the rest of the world in terms of human rights, the practice of democracy, or economic performance? Few Americans are willing to go that far or to countenance regimes that, in the name of doing it "their way," abuse human rights, commit atrocities, or repress their own peoples. But if we are not willing to take a completely cultural-relativist position, where *do* we draw the lines between universal beliefs and rights on the one hand and local or indigenous ways of doing things on the other?

Splendid Isolation?

Countries that opt for an indigenous model of development (e.g., Cambodia, Iran) run the risk of being cut off from the rest of the world. Is that wise? Other countries, particularly in Asia, that were initially attracted to the idea of an indigenous model of development have backed away from it. These countries, whatever their pride in indigenous ways, do not wish to be entirely cut off from Western social, political, and cultural influences, and certainly not from the international trade and commerce vital to their economies. So on this as on the previous point, the issue may not be the either-or one of indigenous-versus-universal but of tough choices on specific issues of where precisely one draws the lines between what is valuable "out there" in the global village versus what is worth preserving of local traditions.

As we see, therefore, the idea of an indigenous theory of development—obviously attractive at some levels—also has in it romantic, naive, and perhaps overly idealistic elements. Indigenous theories were the product of a particular time and place: of growing disillusionment with the older Western theories that in the 1970s and 1980s didn't seem to work well and of the opportunity provided by the parity between the superpowers to maneuver between them. But when faced with the harsh realities and tough choices listed above, many countries became less enamored of the indigenous route and backed away from it. This is not to say that the indigenous path to development represents a totally false start, only that it probably needs to be reined in, viewed more pragmatically, and combined with other useful models of development. Within the social sciences, similarly, indigenous theories of development are being treated less romantically now but nonetheless still seriously as *one* approach among several (the others being liberal developmentalism, political economy, Marxism, dependency, corporatism, organic statism, bureaucratic-authoritarianism) deserving both of detailed scholarly study and of consideration for adoption by Third World countries.[1]

But while criticism of the indigenous path gradually intensified in the 1980s and a variety of countries were moving away from it or combining it with other approaches, a series of cataclysmic events in the late 1980s and early 1990s completely changed the global situation and forced once again a reassessment of the indigenous route.

The New World Order and Indigenous Theories

Between 1989 and 1991—precisely when the idea of indigenous theories of development had come to be viewed more skeptically, as one possible solution among several—a series of cataclysmic events changed the world power balance and had a major effect on thinking about indigenous solutions. The fall of the Berlin Wall and the reunification of Germany, the dissolution of the Warsaw Pact, and then the collapse of the Soviet Union itself were among the most important, even ground-shaking, events of the late twentieth century. These events not only changed the climate, making indigenous theories of development seem less attractive; but, because the Soviet Union had disintegrated, also diminished the capacity of the Third World to maneuver between and play off the two superpowers against each other. A new post–Cold War world order began to emerge.

These world-transforming international events came at about the same time that a world revolution took place in communications—VCRs, cable television, the Internet, satellites, electronic money transfers, new radio and television broadcasting systems, CNN, computers, E-mail, and faxes were coming into everyday use. The communications revolution brought even the remotest Third World villages within the range of global television and, accelerating a trend begun earlier, drastically changed the tastes and preference of *billions* of people. Put briefly, once you've seen the attractive lifestyles portrayed on American and European television—nice homes, cars, affluence, consumerism—who wants to continue in a poor Third World lifestyle, however "indigenous" it may be?

A third factor, stemming from the mid-1970s, was the equally revolutionary spread of democracy throughout the globe. The democratic revolution began in 1974–1975 in Portugal, Greece, and Spain; it then spread to Latin America, then influenced Asia, has by now spread to Russia and Eastern Europe, and includes some countries in Africa and the Islamic world. Polls in these areas indicate that democracy enjoys widespread and almost unanimous support and legitimacy (85–90 percent, depending on the region). All other solutions—military authoritarianism, Marxism-Leninism, *and* indigenous models—seem to have fallen by the wayside. In contrast to the situation a decade or two ago, few people seem to want an indigenous political formula anymore. Democracy and the democratic idea seem to have triumphed almost everywhere.

Not only has democracy become virtually the only legitimate political system globally, but with the collapse of the Soviet Union and other communist states coupled with the phenomenal success of the east Asian nations, capitalism seems to have become the only viable economic system. The neoliberal model of free, open-market economies seems to have triumphed everywhere. It alone, despite the problems and inequalities to which capitalism gives rise, seems to be capable of delivering the goods and services that people, including those in the Third World, want. Our purpose here is not to make moral, ideological, or political judgments about these developments, but simply to report what is happening, which is that free, open markets are now seen almost universally as the most effective way to achieve economic growth. So there we have it: democracy (mainly Western-style) has triumphed in the political sphere and open-market capitalism or neoliberalism has emerged victorious in the economic sphere. Where in this new globalism is there still room for an indigenous theory of development?

When these factors are combined, they add up to an even stronger picture of the triumph of the Western model—for good or ill. The spread of the global communications revolution, for example, means that what most people want is not some new and unproven indigenous theory but instead such "universals" as Coca-Cola, rock music, blue jeans, consumerism, and—not least—democracy, human rights, and free markets. The collapse of the Soviet Union not only means less freedom of maneuver for the former so-called "nonaligned" nations but also demands a whole new set of terms because the "Second World" of developed communist states has ceased to exist and therefore the term "Third World" makes no sense anymore. Moreover, among developing nations we need to distinguish newly industrializing countries (NICs—China, South Korea, Taiwan, Singapore, Indonesia, Brazil, Argentina, Mexico) that are making it into the modern world from others that continue to lag. We also should understand that this is not just an abstract intellectual argument: the United States not only favors democracy and free markets but it is also prepared to use the force of its diplomacy, economic strength, and even military/strategic might, as in Haiti or Bosnia, to ensure these outcomes.[2]

The result of all these influences combined is to strengthen once again the impact of the Western model (democracy, free markets) and to reduce the influence and attractiveness of indigenous models. What then is left or salvageable in the idea of an indigenous theory of development?

Mixed Forms and Fusions

In 1996 Professor Samuel P. Huntington of Harvard University published his provocative *The Clash of Civilizations*.[3] In this book Professor Huntington argues that, with the Cold War over, future conflicts in international affairs would be more between major *cultures* and *civilizations* and less between nations. Huntington also seems to be arguing that with the rise of a diversity of conflicting civilizations, the idea of a universalist global civilization based on the Western model is dead. Huntington's concept of "civilization" corresponds closely to our use of the term "culture area."

However, in this book we find little support for the Huntington thesis of inevitable clash between civilizations. First, while there are clearly cultural differences and political and rhetorical clashes among the regions and countries surveyed here, our authors offer no evidence of a future, full-scale conflict, let alone war between them. Second, we have seen extensive differences *within* each of these areas as to what route to follow, internal differences that militate against clashes *between* culture areas. Third, what our authors highlight is not the monolithic character of these cultural traditions but instead the incredible overlap and mixes of indigenous with Western. Fourth, it is clear that even the strongest proponents of an Asian or Islamic model do not wish to cut themselves off entirely from the West or from Western influences but would prefer to combine the best of the West with the best of their own traditions. And fifth, we have seen the power of the new "world culture" (Lucian Pye's term) of Western music, fashion, lifestyle, democracy, and consumerism and how it serves as a crosscutting corrective to the more flamboyant claims of separate, indigenous routes to development. In short, Huntington has a point: there is a new cultural assertiveness on the part of diverse countries and regions that will produce differences and clashes, but the extent of these differences should not be exaggerated nor should one ignore the tremendously powerful *global* forces pushing toward greater uniformity among regions.

More likely than a full-scale clash or conflict between civilizations is an incredible mix of blends, fusions, and combinations both of conflicting internal cultural currents and of combined Western and local influences. These are likely to take "crazy quilt" patterns of unusual, shifting, and crosscutting combinations, or to represent "halfway houses" located at various points between Western and indigenous poles. In other words, we will see particularly African, Asian, Islamic, Latin American, and Russian ways of doing things combined with foreign influences and models in all sorts of imaginative and unusual ways.

But some culture areas are stronger than others in these regards. Or else their economics or political power is of such importance—e.g., China, Japan—that we are obliged to consider their cultural claims seriously. Japan is the paradigm. It is not only the most successful of the non-Western countries but it also has a remarkably uniform and coherent internal culture that is uniquely Japanese. Among the many reasons that Japan is admired is its *selective* borrowing from the West. It has taken the best that the West has to offer (and often improved upon it) while also taking great pains to preserve Japanese culture and traditions. One suspects that parallel developments will occur in other powerful and important countries that have strong internal cultures: China, India, Mexico, maybe Russia, maybe Brazil.

Other smaller, weaker countries and areas present more mixed outlooks. In Africa there are frequent internal divisions over culture and ethnicity, few examples of successful economies (certainly not on the east Asian scale), and no countries of potential superpower status. So, while there will always be an "African" way (actually a great diversity of ways) of doing things, the capacity of African states to selectively resist or filter outside influences in the same way Japan has will be limited.

Similarly with Latin America. Here we have some large, important countries (Argentina, Brazil, Chile, Colombia, Mexico, Peru, Venezuela) but none of them as big or important as China or Japan. Here we also have Western cultures but often thinly institutionalized and representing a particular historical fragment of the West. While there will continue to be uniquely Latin American ways of doing things (Rousseauian democracy rather than Lockean, for example), at this stage Latin America seems to have thrown in its lot with the West and has little current interest in advancing its own, distinct theory of development.

An especially interesting test case is the Islamic world. Here we have perhaps the clearest instance of a separate, distinct, indigenous theory of development, grounded in Islam—and a certain aggressiveness in some cases in asserting it. But there are widely divergent conceptions of what an Islamic state or developmental model should look like (Iran versus Saudi Arabia, for instance) as well as great differences over the issues within countries. In addition, we do not think of the Islamic models as being especially successful (unlike Japan), nor are there any current or future great powers among the Islamic states able to *enforce* their views on these issues. Moreover, even previously do-it-our-way nations like Iran and Iraq recognize they cannot entirely go it alone in the world, and are increasingly reaching out for trade and other purposes to other nations and culture areas, which almost certainly implies greater compromise with their own indigenous principles. Even the Islamic world is thus liable to end up as a mix with a variety of overlapping influences.

There will, therefore, always be distinct cultural differences among nations and particular, often culturally conditioned ways of doing things. Development and change will follow global patterns, but at the same time these changes will continue to be filtered through the prism of local or indigenous practices and institutions. Some countries and culture areas will doubtless continue to assert these differences and even advance their own "models" more strongly than others. But our prognosis is not so much for each global region to take up its own distinctive, culturally conditioned "model" of development but for varying mixes, blends, and overlaps of indigenous and global—e.g., caste or ethnic associations that function like interest groups, extended families and patronage networks that function like political parties, and so on. Meanwhile, at present and as far into the future as we can see, global currents appear to be ascendant, breaking down old cultural behaviors and stereotypes and often giving them radically new forms, insisting on universally recognized norms in such areas as trade and commerce, and combining and fusing with indigenous traditions in many confused, crosscutting ways.

This study and these comments also carry important policy implications. First, they suggest that future global leaders, if they are to succeed, must be adept at maneuvering both in their own societies and in the broader global one. Second, our study has implications for economic development. We now *know* pretty well the formula for economic development (open markets, an emphasis on education and infrastructure, legal guarantees, an honest and efficient state) but within that well-nigh universal formula there can still be some variation in state size and the public-private balance.

Third, our study has major implications for democracy and human rights. Democracy and human rights are no longer just Western creations but now enjoy near-universal popularity and legitimacy. It is no longer so easy for a regime to blatantly run roughshod over human rights; moreover there is an emerging body of democratic human rights laws and sanctions which few countries can afford to ignore. But at the same time there are still numerous culturally conditioned differences over the precise meanings of *human rights*, *democracy*, and other broad terms, as well as different priorities in different culture areas among the several categories of rights. Democracy is the preferred political formula but within that system there is room for distinct, culturally shaped types and forms of democracy. Policy makers will still need to be both cognizant of these global trends toward democracy and free markets, and at the same time sensitive to the local, indigenous ways of organizing and running their political and economic systems.

Endnotes

1. For detailed treatment and assessments of these alternative models see Howard J. Wiarda, ed., *New Directions in Comparative Politics* (Boulder, CO: Westview Press, 1992); and, by the same author, *An Introduction to Comparative Politics* (Belmont, CA: Wadsworth, 1993).

2. David Sanger, "Playing the Trade Card: U.S. Is Exporting Its Free Market Values through Global Commercial Agreements," *New York Times*, February 17, 1997, 1.

3. Samuel P. Huntington, *The Clash of Civilizations and the Remaking of World Order* (New York: Simon and Schuster, 1996).

Suggested Readings

—Compiled by Lana Wylie

Aguilar, Luis, ed. *Marxism in Latin America*. New York: Knopf, 1971.

Ahmad, Leila. *Women and Gender in Islam: Historical Roots of a Modern Debate*. New Haven, CT: Yale University Press, 1992.

Ake, Claude. *Democracy and Development in Africa*. Washington DC: Brookings Institution, 1996.

Almond, G., and James S. Coleman, eds. *The Politics of the Developing Areas*. Princeton, NJ: Princeton University Press, 1960.

Anderson, Charles W. *Politics and Economic Change in Latin America*. Princeton, NJ: Van Nostrand, 1967.

Apter, D., and C. Rosberg, eds. *Political Development and the New Realism in Sub-Saharan Africa*. Charlottesville: University Press of Virginia, 1994.

Ayittey, George. *Indigenous African Institutions*. Ardsley-on-Hudson, NY: Transnational Publishers, 1991.

Bill, James A., and Robert Springboard. *Politics in the Middle East*. New York: HarperCollins, 1990.

Binder, Leonard. *Islamic Liberalism: A Critique of Development Ideologies*. Chicago: University of Chicago Press, 1988.

Binder, Leonard, James S. Coleman, Joseph LaPalombara, Lucien W. Pye, Sidney Verba, and Myon Weiner, eds. *Crisis and Sequences in Political Development*. Princeton, NJ: Princeton University Press, 1971.

Black, C. E. *The Dynamics of Modernization*. New York: Harper and Row, 1968.

Boilard, Steve. *Russia at the Twenty-First Century: Politics and Social Change in the Post-Soviet Era*. Fort Worth: Harcourt Brace, 1998.

Butterworth, Charles E., ed. *The Political Aspects of Islamic Philosophy: Essays in Honor of Muhsin S. Mahdi*. Cambridge, MA: Harvard University Press, 1992.

Camp, Roderic Ai, ed. *Democracy in Latin America: Patterns and Cycles*. Wilmington, DE: Scholarly Resources Inc., 1996.

Chazan, Naomi et al. *Politics and Society in Contemporary Africa*. 2nd ed. Boulder, CO: Lynne Rienner Publishers, 1992.

Cohen, Leonard J. *Broken Bonds: Yugoslavia's Disintegration and Balkan Politics in Transition*. 2nd ed. Boulder, CO: Westview, 1995.

Coleman, James S., ed. *Education and Political Development*. Princeton, NJ: Princeton University Press, 1965.

Conde, Roberto Cortes. *The First Stages of Modernization in Latin America.* New York: Harper and Row, 1974.

Crawford, Rex W. *A Century of Latin American Thought.* New York: Praeger, 1966.

Davidson, Basil. *The Black Man's Burden: Africa and the Curse of the Nation-State.* New York: Times Books, 1992.

Davutoglu, Ahmet. *Alternative Paradigms: The Impact of Islamic and Western Weltanschauungs on Political Theory.* Lanham, MD: University Press of America, 1994.

Diamond, Larry, ed. *Political Culture and Democracy in Developing Countries.* Boulder, CO: Lynne Rienner, 1994.

Enayat, Hamid. *Modern Islamic Political Thought.* Austin: University of Texas Press, 1982.

Esposito, John L., ed. *Voices of Resurgent Islam.* New York: Oxford University Press, 1983.

————. *Islam and Politics.* Syracuse, NY: Syracuse University Press, 1987.

Evans, Peter. *Embedded Autonomy: States and Industrial Transformation.* Princeton, NJ: Princeton University Press, 1995.

Faletto, Enzo, and Fernando Henrique Cardoso. *Dependency and Development in Latin America.* Berkeley, CA: University of California Press, 1978.

Farsoun, Samih K., and Mashayekhi Mehrdad, eds. *Iran: Political Culture in the Islamic Republic.* New York: Routledge, 1992.

Fisher, Sidney N. *The Middle East: A History.* New York: Alfred A. Knopf, 1979.

Fukuyama, Francis. *The End of History and the Last Man.* New York: Maxwell Macmillan International, 1992.

Gendzier, Irene. *Managing Political Change: Social Scientists and the Third World.* Boulder, CO: Westview Press, 1968.

Gibson, Charles. *Spain in America.* New York: Harper and Row, 1966.

Haddad, Yvonne, ed. *The Islamic Impact.* Syracuse, NY: Syracuse University Press, 1984.

Haggard, Stephen. *Pathways from the Periphery: The Politics of Growth in the Newly Industrialized Countries.* Ithaca, NY: Cornell University Press, 1990.

Hall, John A., and I. C. Jarvie, eds. *Transition to Modernity: Essays on Power, Wealth and Belief.* Cambridge, England: Cambridge University Press, 1992.

Halperin, Tulio Donghi. *The Aftermath of Revolution in Latin America.* New York: Harper and Row, 1973.

Han, Sang-bok, ed. *Asian Peoples and Their Cultures: Continuity and Change.* Seoul: Seoul National University Press, 1986.

Harbeson, J., and D. Rothchild, eds. *Africa in World Politics: Post Cold War Challenges.* Boulder, CO: Westview Press, 1995.

Heilbroner, Robert J. *The Great Ascent.* New York: Harper and Row, 1963.

Himmelstrand, Ulf, Kabiru Kinyanjui, and Edward Mburugu, eds. *African Perspectives on Development: Controversies, Dilemmas and Openings.* New York: St. Martin's Press, 1994.

Huntington, Samuel P. *The Clash of Civilizations and the Remaking of World Order.* New York: Simon and Schuster, 1996.

———. *The Third Wave: Democratization in the Late Twentieth Century.* Norman, OK: University of Oklahoma Press, 1991.

Ike, Nobutaka. *A Theory of Japanese Democracy.* Boulder, CO: Westview Press, 1978.

Johnson, Chalmers. *MITI and the Japanese Miracle: The Growth of Industrial Policy.* Stanford: Stanford University Press, 1982.

———. *Japan: Who Governs? The Rise of the Developmental State.* New York: Norton, 1995.

Jorrín, Miguel, and John Martz. *Latin American Political Thought and Ideology.* Chapel Hill, NC: University of North Carolina Press, 1970.

Jowitt, Ken. *New World Disorder: The Leninist Extinction.* Berkeley: University of California Press, 1992.

Kantor, Harry. *The Ideology and Program of the Peruvian Aprista Movement.* New York: Cotagon Books, 1966.

Kebschull, Harvey G., ed. *Politics in Transitional Societies: The Challenge of Change in Asia, Africa, and Latin America.* New York: Appleton-Century-Crofts, 1968.

Kerr, Clark. *The Future of Industrial Societies: Convergence or Continuing Diversity?.* Cambridge, MA: Harvard University Press, 1983.

Lampe, John R., and Daniel Nelson, eds. *East European Security Reconsidered.* Washington, DC: The Woodrow Wilson Center, 1993.

LaPalombara, Joseph, ed. *Bureaucracy and Political Development.* Princeton, NJ: Princeton University Press, 1963.

——— and Myron Weiner, eds. *Political Parties and Political Development.* Princeton, NJ: Princeton University Press, 1966.

Lasswell, Harold, Daniel Lerner, and John D. Montgomery, eds. *Values and Development: Appraising Asian Experience.* Cambridge, MA: MIT Press, 1976.

Leff, Carol Skalnik. *The Czech and Slovak Republics.* Boulder, CO: Westview, 1997.

Lieven, Anatol. *The Baltic Revolution.* 2nd ed. New Haven, CT: Yale, 1994.

Loveman, Brian. *The Constitution of Tyranny: Regimes of Exception in Latin America*. Pittsburgh: University of Pittsburgh Press, 1993.

Macridis, Roy. *The Study of Comparative Government*. New York: Random House, 1955.

Mahmood, Norma, ed. *Rethinking Political Development in Southeast Asia*. Kuala Lumpur: University of Malaya Press, 1994.

Maryanov, Gerald Seymour. *Conflict and Political Development in Southeast Asia: An Exploration in the International Political Implications of Comparative Theory*. Athens: Ohio University, Center for International Studies, 1969.

Mazrui, Ali A. *The African: A Triple Heritage*. London: BBC Publications, 1986.

McAlister, Lyle. *Spain and Portugal in the New World, 1492–1700*. Minneapolis: University of Minnesota Press, 1984.

Millikan, Max F., and W. W. Rostow. *A Proposal: Key to an Effective Foreign Policy*. New York: Harper, 1957.

Moody, Peter R., Jr. *Tradition and Modernization in China and Japan*. Belmont, CA: Wadsworth, 1995.

Moore, Barrington, Jr. *Social Origins of Dictatorship and Democracy: Lord and the Peasant in the Making of the Modern World*. Boston: Beacon Press, 1960.

Moran, T. *Multinational Corporations and the Politics of Dependence*. Cambridge, MA: Center for International Affairs, Harvard University, 1975.

Morley, James W., ed. *Driven by Growth: Political Change in the Asia-Pacific Region*. Armonk, NY: M. E. Sharpe, 1993.

Moten, Abdul Rashid. *Political Science: An Islamic Perspective*. New York: St. Martin's Press, 1996.

Ndegwa, Stephen. *The Two Faces of Civil Society: NGOs and Politics in Africa*. West Hartford, CT: Kumarian Press, 1996.

Needler, Martin. *Political Development in Latin America*. New York: Random House, 1968.

O'Donnell, Guillermo. *Modernization and Bureaucratic-Authoritarianism in Latin America*. Berkeley: Institute of International Studies, University of California Press, 1973.

————, Philippe Schmitter, and Laurence Whitehead, eds. *Transitions from Authoritarian Rule: Prospects for Democracy*. Baltimore: Johns Hopkins University Press, 1986.

Palmer, Monte. *Political Development: Dilemmas and Challenges*. Itasca, IL: F. E. Peacock, 1997.

Pelletiere, Stephen C. *A Theory of Fundamentalism: An Inquiry into the Origin and Development of the Movement.* Carlisle Barracks, PA: Strategic Studies Institute, U.S. Army War College, 1995.

Pike, Frederick B. *Hispanismo 1898–1936: Spanish Conservatives and Liberals and Their Relations with Spanish America.* Notre Dame, IN: Notre Dame University Press, 1971.

Piscatori, James P., ed. *Islam in the Political Process.* New York: Cambridge University Press, 1983.

Potholm, Christian. *Theory and Practice of African Politics.* Englewood Cliffs, NJ: Prentice-Hall, Inc., 1973.

Pye, Lucian W., ed. *Communications and Political Development.* Princeton, NJ: Princeton University Press, 1963.

———— and Sidney Verba, eds. *Political Culture and Political Development.* Princeton, NJ: Princeton University Press, 1965.

Randall, Vicky, and Robin Theobald. *Political Change and Underdevelopment.* Durham, NC: Duke University Press, 1985.

Robinson, Thomas W. *Democracy and Development in East Asia: Taiwan, South Korea, and the Philippines.* Washington, DC: AEI Press, 1991.

Rodó, José Enrique. *Ariel.* Austin: University of Texas Press, 1988.

Rosenberg, Tina. *The Haunted Land: Facing Europe's Ghosts after Communism.* New York: Random House, 1995.

Rostow, W. W. *The Stages of Economic Growth: A Non-Communist Manifesto.* New York: Cambridge University Press, 1960.

Rothchild, Donald, and Naomi Chazan. *The Precarious Balance: State and Society in Africa.* Boulder, CO: Westview Press, 1988.

Samanta, I. *Theories of Government in Islam.* New Delhi: Enkay Publishers, 1988.

Scalapino, Robert A. *The Politics of Development: Perspectives on Twentieth-Century Asia.* Cambridge, MA: Harvard University Press, 1989.

Shams, Feraidoon, ed. *State and Society in Africa: Perspectives on Continuity and Change.* Lanham, MD: University Press of America, 1995.

Shaw, Timothy, and Kenneth Heard, eds. *The Politics of Africa: Dependence and Development.* New York: Africana Publishing Co., Dalhousie University Press, 1979.

Silvert, Kalman. *The Conflict Society: Reaction and Revolution in Latin America.* New York: Harper and Row, 1968.

Solomon, Susan Gross, ed. *Pluralism in the Soviet Union: Essays in Honour of H. Gordon Skilling.* New York: St. Martin's Press, 1983.

Solzhenitsyn, A. *The Russian Question: At the End of the Twentieth Century.* New York: Farrar, Straus and Giroux, 1995.

Somjee, A. H. *Democracy and Political Change in Village India.* New Delhi: Orient Longman, 1971.

———. *Development Theory: Critiques and Explorations.* London: Macmillan, 1991.

———. *Parallels and Actuals of Political Development.* London: Macmillan, 1986.

——— and G. Somjee. *Development Success in Asia Pacific: An Exercise in Normative-Pragmatic Balance.* New York: St. Martin's Press, 1995.

Stokes, Gale. *The Walls Came Tumbling Down: The Collapse of Communism in Eastern Europe.* New York: Oxford, 1993.

Syed, Anwar. *Pakistan: Islam, Politics and National Solidarity.* Lahore: Vanguard, 1983.

Tamadonfar, Mehran. *The Islamic Polity and Political Leadership: Fundamentalism, Sectarianism, and Pragmatism.* Boulder, CO: Westview Press, 1989.

Tilly, Charles, ed. *The Formation of the National States in Western Europe.* Princeton, NJ: Princeton University Press, 1975.

Van Cott, Donna Lee, ed. *Indigenous Peoples and Democracy in Latin America.* New York: St. Martin's Press, 1994.

Vanden, Harry. *National Marxism in Latin America: Jose Carlos Mariategui's Thought and Politics.* Boulder, CO: Lynne Rienner, 1986.

Veliz, Claudio. *The Centralist Tradition in Latin America.* Princeton, NJ: Princeton University Press, 1980.

Vogel, Ezra. *Japan as Number One: Lessons for America.* Cambridge, MA: Harvard University Press, 1970.

Ward, Haskell G. *African Development Reconsidered: New Perspectives from the Continent.* New York: Phelps-Stokes Institute, 1989.

Ward, Robert E., and Dankwart A. Rustow, eds. *Political Modernization in Japan and Turkey.* Princeton, NJ: Princeton University Press, 1964.

Watt, W. Montgomery. *Islamic Political Thought: The Basic Concepts.* Edinburgh: Edinburgh University Press, 1980.

Weber, Max. *The Religion of China: Confucianism and Taoism.* New York: Macmillan, 1964.

Weidemann, Deithelm, ed. *Nationalism, Ethnicity, and Political Development: South Asian Perspectives.* New Delhi: Manohar Publications, 1991.

Wiarda, Howard J. *Corporatism and Comparative Politics: The Other Great "Ism."* New York: M. E. Sharp, 1966.

———. *Corporatism and National Development in Latin America.* Boulder, CO: Westview Press, 1981.

————. *Democracy and Its Discontents: Development, Interdependence, and U.S. Policy in Latin America.* Lanham, MD: Rowman and Littlefield, 1995.

————. *The Democratic Revolution in Latin America.* New York: A Twentieth Century Book, Holmes and Meier, 1992.

————. *Ethnocentrism in Foreign Policy: Can We Understand the Third World?* Washington, DC: American Enterprise Institute for Public Policy Research, 1983.

————. *Introduction to Comparative Politics.* Belmont, CA: Wadsworth Publishers, 1993.

————. *Latin American Politics: A New World of Possibilities.* Belmont, CA: Wadsworth Publishers, 1995.

————. *New Directions in Comparative Politics.* 2nd ed. Boulder, CO: Westview Press, 1991.

————. *Politics and Social Change in Latin America.* Boulder, CO: Westview Press, 1992.

———— and Harvey Kline, eds. *Latin American Politics and Development.* Boulder, CO: Westview Press, 4th ed. 1996.

Woodward, Susan L. *Balkan Tragedy: Chaos and Dissolution after the Cold War.* Washington, DC: Brookings Institution, 1995.

Young, Crawford. *Ideology and Development in Africa.* New Haven, CT: Yale University Press, 1982.

Index